STRAIGHT
TO THE
TOP

BEYOND LOYALTY, GAMESMANSHIP, MENTORS, AND OTHER CORPORATE MYTHS

PAUL G. STERN
and Tom Shachtman

WARNER BOOKS

A Warner Communications Company

To Patricia, Andrew, Andrea, Alexander, and Tante

Warner Books, Inc., 666 Fifth Avenue, New York, NY 10103

A Warner Communications Company

Printed in the United States of America
First printing April 1990
10 9 8 7 6 5 4 3 2 1

Library of Congress Cataloging-in-Publication Data
Stern, Paul G., 1938-
    Straight to the top / by Paul G. Stern and Tom Shactman.
    p.   cm.
    ISBN 0-446-51518-3
    1. Executives—United States.   2. Career development—United
States.   3. Managing your boss.   4. Industrial management-
-Vocational guidance—United States.   I. Shactman,   Tom.   II. Title.
HD38.25.U6S74   1990
658.4'09—dc20   89-40455
                                                                                      CIP

Book design: H. Roberts

Acknowledgments

My appreciation to Pam Bernstein of the William Morris Agency, who encouraged and promoted this project. I would also like to express my gratitude to my aunt in Switzerland who has been an ardent cheerleader all along, and my thanks to my wife and three children for their abiding faith in my career, and for their help, love, and encouragement throughout our exciting times together in the corporate world. This book is written with particular hopes for my children, to whom the future belongs.

—Paul G. Stern

Table of Contents

Foreword

BEGAN this book shortly after I had left the presidency of Unisys at the close of 1987. I wrote it then because I felt free and had the time to finally give shape to a manual of strategic career planning that would encourage individual managers to chart their own course toward the top according to their needs and abilities. Before that time, I had thought that a book on how to manage your own career could not be written by a sitting top executive officer of a large multinational company. There were too many notions in it that would run counter to the usual line that top executives tend to espouse. For instance, I held the firm belief that there was no such thing as company loyalty. Another—perhaps more radical notion—was that I believed managers could and should control their own futures; that sort of thinking is anathema to most top executives who want to closely control their subordinates' careers. Most CEOs, in fact, still believe loyalty to the company should be unquestioned, the corporate hierarchy unchallenged, and that careers cannot (and perhaps should not) be planned, even by the most ambitious of managers. I don't think that way—but I waited until I'd "retired" to put my ideas down on paper.

At that time, I thought I would never return to the corporate world I had inhabited for a quarter-century; I considered going into a start-up company, or being part of a group that acquired a private or public company, or, more likely, devoting myself entirely to personal interests or to public service, perhaps in education. And while I considered my options, I wrote this book. During 1988, however, in addition to all my other corporate and civic activities, I was asked to join the board of Northern Telecom, a multibillion-dollar telecommunications company with dual headquarters in Toronto and Nashville, and extensive operations in Canada, the United States, Europe, and the Far East. Through work on the board, I became more involved with Northern Telecom, and as I did, a fascination with corporate processes began again to take hold of me. When the opportunity was presented for me to become the company's CEO and chairman-designate, I considered it carefully. I began to see that here was an exciting opportunity to direct an entire corporation that had some challenges, but more importantly, enormous potential with the clear chance of becoming the leader in the telecommunications industry during the next decade. And so in January of 1989, I accepted the CEO and chairman-designate positions with Northern Telecom, and began work in March of 1989, after finishing the manuscript of this book.

Now that I am CEO of a multibillion-dollar, multinational company, I see that my earlier worries were not entirely justified. While there are still many top corporate executives who will find this book's lessons difficult medicine to swallow, as a CEO I embrace the notions described in these pages. They may be radical, but if key employees act in the ways I suggest in these pages, they will only help their companies as they help themselves. As a CEO, I wouldn't be afraid of those employees who, while in the ranks of my managers, capitalized on these lessons about getting ahead rapidly; rather, I'd be glad to have such hard-chargers aboard.

Paul G. Stern,
October 1989

PART ONE

Forming a Career Strategy

1

Do You Want to Manage Your Career?

*D*O you really want to manage your own career? If so, you have to make an active decision to take charge of your future, and this book can be a big first step. *Straight to the Top* is addressed to those involved in management who want to reach the inner circle of high-ranked executives in a large public American-based company. It should empower people at any level, from the first-line manager on up. If your dream is to attain a high position in a big company and what comes with it—personal financial success and independence, power and recognition of one's abilities and achievements—welcome to the club. Those were my goals and I reached them; now I'm determined to show others how to do as I have done—to manage their own careers in the world of multinational companies.

In universities, in business schools, and even on the job many people have been brainwashed to believe that a career can't be planned and managed. We're conditioned to accept the idea that in a big corporation an individual's path to the top is a matter of circumstances, lucky breaks, accidents, the presence or absence of mentors, even of the interplay of planets in the heavens. That's ridiculous. A career can and should be managed, and in the following chapters of this book I'm going to show you, step by step, how it can be done.

The world of big, multinational corporations is a strange one, in many ways hobbled by outmoded ideas and myths that combine to prevent most managers from getting to the top. In this book I'll expose those crippling notions and refute those myths. I am emboldened to do so because I have been successful in my own career. In the past twenty-two years I worked for six of the world's largest companies (DuPont, IBM, Braun, Rockwell International, Burroughs, and Unisys), and was president or CEO of three of them. I did what you're not supposed to be able to do: I changed companies frequently, and in the process received promotions and raises at a tremendous rate. By refusing to fit the mold of the usual employee, by staying only as long with one company as the job challenges and its rewards were good for me and for the company, I went straight to the top. I achieved financial independence while still in my early forties, and then voluntarily left the presidency of Unisys at age forty-eight.

In the chapters of this book, I'll suggest strategies and tactics to help you attain similar goals. You'll learn how to package, present, and position yourself for frequent promotions and a fast-track career.

There's nothing devious about the strategies I'll suggest. This is not a book about shortcuts, or about games that can be played to avoid doing the real work of getting ahead. If you follow my advice, you'll have to work hard, in fact, very hard; it will require you to be talented and to apply your intelligence to many and varied tasks. Above all, you'll have to produce results. And you'll have to have a fire in your belly, a desire that's with you all the time; that fire, too, takes work to spark and stoke. But even if you don't start out with that desire within, it can be developed. I was never afraid of being fired; you can develop this attitude just as easily.

I can't promise you that the road to the executive suite will be easy, but the philosophy that I recommend and detail will guide you and put you in control of your own progress as you aim high and make it to the top.

2

If I Can Do It ...

I *WAS* born in Europe shortly before the beginning of World War II, the only child of professional parents both of whom had come from Czechoslovakia. My first schooling was conducted by Italian nuns, and my native languages became German and Italian. I remember very little of the early war years in Italy; in fact my first memories are of the bombing of Italy by the Allied forces. Once, after the Allied invasion, I was playing on the street during an air raid and an American officer swooped me up, together with a friend, and took us to an underground bomb shelter; I recall this not because of the bombs or the soldier's heroics, but because in that shelter I received my first taste of ice cream. That and the wonder of my first piece of white bread—I thought it was cake—anchor my early childhood memories. The combination of the war and my father's philosophies and desires had us moving frequently, to Northern Africa, the Middle East, and Europe. By the time my father died at a relatively young age, we had lived on three continents, settling in Mexico, and it is the years and experiences there that I consider to have been my most formative.

My mother and I lived in Mexico City, where the family had thriving businesses. Once again I was confronted with a new country, a new language, and new schools. This time, however, the change was accompanied by a dramatic shift in lifestyles to what then seemed to me luxurious surroundings. In the early 1950's Mexico City was beautiful, and a microcosm of the cheek-by-jowl extremes of wealth and poverty that characterize most of Latin America. I became one of the fortunate few, and, at first, the change was so great that I didn't like my new environment at all. A big house with many servants? A plentiful supply of food? A private school where many of the students drove to classes in their own cars? Vacations in Acapulco? I'd never had a meaningful vacation, and hardly knew how to deal with these other elements. I was completely unprepared for this luxurious world because it was the obverse of everything I had known, and also because it was not reflected in any of the books and newspapers I'd read or in the movies I'd seen. I soon learned that the fathers of many of my wealthy classmates at the American High School in Mexico City were either very successful Mexican businessmen, Europeans whose permanent residences were in Mexico, or expatriate American employees of large corporations or those who represented American or international corporations in Mexico. As with many of my non-American classmates, I studied English as well as Spanish; the goal was to prepare us to go on to universities in the United States or in Europe.

By the time I went to Boston to spend a year in a prep school prior to applying to colleges, I had already formed some notions about wealth and its creation. During my formative years I had never realized how difficult things had been for my family—the moving around, the sometimes harsh conditions we had to endure. I now knew what wealth could bring, and that its most important and appealing aspect was independence, the freedom to do what you wanted in life. Unlike my Latin American classmates at the Boston prep school, however, I was not a wealthy young man and would have to make my own way in the world. They had grown up coddled; their worries and concerns seemed trivial when compared to what I'd been able to deal with. I felt much older than my contemporaries, much more mature. I had learned to fend for myself and, when encountering new situations, to land on my feet. I wasn't afraid to take risks; indeed, I had been brought up to accept managing risk as a part of life.

At the American High School in Mexico City and at prep school in Boston I adjusted easily, learned the mannerisms and styles of my classmates and how to capitalize on their forms of power. What impressed me most about these young men was how independent they were. They could choose what to study, what sort of business to enter, where to live in the future—because their families' financial means (and the fact that their businesses were family-owned) freed them from the necessity of sticking to a narrow path. I had always been subject to forces over which I'd had no control: geographic changes, the loss of my father when I was relatively young, the continual shifting of languages, systems, and procedures for living.

By the time I had finished prep school, I had become imbued with the determination to live in a manner that would bring stability and control to my life, and—equally important—would gain for me independence of choice, an independence that I had come to believe could be achieved by generating wealth. I wanted to be able to do, within reason, whatever I wanted to, and whenever I wanted to do it. I had a dream of getting to the top, a dream that would later become an obsession. But how or where to take the first step toward making my dreams a reality? At that moment, I had no strong feelings about a career path. I was willing to go in any number of different directions, as long as the one I picked would fulfill my objectives. As I searched for that path, it seemed to me that engineers were in short supply, that the demand for them was great, and that they were better paid than other professionals. The elite of the engineers were electrical engineers, and I set out to be one.

During my undergraduate engineering studies at an American university, I became thoroughly convinced that the United States was the land of opportunity and I wanted to live here permanently, rather than return to Mexico where my family continued to live. I also became fascinated by corporate America—the employer of most electrical engineers—and by the idea of being a manager within the corporation; that seemed like a fine path to wealth, security, and control. Upon graduating, I accepted a job at AT&T, in the Bell and Western Electric division in New Jersey, and simultaneously began graduate courses at night. I found the job uninteresting, but was keen on pursuing a master's degree in thermonuclear (plasma) physics; shortly, I left my job and took a research assistantship to pursue my studies full-time. We had a strong team working on a project funded by the Atomic Energy Commission. When I began graduate studies, I was in awe of the professors; like most of my childhood friends, I had a deep respect for such learned men, and thought that to earn a doctorate you would have to produce a work of genius or, at least, of considerable innovation. As I went forward, I realized that the professors didn't have a corner on brain power, and began to believe that if they could do the research, so could I—and I was no longer scared of earning a doctorate. In a hurry, I accelerated my studies. Time was precious to me, and so I worked seven days a week, not stopping even for holidays, in order to complete my studies as quickly as possible. I received a Ph.D. in solid-state physics in two and a half years rather than the four to five years my colleagues took to do it, and was immediately snapped up by E.I. DuPont. As I later learned, Ph.D.s are of interest to corporations not only for their specialized expertise, but also because they have already proven their capacity for independent work.

DuPont sent me to their Richmond, Virginia, facility to help develop a product called TYVEK, still sold today. It was a very exciting project, technically the most interesting one of my career, but I didn't like the environment at DuPont. As a research physicist, I saw that my team and immediate boss worked extremely hard, but that managers two and three levels above us would sit in their offices and shuffle papers while we were working; they'd get to take interesting trips while we stayed in Richmond; moreover, they took the credit for our work. I also learned that managers earned much more money than we did.

I often went to the libraries, took out proxy statements, which list the top handful of salaried employees for publicly held U.S. companies, and discovered the extent of the disparity in incomes between scientists, engineers, and managers. Large companies began to fascinate me; I studied them by reading their annual reports, 10K reports, the analyses of financial experts, and other published literature. I had already recognized my own limits as a scientist. Now, knowing that I wasn't going to be an Einstein or a Fermi, and wanting to be at the top of whatever I did, I decided to switch careers. In the United States, the title of manager had a great deal of cachet; as with the title of professor in Europe, it, too, was looked upon with respect. I'd be a manager.

One key reason for leaving DuPont was that I had come to understand that DuPont's decision-making process was cumbersome, bureaucratic, and slow, and that if I became a manager at DuPont (a distinct possibility), it would probably take me years to advance. And so, after two years at DuPont, in December of 1968 my wife and two children and I moved to Poughkeepsie, New York, and I started at IBM as a first-line, or lowest-level, manager.

In those years IBM was on top of the world, the leader in the emerging computer industry, and a dynamic, fast-growing company. For me, it was the perfect environment. I spent seven years there, during which I had nine bosses, five significant promotions, and twelve salary increases. (Two of those bosses I later hired to work for me at Burroughs; both stayed on through our acquisition of Sperry, when the company became Unisys.) I attended five management schools, from the lowest-level one to a summer executive course at the Sloan School of Management at M.I.T. and eventually to IBM's own Advanced Management School at Sands Point on Long Island, which was at that time open only to those considered by the company to have high potential, that is, the ability and talent to eventually lead one of its major operating units. I was a "rising star," shooting up through the ranks like a rocket. I seldom spent more than a year in a job before being asked to move on to larger responsibilities.

I'll explain in later chapters some of the ways in which I worked to leverage my potential, but for the moment, let me just point out a few interesting aspects of my years at IBM.

Poughkeepsie was an IBM ghetto. We lived in an area where many other managers and their families also lived, and, for a dollar a year, we belonged to the IBM country club, whose entire membership worked for the company. Once my wife was asked by neighbors what sort of furniture I had in my office. The answer to that seemingly innocent question would have let the neighbors know my precise status in the company as well as my salary range, for at IBM, furniture and office size went hand in glove with job level and, of course, salary, so as a result, everyone was able to know everyone else's business. I wasn't crazy about this arrangement. I did have interests outside of IBM and wanted to continue to cultivate them; in such an all-enveloping environment, that was made difficult.

I was different from the rest of the IBMers. I soon discovered that most managers at IBM had come from various places in the United States, and were experts in their own fields, whether technical, marketing, or finance—but they only knew what they'd learned in school. They were middle Americans, I was not. My background set me apart from them in many ways. For one thing, my calling card, my Ph.D., put me in somewhat exclusive company: my first three bosses also had doctorates, and being certified as an engineer and scientist I became "one of them." For another, I spoke several languages; once, early in my days at IBM, a senior executive asked me to accompany him on a trip to some research facilities in Germany—a trip on which I was able to display not only my knowledge of German but also my worldliness (an important thing when traveling with senior executives who had not had similar experience). I was helpful, and it brought me to the notice of managers who could and did boost my career. Because I'd lived through so much, and seemed more mature than my years, I usually had older friends who happened to have more senior positions, and these, too, assisted me.

IBM was growing rapidly, hiring thousands of people, empowering managers all over the place. Almost anyone who wanted to be a manager could obtain a first- or second-level job. To shoot quickly beyond other managers, to break out of the lower levels of management, I had to build a reputation as a manager who got things done—a "can do" person rather than one who just talked a good game and could not deliver what he had promised. I learned early not to make excuses; what counted was performance. IBM's environment of constant growth helped provide opportunities for me to demonstrate my abilities. Although I'd never had a course in business before I came to IBM, I managed high-technology areas, ranging from semiconductors (chips) to factory automation (Future Manufacturing Systems). I served as group director of organization, and as executive assistant to the chief financial officer (CFO), who was also a member of IBM's board of directors; working with him afforded me exposure to the top management of the company.

This last-named position was perhaps my biggest break, and it came after I'd been with IBM only four years. I was able to force my superiors to take me out of operations and to apprentice me to the CFO; this move allowed me to make my mark in finance, a big differentiator for anyone who aspires to be a top officer of a multibillion-dollar corporation. (I'll amplify this and other career-choice points in later chapters.)

In many respects the company was very good to me, and I was a great fan of IBM and a cheerleader for the company both within it and when in the outside world. I liked the company's egalitarian ways: I don't think that even the most senior executives had company cars; offices were nice, but spare. The company both preached and practiced respect for the individual, and as a business entity IBM had a lot of character and integrity—all things which I personally found important. I had misgivings about the decision-making process, which I considered cumbersome and overly burdened with support staffs, committees, and task forces; I had similar worries about the waste rate of the research and capital investment dollars we were so generously spending; but, on the whole, in those days I was a thoroughgoing IBM man.

As my reputation and abilities grew, I was increasingly handed assignments in troubled areas, and was soon considered a managerial Mr. Fix-it. One such assignment was called Future Manufacturing Systems. FMS, which had thousands of people and an enormous budget, was in the process of developing automated factories that would produce the components for a new series of computers. I was told to salvage what I could of this expensive and complicated long-term project. By the end of seven years, I was getting tired of cleaning up such messes. By then, too, I had learned enough about management to know I wanted to work in a corporation that would have a management structure different from the functional one employed by IBM. By a functional structure, I mean that there were separate divisions for engineering, manufacturing, sales, customer service, and so on, rather than fully integrated business units that were responsible for profits and losses. Because of its functional structure, IBM had almost no managers who had total responsibility for a bottom line; to assess profitability, one had to combine the efforts of engineering, manufacturing, sales, marketing, and a few more parts. At that time, I thought being functionally organized was just fine for IBM—but it no longer suited the career path or the sensibilities of Paul Stern. I had a burning desire to run an integrated business unit in which I would have my own engineering, manufacturing, marketing, sales, service, and support staff, and where my performance—my results—would be measured strictly in terms of profits and losses and the balance sheet.

Occasionally, during my seven years at IBM, I'd been approached by recruiters, and had at times interviewed outside for jobs—principally to see what my market value might be. I had been offered loftier titles and much greater income than I was earning at IBM, but from companies that were also functionally organized. I'd turned down those jobs, although I concluded that I'd outgrown both IBM and the functional organization. I also knew that my market value was considerably higher than what I was then earning. In large organizations, I now knew, it was the general managers, the people who ran integrated business units, who held the true power and earned the highest incomes; they were the candidates from whom were usually chosen those who would hold the top five jobs in big companies. If I could find a job managing a good-sized business unit, it would be a springboard for me, a way to get into the inner circle at a big company.

It was difficult for me to leave a company that had been so good to me in so many ways, but corporate loyalty was not a concept in my vocabulary. I didn't believe it existed—in regard to IBM or to any other industrial institution. In any event, an offer from the electrical consumer products company Braun A.G., then a company controlled by Gillette, had all the ingredients to excite me.

I was to go to Germany and join the upper-management team, known formally in German as the *vorstand*, or VO; the opportunity to become chief operating officer (COO) and, later, CEO of Braun was held out to me in terms that allowed me to believe those goals to be realistic. The company had troubled divisions and product line problems that had caused its profits to fall below expectations—so Mr. Fix-It would have a chance to participate in turning it around while at the same time gaining international experience and receiving good pay as well as the considerable benefits and perks of being an expatriate employee of an American concern. In short, I saw that jumping to Braun would augment my résumé and would someday provide an outstanding ticket to a top job in a very large American corporation. I thought Gillette was taking a substantial risk to hire me when they could have hired any number of German nationals who had spent time working in their industry in the U.S.—especially since I had had absolutely no experience with consumer products. I didn't know Braun's electrical shavers, for instance; as a matter of fact, I shaved wet, that is, with a blade, and knew absolutely nothing about the technology or marketing of electrical shavers. Or coffee-makers and other kitchen appliances, which Braun also manufactured. But I went to Germany, and in four and a half years managed to accomplish nearly everything I'd set out to do. We turned the company around; I became the COO (chief operating officer) and then served as both the chairman and the CEO.

At Braun I established a cadre of managers to whom I could turn over the company and feel confident that its success would continue. My oldest child was about ready to enter high school, and my wife and I felt that the education all three of our children had been receiving at the Frankfurt International School was not adequate to their needs. So when I was recruited for a high-level job at the corporate headquarters of Rockwell International, I jumped at it—with what, in retrospect, seems to have been mistaken haste. I wanted a ticket back to the United States, and this job at Rockwell appeared to be just the thing. I was to be Vice President for Strategic Management, to report directly to the chairman and CEO, and to be responsible for acquisitions, divestitures, and joint ventures— areas new to me that would enhance my portfolio of skills. It was the era when big deal-making was coming into flower, and I would be able to participate in its blooming. The company was widely diversified, and manufactured power tools, water meters, valves, automotive products, and sophisticated commercial and defense electronics as well as the B-1 bomber and the space shuttle.

We moved to Pittsburgh. After a few months at Rockwell, in addition to my other tasks I was asked to take on the position of president of its troubled Commercial Electronics Operations, whose headquarters was near Dallas. Corporate headquarters was in Pittsburgh, but the upper management had taken to having many important meetings in what was styled the Corporate Office at El Segundo, California, and of course I frequently had to be in Texas to oversee parts of some of the troubled divisions that now reported to me. I bounced back and forth from Pittsburgh to Dallas to California to other locations for my division—so much that I was hardly ever at home. Moreover, there were problems in the upper management that I hadn't known existed. I should and could have known about these if I'd done more research, but I hadn't done enough homework on Rockwell because I had been too eager to return to the States. Almost as soon as I'd taken the job I'd learned that their style might be good for them, but it wasn't healthy for me. I decided to leave. Rockwell might have turned into a costly mistake for me, because to take such a big job and then to bail out after a short stay is not looked upon favorably in many circles. However, the company fit neither my style nor my future plans, and so I needed to leave quickly. Through contacts I'd made in the investment community in the course of my deal-making for Rockwell, and through executive recruiters I'd befriended in the past, I began to finesse my way out. I wanted to find a job that would put me back on my career path in terms of job level, income, and opportunity to reach the top.

The right job came along in an offer from W. Michael Blumenthal, who had recently resigned as President Jimmy Carter's secretary of the treasury and had become CEO of the Burroughs Corporation of Detroit. I joined Burroughs in January of 1981 as executive vice-president for engineering and manufacturing, with a very good chance of becoming president and COO in the near future. I worked hard, and because I'd produced the desired results while restructuring and rebuilding the engineering and manufacturing operations, I was chosen in May of 1982 to be president, COO, and a director of the company. In my own terms, I had now arrived. My salary as president, the short- and long-term bonuses, substantial stock options and the like had at last afforded me the independence I had sought.

Because the atmosphere was collegial and the business environment was stimulating, I continued on at Burroughs; we were making great progress and having fun while working very hard. Soon after I began there, the company set out to grow internally and also by acquisitions, and did so in the years between 1981 and 1985. We bought the System Development Corporation, which strengthened our markets in government-related systems and with other systems integration customers. Then we bought three smaller companies, one that produced communications processors, another that developed applications software for educational institutions, and the third, which was in computer-aided design. The largest acquisition of the era was, of course, Memorex, whose disk drive technology we urgently needed. By 1985, through internal growth and acquisitions, Burroughs had grown from a company with just over $2 billion a year in sales to a $5 billion corporation that also had significantly improved profitability and a very respectable balance sheet.

To challenge IBM at all levels, though, Burroughs would have to be even larger, and that was the prime reason Blumenthal and I met with the top officials of Sperry in April of 1985 to discuss a merger of our two companies that would result in a $10-billion-a-year giant, a company big enough to make a dent in some of IBM's markets. Sperry resisted our offer. News of our discussions leaked out and the stocks of both companies swung wildly. The merger idea was dropped, and we went back to the drawing board, but kept coming up with the necessity of growing larger by affiliating Sperry and Burroughs—and so, a year later, in May of 1986, we acquired our rival outright, in a deal that was at that time one of the three largest in industrial history, alongside Allied-Signal and GE-RCA.

For many reasons, the acquisition was dubbed a merger, and for me it created as many problems as opportunities. In the aftermath of any large acquisition, especially in the data processing industry, there exists a good deal of nervousness among both employees and customers. Former Sperry and Burroughs customers wanted to know whether existing product lines would be continued, so they would not have to change or place at risk their investments in costly systems architecture. Customers also sought reassurance that their contact people from the old companies would stay on and be of service to them. Employees, of course, wanted to know if they would retain their jobs, or get new ones, or be pushed out altogether in the inevitable elimination of redundant positions and facilities. For Mike Blumenthal, chairman of the new company, this unease translated into difficulty in senior management. He was fortunate in that Sperry's former chairman, Jerry Probst, announced his intention to retire. However, Blumenthal was faced with the problem of having two presidents on hand: Joe Kroger had been president of Sperry, and I, of Burroughs. How could Blumenthal keep us both in harness—and, by extension, keep those that were loyal to us? If he appointed one of us to be president and COO, the likelihood was that the second man would resign. Further, he must have felt that neither of us would readily agree to work under the other man.

Blumenthal's solution was to propose an Executive Office to run the company, an office that would consist of himself, Joe Kroger as vice-chairman, myself as president (but not as COO—a title which the terms of my contract guaranteed me), and Jim Unruh, former CFO of Burroughs, as Executive Vice-President and the fourth member. Since Blumenthal's style had been very much hands-off, I think Unruh was asked to join to be a tie-breaker if Kroger and I couldn't agree on an issue. The Executive Office was to meet at least once a week to discuss and decide matters of general importance; in addition, each of us was to be contact executive for various parts of the business. Unruh's domain was all the corporate staffs, such as the financial, legal, and human resource people. He was also to manage the divestiture of "nonessential" businesses for cash to pay down the substantial debt generated by the acquisition of Sperry. Kroger was to deal with commercial sales and service of all nondefense business products worldwide. I was to be responsible for the company's defense businesses; its nondefense work for other government agencies; the manufacturing, engineering, and development of all our products; and the product management functions that oversaw our product lines. In addition, as president I was to be held responsible for the overall profitability of the company. I was the one who managed the quarterly and annual financial results for the entire corporation, and was also in charge of putting together the company's annual budget.

I hated the concept of an Executive Office. It was a bad idea, a committee with no real purpose but to hamper the decision-making process and diffuse responsibility among its members. I had lived with such a committee at Braun, the *vorstand*, because it was required by German law, but I didn't think any such committee ought to exist when there was no legal requirement for it. In the EO, we had imposed on ourselves a form of governance that most companies in the world longed to shed.

It was time for me to leave. I had a nice golden parachute, and would open it. Blumenthal and several members of the old Burroughs board prevailed on me to try the committee concept for a year; they said I owed it to them, and to the many people I'd brought into Burroughs, to stay through the transition period. I agreed, and moved immediately to the suburbs of Philadelphia, near what we were billing as one of the new company's dual headquarters, the former Sperry facility in Bluebell, Pennsylvania.

As I had suspected, the EO system didn't work. Blumenthal soon found it impossible to attend our weekly meetings, and direction was left to Kroger, Unruh, and me. But since I had responsibility for budgets and profitability, I constantly had to drive the company forward. To accomplish that I had to constantly convince and direct managers who were supposed to report to Kroger and Unruh and give them direction as well as monitor their programs. My efforts to assure profitability thus had the side effect of sabotaging the committee, although this had not been my intent. However, I continued to do it, believing that if I did not take this sort of direct charge, the company would not achieve its objectives. During this transition period we consolidated facilities, people, and resources and made the new company more profitable than the two old ones had been; in 1987 Unisys stock jumped ahead substantially.

However, the committee structure kept hampering all of us. Working at Unisys was no longer fun. For the first time in my career, I was not looking forward each day to going to my job. Having been successful at managing companies, I wanted, and believed I had earned, the luxury of operating a business my own way or not being part of it at all. Joe Kroger admitted to me privately in March of 1987 that the current structure wasn't working. He said he'd told Blumenthal that I had done a terrific job as president and that he, Kroger, ought to be reporting to me as COO. Later, I braced Blumenthal about that conversation, and expressed my unhappiness. He verified that Kroger had said all those nice things about me, but counseled patience, saying he'd reorganize in the fall of that year. By this time, outsiders learned that I was restive; headhunters and large companies tried to recruit me. Some offers were very attractive. I informed Mike that I wasn't inclined to take any of the jobs, good as they were, but I had to know what he planned to do about the intolerable working environment at Unisys.

At this point, I held almost all the cards. Since the formation of Unisys, I had exceeded all of our objectives; Joe Kroger and Jim Unruh had both admitted that the structure didn't work; further, Joe was willing to report to me; also, I had outside offers; last of all, the contract given to me by the Burroughs board of directors read that I would be president and COO of the Burroughs Corporation or its successor, and that if these titles and responsibilities weren't awarded to me I was to receive a large financial settlement.

This created an impasse for Blumenthal, who likes to be in control of every situation and often becomes personally offended if someone wishes to leave "his" company. After asking me not to leave, he agreed to work closely with me over the next few weeks to develop an organizational structure which would do away with the EO and make me president and COO. I outlined a few organizational concepts and refined them with him before the May board meeting, to be held in London. We had already agreed on the structure but had yet to finish deciding precisely which people were to get what jobs, and this last hitch prevented the document from being finished in time for the May meeting. We agreed to meet during the second week of June, in our Pennsylvania headquarters, to tidy up the final details. By this time, and especially after having worked with Blumenthal for seven years, it was clear to me that he was dragging his feet, aggravated because I had the upper hand and was forcing him into a decision he had hoped to delay. The rift between us had widened considerably, but I was determined to bring the matter of the structure to a head, no matter what the consequences. As far as I was concerned, I had fulfilled my obligations to those who had asked me to stay through the transition. It was time to go. During the first week of August 1987, Blumenthal and I agreed to part ways. I insisted on staying on as president until December 31, 1987, because I wanted my tenure to extend through the first full year of the new company, a year of successes for which I wished to take the credit I knew was due to me.

As I had believed would happen, after the announcement of my impending resignation was made public Blumenthal did not appoint anyone else to the presidency of Unisys, but, rather, changed the name of the EO to the Board of Management, and expanded it to seven people—a bigger committee. Then, as I was winding things up in December, Unisys was further shocked by Joe Kroger's apparently sudden decision also to leave the company as of the end of 1987.

I didn't look back. I was forty-nine, in good health and financially independent enough to do whatever I wished to do for the rest of my life. I decided to take a breather, not even entertain thoughts of joining another company in the near future. And "retirement" proved good to me; it was the first time in years that I had the leisure to pursue personal and family interests—I took up painting, improved my tennis, traveled extensively with my family. I write this chapter while aboard the *Queen Elizabeth II*, cruising through the Strait of Magellan off the coast of South America, gazing at some of the most beautiful scenery in the world, thankful to have earned the money and time to enjoy it, and blessed with conviction and enough philosophical distance from the corporate world to set guidelines to help readers of this book go straight to the top—as I did.

3

The Three
Key Tasks

A *PERSON* who is serious about managing his or her own career will have three tasks always in mind. Everything else a manager does is secondary and subservient to these three major ideas.

CREATE AN IMAGE OF PROFESSIONALISM

Corporations are large, highly impersonal places. To advance rapidly, you need to create an image that will distinguish you from your colleagues, a positive, can do image that will force people around you—and several ranks above you—to know who you are. In corporations, what helps you to advance is not only what you do, but how you are perceived. Your reputation is of the essence, and you must do everything in your power to be thought of as a person of quality. The image has to do with virtually every detail of the way you conduct your life, including your manners and lifestyle, even the clothes you wear.

The externals part—how you dress—is the most easily discernible. However, your style must be consistent with the environment in which you find yourself. At IBM, where the dress code was conservative, it would have been silly to wear patterned shirts and loud sports coats when everyone around me wore button-down white shirts and dark suits. (Woe to the person who stands out—in a negative sense.) I had to conform. However, I was determined to dress in my own style. I wore the dark suits, but they were European tailored; I wore white shirts, but only those that were a bit different from the norm: mine had French cuffs. In my office furnishings (and home, too), I tried for quality and excellence in everything: where my colleagues had framed posters on their walls, I scrimped to buy and display original works of art, some from the Renaissance period, and Oriental rugs, all of which we still have at home. When my colleagues drove Chevrolets, I put my money into sports cars—they were much more fun. In all these instances, I considered my purchases as investments of the best sort, investments in my future.

> Always remember to treat your image—indeed, your whole career—as a product that you are managing and marketing.

Was it pretentious for me to display Oriental rugs and drive sports cars? No, I don't think so. My goal was to stand out from the crowd; if I failed to do so, I'd be unable to advance as rapidly as my private career plan required, something I wouldn't allow. So, if I wore European clothes, well, I had a background that differed from that of my colleagues, and could show it. It also helped that I liked this particular style—and that era in art—and cavorting in a sports car—for if I'd simply had such things around as props, they would have been meaningless.

As I look back on it now, I define what I was doing in my image-building as showing my colors as a true internationalist at a time when many American companies were fixated on this country alone. I spoke several languages, and saw no reason to hide that; rather, I wanted to use my knowledge to further my career. I appreciated products and styles that originated or were celebrated beyond the borders of the United States—French wines, Italian tailoring, Mexican hot peppers, Persian rugs. I learned to enjoy the best in everything, and to insist on it in every area of my life.

There's a German word, *korrekt*, which isn't quite translatable into English—the dictionary suggests "irreproachable," but that is only an approximation—that sums up how I envisioned my behavior toward other people. *Korrekt* is also a synonym for having integrity, but in German the concept goes beyond the mere possession of integrity to indicate a person whose integrity has never been compromised and will not be, even in the future. A *korrekt* person will protect other people's property and integrity perhaps even more fiercely than he does his own, and behaves toward others in a manner that assumes and champions at all times the other person's basic dignity and humanity. For instance, there are some people who, in their conversations, never come right out and lie, but nonetheless say things that lead their listeners to wrong conclusions; a *korrekt* person won't countenance such behavior.

One outward manifestation of a person's behavior is manners. They are a visible way in which others perceive you. Let me provide . . .

> Bad Example # 1: If My Mother Could See Me Now . . .
> I've seen some powerful corporate executives who'll take their shoes off while they're in a meeting, or light pungent cigars without asking others if it's all right to do so. (I enjoy a good cigar, too, but only in the right circumstances.) Of course no one junior to them is going to voice their displeasure at shoeless feet, even if the feet are then put up on the conference table or desk, or at the cigar, because the juniors don't wish to offend the boss. But the boss is offending them; in fact, the boss may be doing these things partly as a demonstration of his power. Other such demonstrations: keeping people waiting for appointments; failing to answer correspondence or to return telephone calls.

Would the boss put his shoeless feet on the dining table at home? Would he wish a still higher executive to blow cigar smoke in his face as an irritant? Or not return his phone calls? Probably not.

> Courtesy toward others must not be altered in relation to the status or power of the person with whom you're dealing.

You should act in the same courteous manner toward a junior as toward a senior. And such courtesy must extend through a whole range of behavior. Courtesy must be the guiding principle behind those actions you take which might seem ordinary but which can add up to a positive image. For example, don't have your shoes shined when you're in a meeting with others, even if it's convenient; it shows a disdain for everyone else in the room. If you're in a one-on-one session with a colleague (either senior or junior), don't take any phone calls. Devote your wholehearted attention to the person across the desk; it's common courtesy. Or maybe, these days, it's uncommon courtesy.

Courtesy isn't an affectation, it's a mirror of character. Although good manners don't always prove that the person who displays them is a good person, the opposite—a display of bad manners—is a more reliable indicator of character. Unfailingly, when I've run into someone who's purposefully discourteous (as opposed to one who doesn't know better and makes honest mistakes), sooner or later, in their business dealings, that person reveals still more offensive personal actions; they show themselves to be bad characters.

One of the worst consequences of bad behavior or discourtesy is that such a style of behaving toward others on the part of a top executive is almost always replicated down the line. For instance, some top executives are notorious for their foul-mouthedness. Their obscenities are echoed by those who attend meetings with the chiefs, and then repeated to the troops so that they become a part of the corporate culture—often with unfortunate results when those executives interact with others who don't salt their conversation with four-letter words.

Beyond obscenities lurk ethnic jokes and slurs, which are equally dangerous and offensive. Yes, I know that some people like to make such jokes as a way of loosening up a conversation, getting a laugh, establishing a sense of camaraderie, but often the demeaning of a culture or a nationality can have unforeseen consequences:

Bad Example #2: Did You Hear the One About . . . ?
I was recently at a high-level meeting of an international company with a man I'd never met, and he was talking lightly about
the propensity of Jews for business. I could feel that some of
the participants found this offensive, and I knew that such behavior invariably colored my own view of a new acquaintance
and would continue to do so for some time to come. The man
didn't know that yet; in fact, he might never catch on that he
had offended other people—but the damage was done.

Remember that when you make an ethnic joke, people may laugh,
but long after the laughter is gone the person you've offended will
still recall the slight.

And then there's gossip. The same formulation applies to be-
hind-the-back talk about employees' private lives. I've often been
in the position where someone tells me tales about a mutual
acquaintance. I try not to pass them on, and, indeed, often say that
I'd rather not be privy to such stories at all. My strong feeling is that
those who revel in gossip will themselves one day be the subject of
equally noxious rumors.

By gossiping or telling ethnic jokes, what the joke-teller is trying
to do is be "one of the guys." Now, demonstrating your common
humanity with your peers, subordinates, and superiors is an essential
thing to do in business, because the manager who is considered
humorless, unable to let his hair down, or unbearably inflexible will
be shunned. But there are other ways to be a good companion.

Looking into the subject a bit more deeply, we can see that the
essential in being one of the guys is generating *trust* between yourself
and those around you. Making gossip and telling ethnic jokes just
aren't the right ways to go about building trust.

> Trust in business is a serious and delicate matter; it is also a form of
> risk-taking—to trust someone, you must surrender some of your au-
> tonomy.

In a large, integrated company, the managers and executives
are continuously interdependent. Each department and division

must pursue not only its own goals, but the goals of the other parts of the company and of the company as a whole. All the managers must understand that any one of them, acting alone, cannot really succeed unless he or she helps the other managers to succeed. And that takes trust among the managers. Successful managers will trust not only in themselves and in their colleagues, but also in the corporation's priorities. It's been my experience that most managers who make it to the top do so by always putting the company's interests first—by putting their trust in maximizing those interests —even if that sometimes means sacrificing group or personal ambitions.

It's imperative that your colleagues believe in their hearts that you will act properly toward them; they need to *trust* you to do so. How do you make them feel that way? By being trustworthy! It's the classic chicken and egg problem—which came first, the trust or the trustworthiness? To get at it, redefine trust as being of two sorts or existing on two levels. The first is, "I trust you to do the job." That means that I believe you're competent enough to take on the tasks in your bailiwick. A résumé or a quick meeting may show that an employee is worthy of this sort of trust. The second meaning or level might be represented by the phrase, "I trust you not to hurt me by your actions." This is what I consider to be *real* trust.

Here's the paradigm: I tell you something in confidence. I know, though I probably don't say so, that if you misuse this information, I stand to lose much more than you will gain if you use it irresponsibly. So I'm counting on you—indeed, I'm quite dependent on you—to keep the trust and not divulge what I've said to third parties. Once the information-giver sees that the sensitive material hasn't been compromised, a trusting relationship is established. If you act so that people have reason to believe you won't hurt them, others will feel comfortable with you and will stick by you; further, they'll act in a trustworthy manner toward you.

To state it another way: *the real litmus test of trust is to be as good as your word.* For example, when I promise something to a subordinate—say, a pay raise or a transfer to take effect within eighteen months, contingent upon he or she completing a particularly onerous task—I put it in writing. Some managers blanch at doing this, because they make idle promises to get people to perform, and never expect to have to pay off. But if you are sincere about a promise, it won't hurt you to put a memo in the office files. And on the other side of the coin: if you set a demanding pace and expect it of others, if you insist on performance from your subordinates in terms of target dates when production schedules are supposed to be met, or sales quotas to be achieved, or percentages of overhead to be pared, then you must be as tough as your word. Some people equate toughness with being a nasty and uncaring person. I don't. You can be tough by being fair, by setting out expectations, rewarding achievement, and punishing inadequate work with an even hand. (More about being tough in Chapter Sixteen.)

So: creating an image is the first task. If this were a book on "getting ahead in business without really trying," I could stop right there, or go on to demonstrate little tricks on burnishing your personal image and avoiding the essential work of business. But it's not a book on image alone. Image won't get you to the top. Nor will "gamesmanship." Such things will get you ahead, but not very far. The point is that to truly inhabit the image of a manager who stands out from the crowd, you have to perform your work well, spectacularly well. And that's why I say that the second task is to . . .

DELIVER . . . BETTER THAN EXPECTED

In my terminology, to deliver means to do the tasks that have been set in front of you better than anyone else in your position is expected to—to exceed the sales quota, increase profits beyond the planned amount, manage expenses so that you keep them below budgeted targets, develop the product ahead of schedule, build the best team, give the best service. As a manager, you will be judged on your *performance*. Most people think they know what performance means in these contexts, yet in business it often seems hard to achieve the kind of results that make you stand out from the pack. An inability to do so may derive from an incomplete understanding of how performance is evaluated. It's not only how you perform, but how those who are weighing your performance evaluate what you have done and are capable of doing.

In an ideal world, high performers would invariably be rewarded just because they were good at what they did. Unfortunately, the world of big corporations isn't an ideal one, and so you must . . .

LEVERAGE YOUR PERFORMANCE

To "leverage" means to do those things that will bring your efforts to the notice of your superiors and that will result in added rewards and promotions for you. Thus the second task is interlinked with the third. I'll discuss them together.

I've found, to my chagrin, that in business many employees don't know what hard work is. In terms of what is expected from managers, hard work is lots of mental labor of the sort that computers can't replace, the brain work of trying to figure things out. Hard work does not simply consist of putting in long hours, though long hours are an element of the mix. For the most part, hard work has to do with an insistence on excellence, an insistence on professionalism, starting with a manager's demanding high personal standards. *Hard work is mental labor that is measured not only in terms of hours, but also in terms of productivity, output, and quality of results.*

Even as a relatively junior manager, I always insisted on doing things well myself, and, certainly, on making sure that everything that came out of my domain was as near perfect as my team and I could make it. In contrast, I present . . .

Bad Example #3: Sorry About That, Folks . . .
Have you ever gone to a meeting and found that your copy of an important document had several pages missing, or important data was copied aslant or half-off the page? That's not only annoying, it's an indication that the person in charge of the department that issued the report hasn't insisted on quality in everything his or her department does. There's no excuse for mediocrity in business, and sloppiness is one sure symptom of mediocrity, of letting things slide, of doing a half-good job when only a superb job will do. It costs no more to prepare proper copies. Inability to do so demonstrates a willingness to settle for mediocrity. Other examples: sending out correspondence full of typographical errors, or not having the department's phones answered after the first few rings. Or not instructing secretaries to handle complaint calls from customers properly —that is, putting them through to the manager whom the caller is really trying to reach, rather than automatically referring them to the complaint department.

> The antidote to mediocrity is to be an example of excellence yourself and to demand it from your subordinates, even in the matter of small, supposedly inconsequential details.

If you demand that tasks be done properly, and reward those who accomplish that and express your displeasure to those who don't, you'll raise your quality quotient.

Let me take a moment to define quality. In America, quality has often seemed to mean only an aura of luxury that's associated with a finished product. That definition is too narrow. For me, *quality is the expression of professionalism in all areas of business.* As a manager, by insisting on quality and hard work, you can create the actuality, in addition to the image, of a well-run department. For instance, you can use superior materials, insist on superior workmanship, and eliminate second best practices in every area of the business. When I was at Burroughs, we instituted the first vice-president for quality at the corporate level of a multibillion-dollar high-technology company in the United States. He reported directly to me as president. The high level of his job sent a signal to our customers that we were serious about our commitment to quality; in fact, it helped us to improve our customer relations. (More about quality in a later chapter.)

Reading and answering all mail overnight was a highly visible way to increase the efficiency level of my own performance. I'd often go home with two full briefcases, sometimes three, and after spending some time with my family I'd read into the night. Customer letters containing questions or complaints were high on my list. If these had been addressed to my superior, and I got copies, I'd try to read them and respond to the problems before my boss could even get to them. Or if they were addressed to one of my subordinates, and it was I who had gotten the copy, I'd digest the material so I could call the subordinate in the morning and find out what he or she was going to do about the difficulty. There were almost no occasions when a colleague of mine would have read his or her copy of a customer letter before I had—and that gave me an edge. I'd do the same with internal progress reports, noting schedules, costs, specifications, and the status of the task, or with copies of internal correspondence—say, a memo from a manager in Europe to someone in production. Reading such documents early would let me know where bottlenecks were and give me an opportunity to do something about them.

Does this sound like a task impossible for you to do? Or does it sound like the calling card of a workaholic? It is neither. Rather, it is an aspect of "working smart," applying oneself to tasks that will most directly leverage your performance. Gaining control over the information flow in your office is one of the most important things you can do. Most people let the paperwork overwhelm them—but if you're intent on getting ahead, you've got to charge into that paper with determination.

I also used to read, as a matter of course and to keep up with what was going on in the world, business and national news publications. This was important to my career in that it added to my knowledge base; it also didn't hurt my image. Other senior executives evidently do the same thing. A survey by Accountemps, reported in *The Wall Street Journal* of September 13, 1988, reports that top executives "find time to know more than their underlings about local, national, international, and business news," while "middle managers are more up on sports."

Another aspect of my improved performance was a trained memory. I was well known for having a prodigious memory, but it wasn't because of mnemonic tricks. Actually, I read rather slowly—as one would read an engineering report, in which every word counts and must be understood. But in reading slowly, I'd take the time to commit important facts to memory. Then I'd ruminate over these almost constantly. Having key facts in memory, say, the early forecast for sales, I'd be able to mentally compare the current sales figures to the budgeted numbers, as well as those for previous years (trend analysis). On airplanes, while waiting for transportation, even while sitting on the beach on vacation, I'd think about important facts and figures from the business and what actions could be taken to affect them. Because I had key facts in memory, I didn't have to carry with me the paper on which the figures were written, and so I could put thought into them at any moment when I had the time. What were the expense categories, and how were they growing from year to year? How much of the overhead was associated with this manufacturing operation versus how much for that? The production team said it could only make nine hundred units this quarter, but three years ago, I remembered, the sales team reported sales of one thousand units during a quarter. Didn't that mean output could be pushed higher?

I would come back from a trip having conjured some permutations on the figures—and be ahead of people who had just glanced at a report and hadn't really taken the time or used the mental energy to consider its implications or to dream up other ways of doing things.

At a meeting, I'd be able to make reference to many matters without need of notes. That impresses people not only because it is a demonstration of memory, but also because it shows that your mind is engaged in understanding all elements of the business and with the most concise details of the company. In later years, when a middle manager would send a report to me and then come in person to discuss it, he or she would know that I'd have retained all the important data from the papers I'd been sent, and so they'd have to be on their toes in discussing their briefs.

> **Always do your homework, especially in areas where other people won't bother to do so, and you will gain valuable perspective.**

When I came into a new job or department or division or company, I'd devote a lot of time to exploring how it worked. What was the history? The past performance? How did the structure evolve? On coming in to Burroughs, I checked out of the company library twenty years of annual and quarterly reports, and read them over a four-day weekend. By steeping myself in the history, I came to know about the company's successes and failures, what they'd told their shareholders, how they communicated to employees, how departments and divisions had been created. I gained a long, historical view of the company; that helped me evaluate the situation at the moment.

For example, in going over some reports, it dawned on me that I didn't know how many of our U.S. employees and managers were working abroad, and how many of our foreign nationals we had brought over to work with us in this country. Both these categories of expatriates were being paid at extraordinary rates, with allowances for housing, schooling for their children, cars, trips home, and other perks. The biggest item was the extra taxes that we paid so that employees' income would not suffer from their being posted in another country. For an employee whose cost to the company when in the U.S. would be $100,000 per year, we were actually spending from $500,000 to $800,000 per year for that employee overseas, the high end of the scale being for employees in Japan or Hong Kong. It turned out that nobody in the company knew how many expatriates we had—not personnel, not the division heads. It took weeks to gather the data; we found there were hundreds of employees in this category, some of whom had been living overseas for periods of up to ten years. One reason for a foreign assignment was to season someone for two or three years before bringing that person back into the fold. But the major reason for having expatriates was the sometimes real, but sometimes only perceived shortage of certain kinds of skills in various overseas subsidiaries. However, a U.S. citizen living and working in, say, France for ten years, with extra salary and perks—and who didn't really intend ever to come back to the U.S., except for vacations and to renew a passport— was virtually an in-country employee. Had we used a French national in his stead, even if we trained him here first and then sent him back to France, it would cost us less, because we wouldn't be obligated to pay for his children's schooling and all the other expenses. At Burroughs, after I'd looked into the matter, we were able to phase down the excessive use of expatriate employees, which eventually resulted in substantial savings, and, in many instances, obtained better levels of performance through the use of foreign nationals in their home countries.

In corporations, we're always concerned with figures. I also developed super-competence by *studying our numbers in ways that many managers never do.* For instance, it's understood that the accounting procedures allowed, demanded, or encouraged by various government agencies can change how a company reports its revenues, its costs of doing business, its profits, and its balance sheet. Generally, though, the perusal of the supposedly arcane documents that regulate a company's accounting are thought to be the province of the financial officers and outside accountants and auditors. I discovered that key documents, such as the FASB reports, are available to everyone and that they could be studied to good effect.

What I found in FASB-II, for instance, was nothing less than the ground rules for the game of corporate hardball that I was engaged in playing. It's not only a background paper; it also has a lot of judgment in it, and the implications to be drawn from it were significant. You wouldn't play baseball or hockey without knowing the rules, would you? Why do less with finance and accounting? FASB-II gave the rules for determining what sort of R&D costs should be taken as current expenses—to be deducted from current year gross profits—as opposed to which of those costs should be capitalized as product development monies and amortized over a longer period of time. Executives of a company oriented toward short-term profit tend to want to capitalize development expenses and amortize them against product cost over the first few years of production. I'd know, however, that such a strategem mortgages the future, and that I'd have to continue using the FASB-II guidelines for some time if I started with them. FASB-1987, for another instance, has a lot to do with pension accounting funds and other matters relating to nontraditional compensation. By reading such reports, I learned new tools. Beyond that, I benefited because when I understood them I was able to participate in discussions with financial officers and outside auditors on the positives and negatives of implementing certain financial guidelines. This allowed me not to be at the mercy of those experts, and to make better-informed choices. Of course, my demonstration of this sort of knowledge also impressed those around me, because it became obvious that I knew more than a man in my position was expected to know.

My concentration on history and figures was part of my concern—some would call it my obsession—with the bottom line. During your own long management career, your bottom line may not always be measured by profits. For some time, in a corporation, you may be at a level where you're not directly impacting the company's profitability. But *there is always a bottom line for any managerial activity, and it is always a measure of performance.* It can be designated in many ways: your boss may see it in terms of meeting a schedule, or building a team, or keeping a weather eye on expenses; you might need to adhere to a production schedule, as gauged by certain milestones. If you're in a staff position, say in a legal department, performance might be measured by progress on an important suit, or by the filing of a significant patent. Some start-up departments might determine success by the speed at which they add to their staff or the quality of the new hires. I always made it my business to beat production schedules; to score higher than my predecessors (or than I had the previous year) on such measures as opinion surveys of employee morale; to cut expenses by more than the target amount; to "grow" sales faster than the expected rate.

Later on, of course, when you're at a higher level, your primary concern ought to be growth, market share, and the actual bottom line; you should gauge whatever your department, division, or other part of the company is doing in terms of the return to the shareholders. Everything else—building a fiefdom, for instance—should be secondary to that prime objective. This may seem obvious, but, given the games I've seen played at all levels in corporations, it appears not always to be the objective that is pursued. In my organization, at whatever level I was, I'd keep the focus on the key objectives to exceed. My subordinates knew that in every conversation I'd have with them, sooner or later I'd ask, "How does the quarter look?" or, "Are you going to make the numbers?" or some other question to find out how their area was going to impact on our bottom line.

I don't like to lose; in fact, I'm proud to say that during all the time I had responsibilities that impacted on bottom lines, I only had a few occasions that weren't as satisfactory as my projections would have had them be. Both of those were at Burroughs, and they were soon eclipsed by better earnings. In those conversations with subordinates, in addition to asking about the bottom line, I'd also invariably inquire, "What else can I do to help you make or exceed your short- and long-term goals?" That, too, came to be part of my image and my performance.

Lest that be taken as an indication that I only thought about the short-term, I want to note that, for example, while at Burroughs I consistently tried also to work toward long-term goals. For instance, I doubled our spending on engineering over five years; I could have done less research and development, and had more money go into the profits column, but chose rather to spend it on development for the future. Similarly, I helped increase our training expenditures from a few million dollars a year to $80 million, and also put a lot of money into upgrading old facilities and building new ones.

To review some of the notions in this chapter:

1. *Differentiate yourself from the pack by the sustained level of your work and the knowledge you've gained.* Mastering various financial guidance documents, accounting procedures, and a reasonable knowledge of finance weren't just perfecting card tricks; these provided me with knowledge well beyond the norm, and did so at a

time—when I was still in lower management—that also said a lot about me.

2. *Concentrate on getting things done in less time than your competitors and colleagues.* Making sure to get every piece of my day's correspondence answered by the next morning was part of sustaining a pace; my subordinates knew that if they sent me a report, I'd go through it right away and ask follow-up questions about it by the next day. I'd act right away on those that required my signature for authorization, although I didn't always approve them. Invariably, I'd want to know how the information or action was going to impact on the entire organization. I never treated business documents as things to file and forget, and I wouldn't let my subordinates do so, either; I wanted forgettable documents eliminated entirely from the system. This drive and fast pace differentiated me from other managers who operated at a more normal pace.

3. *Lose no opportunity to make known both your desires for advancement and your willingness to do virtually anything for the company and your career.* Keep the pressure on your superiors by demonstrating the quality and pace of your work, and your perpetual state of only partial satisfaction. If your superiors perceive that you're satisfied with your current station in life—that you won't ever consider leaving the company—then your upward progress will be slowed if not crippled, because they know you'll stay even if everything isn't to your liking. If, however, you let people know that you understand you're a high-potential employee, and that you'll leave if you're not challenged, rewarded well, and advanced quickly, that creates pressure on superiors to keep challenging, adequately compensating, and advancing you. That pressure on your part has to be accompanied—above all—by results, as well as by repeated indications of your willingness to work hard, to cut short your vacations, to move (even with your family's small children), to subordinate such things as your love for tennis, golf, hunting, music, or other hobbies to your devotion to the company's tasks.

As I went up the ladder in these big corporations, I noticed that in one way or another, there were always people dropping out of the scramble toward the top. This fellow liked his northeastern suburban community, and didn't want to go overseas to start a new subsidiary. That one was so involved in local community activities that he couldn't work late most evenings. A third one's family was fed up with having moved five times in five years, and he was no longer willing to uproot the children. A fourth was counting the days to retirement and wouldn't leap to a new company, even though he was in his prime years as an executive.

To my mind, those people were not clearly pursuing the objective of a management career in which they were trying very hard to get to the top. Now I must take a moment to point out that not everyone in a corporation is oriented the way I was, and the way I hope you'll be. Many people in corporations look at the more senior executives, see how many hours they put in, how much traveling they have to do, and the price they pay in terms of loss of leisure time, pressure on the families, and so forth—and conclude that such a path is not for them. These people decide, in one way or another, that they like what they're doing, and don't want to pay the dues to be in line for one of the larger jobs. They are interested more in what are now called the "quality of life" factors, and make conscious decisions based on their interests. There are also people who have a profession within the company, say, as an engineer or a scientist or an accountant or even as a lawyer. Usually, those who adhere to such professions in a large company are not as well rewarded as people on the management ladder, but some companies such as IBM, DuPont, and others recognize the value of senior professionals by establishing a separate and relatively high compensation scale for them, and recognizing their achievements in a way that gives them almost equal status with senior managers.

I admire people who know what they want and are dedicated to their objectives, whatever they might be. Considering those outside of the corporate world, I think highly of professionals such as teachers, nurses, doctors, and others, for instance, and inside the corporations I have equal regard for the senior engineering fellows at DuPont and IBM who were at the top of their profession. But this book is not directed to teachers and nurses—or for those whose goal is to become senior professional fellows. It is for managers, and in particular for those who want to climb, and climb fast, in the corporate management world.

Does any of this daunt you? It shouldn't. Maybe you've said to yourself that you want to go straight to the top, but haven't sat down and tried to analyze what will be necessary in order to accomplish that goal. Perhaps you haven't really taken the time to examine your own goals clearly, and to understand their ramifications. You know you can be a hard worker, but have you really invested the time to learn how to achieve results? Maybe your desire is intense, but you've been less than fervent about doing things in order to make your dreams become reality. Now is the time to firm up your resolve, and to look for ways to excel.

So, readers, be warned: you can make an ordinary career by working only a regular day, or by not agreeing to move at the drop of a hat, or while maintaining substantial outside interests, or by making the decision to stay with your current company because of its "security" benefits rather than risking uncertainty in a new one. But recognize, too, that refusal to subordinate other aspects of life to the drive to get to the top will, in general, limit your continued advancement.

4

Establishing Long-Term Goals

A *CAREER starts with a vision, a dream.* Mine was to become a top-level executive with a large American corporation. In such a position, I believed, I'd have immense challenge, personal satisfaction, tremendous prestige, and would earn an income that would afford me a high quality of life as well as eventual financial independence. My dream became an obsession. I thought about what life would be like once I got to the top—I never thought "if" I got there, because I knew I would make it, somehow, sometime. When, along the way, I'd hear a comrade-in-arms complain about the actions of a higher executive and how those constrained him, I'd know that this particular comrade might not get very far. On the other hand, if I heard a colleague questioning the senior management's actions and figuring out alternate ways of attacking the issues, I'd know that here was a serious contender for the upper echelon, for that man—like me—was constantly thinking, consciously or subconsciously, about his long-term goal of getting to the top.

FACTORS THAT INFLUENCE CAREERS

Many disparate factors influence your career. Some are external factors that are beyond your control. Among the most important of these is the mentality of Wall Street—a mind-set that continually insists on short-term, quarterly earnings increases in publicly traded corporations. This pressure often cramps a company's latitudes of managing a business in a balanced way, and can affect the individual manager, too. Other similarly controlling agents are the cycles of the economy and the actions of government and regulatory bodies. A few factors are partly external and partly internal, that is, somewhat within your control. In this group I count the image you burnish by doing work in your home community or your professional community.

This book is principally concerned with the internal factors, the great bulk of influences that affect your career. It suggests that you can control these, set long-term goals and achieve them. Is it truly possible to have long-term career goals? Plenty of sages will tell you that in business such goals can't be properly set, that careers are totally subject to external factors beyond your control, such as the vicissitudes of the marketplace, the personalities of individuals ranking above you in the company, and other exigencies which alter the best-laid plans of would-be corporate executives. I disagree. Goals can be set.

> You must make a multiyear plan and work out ways of measuring progress on it.

A good manager is generally able to do a lot of planning for his or her corporation, to take on a big project, work out the proper milestones to mark its progress, the budgets associated with it, the hundreds of details and checkpoints and ways of measuring its progress. You have to be able to do the same thing with your own career. You have to be specific in terms of targets and the time it will take to implement your actions. Perhaps you feel that right now you can't say precisely where you'll be in five years, but you do know that your long-term goal is to be in one of the top five positions of a big company, ten or more years before retirement age. To achieve that goal, you'll have to reach certain milestones. Now, what are they? You can say to yourself, "Knowing where I want to go, what are the next two or three jobs I ought to have?" Conceived in this way, a long-range plan can be made up of evolving shorter-range plans. If you can work out a good-sized project for a company, there is no reason why you can't apply the same zest and intelligence to achieving your own personal goals.

> **Long-range planning is not only possible—it's essential.**

YOU MUST KNOW YOUR GOAL

A crucial moment in regard to vision and dreams came while I was at IBM and still relatively junior in management. Sixteen of us, fourteen men and two women from various parts of the company, had been gathered at an old estate on Long Island for several weeks of intensive management training. It was a standard advanced management course, and, as is usual in such courses, which are a regular feature of many large companies, we played management games; for instance, on a computer we were given control of a hypothetical company and had to operate it for increased market shares. This group of sixteen was distinguished from the regular cadre of IBM managers; we had all spent several years with the company and had had several promotions. We were also distinguished in that we had been selected as having high potential, which meant that upper management expected us someday to hold one of the top fifty slots in the company, to head up divisions or rise to the level of elected corporate officers. At IBM, there were few ways of knowing if you actually had been designated as high potential—but if you were sent to this exclusive management school, you knew you had made the list . . . for now.

One visiting lecturer at the school, an industrial psychologist, put us through an especially critical experience. It was brought out into the open that we had been dubbed as having high potential;

taking that as a given, we were asked to write our professional autobiographies, dividing our lives into several segments, and recounting the events in each segment which brought us our successes to this point. This was difficult for all of us. It took three to four hours to write out our past history in a way that analyzed the strengths—and "lucky" breaks—that had landed us in the high-potential group. Then, just when we thought the inquisition was over, the lecturer asked us to do another, follow-up exercise. We were to imagine that things would continue to break our way, and that, a few years down the line, we had arrived at whatever exalted station in corporate life we wanted to reach; now we were to describe, in the most exacting detail, a typical day in our business life, from the moment we awoke to the moment we went to sleep. Where would we be living? In what type of house? On what sized property? At what hour would we arise? Was our family awake when we had breakfast? Did we read at breakfast a newspaper from a big city close to headquarters, or an out-of-town paper? What kind of car did we drive? How far? What was the office environment like? What did we do all day? How long did we stay in the office? Was the workday full of interest?

Although not stated baldly, the objective was to make us more conscious of precisely what was entailed in holding down one of the top positions in the company. We weren't told to translate what we'd put down into philosophical and emotional imperatives, but the need to do so became apparent. If you had described yourself as living on an estate with servants, were you willing to accept the responsibilities and the demands to earn the money to keep the estate going? And to make the sacrifices that went along with the job and the income? If, on the other hand, you described yourself living modestly at that point in the future, what were your reasons for trying to climb up the management ladder? Power? Control? The exercise rocked most of those in the group, because they had never given sustained thought to where they were going, and, more important, what life would be like once they had "arrived."

What I found interesting was that the exercise held no surprises for me. My dreams, which I had already defined so closely that they had taken on the attributes of an obsession and a commitment, were congruent with the imagined reality I had set down in the exercise for that day when I'd have reached a high corporate position. We were asked to take the study home and discuss it with our spouses, to see whether they shared our ambitions and willingness to sacrifice to achieve them. My wife and I had had continuing discussions about my goals and timetable for reaching the interim steps, and about the sacrifices our whole family was making in order for me to have the best chance to get to the top, so it presented no revelations for us. On the other hand, some of my management school colleagues were upset by this process. As a result of it, one man quit almost immediately. Over the next several years, a few more left IBM—a handful when IBM didn't want to lose them. Of the rest, a fair-sized group must have accepted both the risks and the rewards, for a handful rose to high positions, though, to date, I am the only one to have risen to the ranks of presidency and CEO-ship of a large company. In fact, with four companies, in my case (Braun A.G., Burroughs, Unisys, and Northern Telecom).

If anything, the exercise reaffirmed my values. I rededicated myself to moving ahead quickly so that I could reach the pinnacle soon, becoming independent and able to do whatever I chose to do. Because at the time I went through the exercise I already had a long-term plan for my career with clear checkpoints and time frames, as well as a reasonable understanding of the price that would have to be paid for achieving the interim goals, I could feel at ease with the sort of self-examination that left others upset. I wasn't wandering aimlessly around in the desert of the corporation, and I never felt that my future was being determined by outside elements. I was in charge; I knew where I was going and was continually developing a better sense of what it would take to get there.

Planning your career is essential, for without a plan, you're adrift on the currents, at the mercy of other people's needs and whims.

You may have a sense of the next job you want, but that's not enough of a plan. Where will you be in five years? Ten? How, step-by-step, will you get there? What skills or credits do you need, in addition to those you already have, to attain the objective you've set for five years ahead?

Just as you would plot out milestones for the development, manufacture, and marketing of a new product, make a business plan for yourself. *Your career is the product.* Chart your moves and promotions, and attach approximate dollar signs to them: "I want to keep moving so that I'll be earning $50,000 per year in two years, $100,000 in four years, $200,000 per year in six years." And then, just as you would with your job objectives, set out to beat these goals.

CULTIVATING PROFESSIONALISM

The major goal for every manager aspiring to a high position should be to become the consummate professional. As I define it, professionalism is a quality of the intellect. The professional is a person who *knows*—knows about his or her business, the company's products, the management of people, the problems of the company's customers—everything. Professionalism is not only indicative of a sense of detail, it also fosters attention to detail. Professionalism can be seen in a person's appearance, but is most appropriately reflected in his or her behavior.

Some of the most critical behavioral characteristics of a professional are:

—*An excellent sense of organization.*
—*An enjoyment of people.*
—*Good, logical faculties, a problem-solver.*
—*Tenacity, resourcefulness, and perseverance.*
—*The desire and willingness to work hard.*
—*The willingness to fight for what you believe in and want.*
—*An understanding of the influence of the past, coupled with . . .*
—*The ability to think ahead and to project yourself into the future.*
—*The ability to set far-reaching goals for yourself and your company.*
—*The determination to make your dreams become a reality.*

To state it another way, the professional is one who refuses to tolerate mediocrity and constantly pursues excellence. Just as the archer aims for the bull's-eye even while knowing he or she will seldom hit it, but to keep striving for it is the only way to perfection, the professional continually seeks to approach perfection in all that he or she is and does.

SET OVERALL OBJECTIVES

To *set a good overall objective*, study the publicly available information and compilations on the top executives of large corporations. Proxy statements, for instance, report the salaries, bonuses, perks, contracted arrangements, and other compensation of the top executives of publicly traded firms. Magazines like *Forbes*, *Fortune*, and *Business Week* regularly publish lists of the incomes and backgrounds of hundreds of high-level executives. Scrutinize these lists and determine where the chiefs came from. What was their educational background? To MBA or not to MBA? Did they come out of line positions or from staff? Did taking a law degree help anyone? Do boards of directors still want top officers to have operating experience, rather than only a mixture of staff experiences? Have the executives risen in a straight line through, say, marketing alone? Chances are they've also picked up financial or other staff and operating experience along the way.

This last observation brings up a key point in regard to the backgrounds of senior executives. The three most important legs of any large manufacturing business are: *product operations* (the generating of the product through development and manufacturing), *marketing and sales* (the defining, positioning, and selling of the product), and *finance*. If you have experience with only one leg of the three, to broaden your own background you should try to obtain your next job in one of the other areas—and the sooner the better. Don't stay in one of the legs too long, or you'll risk being viewed as a specialist in a particular function, rather than as a general manager.

Once you have charted where you are going, and how to get the needed experience, you are ready to be more specific about financial goals, and other goals that have to do with the level you want to reach and the power you want to wield. The least well understood of these concepts is power.

In a democracy, many people associate the notion of power with evil. But power is not evil, it is merely part of the equation of government, industry, and services of our country; in corporate terms, power is a useful tool and a legitimate objective. Theoretically, in a public corporation the shareholders hold the ultimate power, and their clout is exercised through a board of directors who are elected by them and are to act for them; in turn, the board is supposed to supervise the actions of the chairman, the CEO, and other senior executives. That concept worked in practice as well as in theory when shareholders were truly owners; nowadays, however, they are more like investors and at times even speculators, rather than owners, and the power has shifted to the boards themselves —or, in some instances, to the chairmen and CEOs of large companies.

There are CEOs who, while nominally reporting to a board of directors, actually control their boards; these men have something that in business approaches *absolute power, power equivalent to autonomy, a free hand in running the corporation.* Many people would like to have that sort of power, especially since it often goes hand-in-glove with another sort of power, that of having the use of the company's resources, such as aircraft, houses, apartments, cars and chauffeurs, expense accounts; this is *power which brings convenience and comforts* with it. And there is also a third kind of power, *the ability to get things done.* In the corporate world, it is this third sort of power which interacts with political power: a high-level executive of a large corporation often has the capability of providing significant employment in a geographical area, and will be on somewhat intimate terms with congressmen, senators, governors, mayors, and other federal, state, and local governmental officials interested in such matters. Lower down on the corporate ladder, this sort of power translates into authority over hiring and firing, the ability to control people in one way or another. In this realm we often come across the power games that executives play. These games relate to spheres of influence, to how to get ahead by seeming to possess more power than you actually do, and so on. I'll be discussing these games in detail throughout the book.

Before going on, however, I need to discuss something that is seldom mentioned: the flip side to corporate power, one of the drawbacks of being in a senior position. In an organization, as you climb up the ladder you have more power—but you also become increasingly more dependent for success upon those who are below you and who report to you; they must successfully accomplish the goals on which your own performance is judged by your superiors. At lower levels, within smaller spheres, managers have more direct control over what is going on—a sales manager knows every day how his people are doing; the engineering manager knows precisely how the product development is coming along. When something goes wrong, that sales or product development manager can reach in and try to fix it, immediately and directly. At higher corporate levels, the need and the ability to have your hands on in that way is reduced, but so is the ability to fix problems before they reach the size of serious difficulties for the company as a whole.

> As you go up the ladder, while you exercise and enjoy your power, you must simultaneously develop a tolerance for ambiguity, uncertainty, and the ability to live with a lot of loose ends.

Your success will have become more dependent, not less, on the solution to complex problems, the elements and solutions of which are provided by those subordinate to you. You'll have the power to reward and punish the individuals directly under your command—but, because of your high level and your distance from the day-to-day operations, you'll be dependent upon your subordinates, forced to rely on them but often unable to truly measure in real time the reliability and quality of the reports they provide to you. The skill to assess and evaluate the quality of information you're given is crucial to your personal success. And that information, in turn, comes mainly from your team.

ARE YOU ON THE RIGHT TRACK?

Keep specific ideas in mind when making an overall plan for your career:

1. *Pick a broad-enough objective.* Don't be too narrow in your aim. It's overly presumptuous to say that the only job you'll be happy in is the presidency of General Motors. It's almost as ambitious, but surely more realistic, to want to become one of the top executives in a major automobile manufacturing company.

2. *Make a plan, and stick to it.* Without a plan, you'll lack reasons for making certain decisions. For instance, if the company won't pay and advance you on your schedule—and you have a plan— you'll know what to do: leave. If you have no plan, you might be tempted to let things develop for another year or two, or not to press so hard and to be satisfied with less. Assess what skills you

currently have, and what skills you need to acquire. Do you have broad experience in several sectors of management, so you can be considered for higher positions which require you to be a businessman rather than someone with only a certain kind of narrow, specialized expertise? How are you doing in your quest to become a true professional, that is to say, a general manager?

3. With such goals in mind, *at the time you're being recruited into a new company, ask questions about career paths and opportunities for advancement.* Upon joining, have an understanding of what the next logical job (and the compensation associated with it) will be, and how long the management envisions it will take before you will be considered for that next step. If such things are impossible to know before you get inside, think twice about accepting the job; or, go ahead and sign up but then make it your objective to quickly determine the location and possibilities of that next opportunity.

4. When you're inside a company, then, work hard to *get a sense of what it takes to get ahead in your particular environment.* Some companies favor operating experience, others financial or marketing expertise. If you don't understand the corporate culture of the company you're in, advancement will be that much more difficult. And if you do know that culture, your next goal may be more easily defined.

5. *Tailor your objectives as you go along.* As you proceed up the ladder in management, update your plan; take into account your new expertise, the changing marketplace, your own needs. Do you know what your needs are now—and how they differ from what they were a few years ago? Avoid getting slotted too narrowly. If you're on the technical side, and eventually want to be in upper management, realize that to avoid being characterized only as a technical person, your next job needs to be in another discipline such as finance or marketing. Keep referring to your schedule, and push yourself. Have I reached that new salary plateau? Is my management horizon expanding? Have I accomplished my objective for this year? Or fulfilled the goals set for me by my superior (or by myself)? Can I now legitimately ask for a higher-level position? Be perpetually looking, perpetually striving.

6. *Help the headhunters.* When they call—and, if you're advancing rapidly, they will—assist them. If you're not thinking of leaving, recommend other people, preferably in a different company. There's no way that recommending competent people can hurt you; rather, it will ensure that when you're ready to change companies,

the headhunters will be there to assist you in your search and provide you with options.

7. *When you do leave for a new company, do it only in the right circumstances.* Don't jump too easily, and don't jump only for an increase in salary. Opportunities with the new company should be considered alongside the income; at times, in order to gain experience, you may even take a job that isn't at a quantum increase in salary. I convinced an executive to leave the company in which he had grown up to join Burroughs, and to go from a line to a staff position—with the promise of having a higher-level line job within eighteen months. The experience he gained on staff soon led to that bigger job, and then to another position as head of a newly acquired Burroughs' subsidiary, where he achieved his own goal of being responsible for an entire business, that is, an entity with its own engineering, manufacturing, marketing, sales, and service organizations.

Also, consider what kind of a company you'll be joining. The size of the company is critical. There are trade-offs involved in choosing a career move into a large or a small company. Do you want to be a big fish in a small pond? Someone who manages $50 million worth of sales in a $100 million company is a big fish, but the man who is in charge of $50 million in a $5 billion company has only 1 percent of annual sales, and is a small fish. Interestingly enough, the man in the smaller company has an exalted title, and may earn as much, if not more, than the man with a similar dollar-amount fiefdom in a larger company; that's because smaller companies have more flexibility in their negotiating terms and are more likely to give large stock options that are at or below current market price. However, if your eventual goal lies in a large company, it's not wise to stay in a small one too long, because in the large companies a manager's ability is often judged by the size of the entity he has been shepherding. Then, too, managers need to know if they are comfortable working in a smaller place; for instance, a smaller company has less staff support, a smaller "cookie jar" of dollars with which to experiment—and, therefore, less tolerance for errors. You may be able to gain financial independence in a smaller company, but equally, the risk of that company losing its independency or going out of business is also greater. Essentially, the answer to what sort of company is good for your next move will depend on your goals.

It is important to make your decision rationally, not emotionally, and when you are in possession of considerable information about the new company. Do your homework about the new company's financial and market position, its product line and cycles of development, its competitors, the salary and benefits structure, people, opportunities, and corporate culture. You'd be surprised how much of this information is available. Consult such reports as *Value Line*, or get a Dun and Bradstreet analysis of the company; look up and peruse its annual reports; find its top executives' biographies in various *Who's Who* publications; also obtain such publications as the company's 10K, 10Q, and proxy reports, prepared for shareholders and available to anyone on written request to the company. Finally, ask the opinions of those who have worked for the company and have subsequently left it.

8. When on the job, always make sure to do your job well, but also, *keep your superiors on edge by making them understand that if you are not continually challenged and rewarded—you'll leave.*

WHY BE LOYAL TO AN INDUSTRIAL INSTITUTION?

Many times, when companies are trying to keep you satisfied with your lot, or asking you not to jump to a new company, or requesting that you be patient and not demand that promotion right away, the heart of your superior's argument is that you must have loyalty to the company and faith in its management. Frankly, I don't understand the concept of loyalty to an industrial institution. *Is the company loyal to you? The answer is definitely no.* Company loyalty is, in most cases, a charade, a term of convenience, a vehicle for holding people to the company. In general, the company is loyal only as long as it needs you, can afford you, and the arrangement is convenient.

I know how some people feel: that after they've been with a company for many years, the company is indebted to them and will keep them on as employees even when they're no longer needed and may in fact be unproductive. That isn't so; the rash of age discrimination suits against companies, and the equivalent number of instances where employees have been severed after decades of service, attest to the accuracy of my view. Companies may hesitate to fire some older employees—or minority employees—because they fear discrimination suits, but that doesn't constitute loyalty on the part of the company; rather, that has to do with enforced obedience to governmental standards. A few companies, able to afford the costs financially, have occasionally (during hard times) been generous enough to offer early retirement plans to long-serving employees, but these actions are the exception, not the rule.

On the other hand, there exist certain geographical and industrial situations in which employees change jobs with alarming frequency, and demonstrate so little fealty to an employer that they endanger their own reputations. I'm thinking here of conditions in Silicon Valley, where people hopped from job to job, company to company, as new start-ups entered the field and engaged in fierce competition for good professional people.

True loyalty is a two-way street. There is loyalty to people, principally to colleagues; I insist on that, cultivate it, and honor it. Keep faith with individuals! (For me, the hardest thing about leaving IBM was my boss's feeling that in going I was being personally disloyal to him; fortunately, that feeling passed, and today we're still friends.) But loyalty to an employing company? In the past few years, while I've been thinking about the ideas expressed in this book, I've talked informally to top executives in dozens of companies about the notion that companies are not really loyal to individual employees. Some resist the idea, but the overwhelming majority agree with me that company loyalty simply doesn't exist in any meaningful way. In John Sculley's book *Odyssey*, about his corporate career, which involved a switch from long-term employment at Pepsico to taking over the reins at Apple Computers, he suggests that the sort of loyalty that saw his father through the Depression years but failed him in the 1950's no longer applies today. The old bond between man and institution, Sculley maintains, "represented a social contract in which the Organization Man [of the 1950's] traded his loyalty for security and lifetime employment. It was a Faustian bargain, which seemed to offer the job holder limitless wishes while robbing him of his freedom, his motivation, his creativity. That social contract is no longer valid. Nor, perhaps, should it be."

Even loyalty to people needs sorting out. *You need to know who are your real friends, and which people are only being friendly so long as you're an important colleague—or their superior.* One key way of separating the wheat from the chaff is noting who keeps in touch after you leave your former division or company.

There is another sort of loyalty, that to a profession such as the law, communications, or engineering; some people want to be lawyers, engineers, programmers, accountants, or advertising experts wherever they go, and they are more apt to adhere to the canons of their professional disciplines than to be subject to company loyalty.

Don't be swayed from a decision to leave, or persuaded to stay where you are, on the grounds of company loyalty. When you come in to discuss your outside job offer or your resignation, and people try to convince you not to go by asking you to "give us time" to make things better here, or beg you to reconsider on the grounds that your departure might hurt them as friends of yours—don't be dissuaded. Many times, you'll be offered a promotion to a job you know that you should have been awarded months or years ago. If you take it, you may be in trouble, for they'll shortly put in a backup person, and they won't forget that you wanted to leave the company. At a later date, when there is a reorganization (and these always occur), the company will place you in an undesirable job or perhaps even suggest that you leave; and this time when you go, it will be on *their* terms. Always leave on your own terms, if you can; when *you're* ready, not when they are. To that counteroffer, you must say, "Suddenly you think I can do this big job—where were you with the offer six months ago? How come you think I can do it now, if you didn't think so then?" Recognize that even if some of your more immediate demands are met, chances are that the higher-ups will not trust you or extend to you further promotions, feeling that you'll leave sooner or later.

Disbelieve all promises whose centerpiece is the false claim of loyalty; make your own path.

One last word about the sort of loyalty that should be demonstrated even after you've decided to leave a company. As a matter of principle, an employee should consider that at this crucial time it is responsible and sometimes legally mandated behavior to:

1. make sure company secrets are not compromised;
2. refrain from raiding your old company in any serious way for the benefit of the new one;

3. not say to outsiders detrimental things about the old company and its management; and
4. offer to stay through a transition period—although actually staying on for any length of time past a few weeks is seldom helpful either to you or to the company.

5

You Need the Right Assignment

UNREASONABLE FEARS

One fundamental reason that many lower-rank managers don't progress very far, or very quickly, is their fear that if they push too hard, something bad will happen to them. They've seen instances in business where a manager sticks his head up out of a crowd, and other people shoot at it. Many believe that taking the sort of actions and having the sort of attitudes recommended in this book will cause them to lose their jobs. They further believe that being fired will mean the end of their careers; they worry about being out of work, out of funds, unable to make their mortgage payments or otherwise to support their families. They fret about the possibility of not having health and other insurance in an era when medical costs have gone through the roof. They start to sweat when they wonder how they'll obtain enough money to put their children through college, or to take care of an aged parent. Examine your own mental attitude closely. Are you in danger of being one of the . . .

Bad Example #4: Fear-Ridden Managers

These are people who, as a consequence of the fear of losing their income and their security, have become managers or executives who often take actions that are cautious, overly conservative, or, worse, are do-nothing actions that merely continue problematic situations without attempting to rectify them. Their fears have translated into timidity in business situations. Such managers become adroit at not rocking the boat, at basing their lives on the wonders of their benefits packages, at being yes-men, at staying around long enough so that they earn promotion only through seniority, at counting the days until retirement.

Fear can paralyze a career; you must learn to manage it or else you'll be forever in its clutches. Here's Step One: *understand that it is not necessary to put your safety and security ahead of all else in order to remain employed and make it to the top.* The perception that companies do not tolerate those who take aggressive actions—even if some turn out to be bad guesses—is wrong. Companies don't automatically punish those who bend the system's rules in the course of trying to do their jobs well. Most companies know that those who take chances will *have* to bend some rules, and subtly encourage this sort of behavior. At IBM—perceived from the outside as a rather rigid company—people were encouraged to be "wild ducks," and not to fly in formation with the rest of the flock. (The idea was good, but wild ducks actually do fly in formation, as critics were fond of pointing out to the company.)

In the second place, *fear can be beaten back so it doesn't overwhelm you.* Take a clue from the intelligence agencies: in the field of espionage, operatives have to deal with fear all the time; recruits are taught that the antidote for fear is information. Here is some information that ought to quiet the fear of losing a job: government statistics show that white-collar managers who quit, are fired, or otherwise lose their jobs, are *unemployed for a period averaging only three to six months; then they usually find employment.* In *The New York Times* (February 21, 1989), employment consultants report that the majority of managers who leave a company find positions that are *better* than those they left! About 35 percent do find it necessary, however, to take a position somewhere other than the city in which they have resided, or to fill a slot other than the one they thought they ought to hold—but the job match is, again on the average, rather good. The article cites one consultant as saying that even managers in the fifty to fifty-five year age group can change jobs as quickly and easily as younger managers.

Now, what about those benefits? When people lose jobs and health insurance benefits, major employers and health insurance providers have plans that for a limited time (three to eighteen months, in most cases) will allow former employees to pay for their own insurance, often quarterly. Should you lose your job, then, the figures suggest that you'd only have to pay for health insurance by yourself for one or two quarters. The sums involved, while not inconsequential, are generally within reach of most people who have been in the management ranks of a large corporation.

Another point: often, when a company wants to sever an employee, the exit benefits are negotiable. Quite a few companies now provide outplacement services that can be helpful. You can argue to have medical benefits continued for an extra six months or a year, or to have loan repayments delayed; you might obtain the use of an office, telephone, and secretary to pursue a job search. Most employees don't even try to negotiate such things, though.

There are other, related fears. You've been at the company for a few years, will soon become vested in the pension plan, and fear jumping to a new company, where you'll have to start all over again and put in at least five years before becoming vested in the new company's pension plan. (This fear operates more among lower-level employees than among middle managers.) Or you don't want to take that new, more high-ranking job because it will mean moving from the Midwest to the canyons of Manhattan, and you believe that it will cost you too much to live in or near the Big Apple. Or, as an operations manager, you refuse an offered lateral transfer within a company to finance or overseas marketing—because, in your eyes, it's not really a promotion, and you don't want to go from a safe and secure job in an operational sector to one in a sector about which you know very little, a sector in which you believe you might fail.

None of these fears are completely unreasonable. But information goes a ways toward relieving some of them. For instance, if you wait until you're vested to leave, and you've only been with that company the minimum time necessary to become vested, the amount that you'll receive years later, upon your retirement, is extremely small, virtually insignificant if judged in terms of what the purchasing power of this pension will be in twenty or thirty years. So, jump to another company if you have to or want to— it won't really adversely affect your retirement years. That *New York Times* article cited just above reports that managers generally change companies five to seven times in their first twenty-five years as managers. As for other fears, many are matters of wrong perception. If you change your perception of what jobs are good for you, you'll see that a job in marketing or finance, while it may not currently be viewed as a promotion, will enhance your skills and résumé more than would the next job in your current operational sector.

To my way of thinking, it's essential for a manager aiming upward not to base any decisions on the job or about the job on the question of whether or not there'll be a safety net that will protect him or her from all the risks. There would be little excitement if everything were safe, secure, and easy.

If you're protected from losing, you're also insulated from the possibility of winning! Nothing in life that holds out the promise of reward is without risk.

Then, too, what appear to others to be risks may actually be actions that are essential for you to take. Suppose you're one of those people who hate meetings so much that you'll do almost anything to avoid them. Suddenly, your company is taken over by a giant, and you're subjected to management by committee and endless meetings. Or suppose that you're in one of those companies that have fallen in love with the team concept, and higher executives talk a lot about "wanting your input" and "having a full, free, and open discussion," but when you voice your ideas you are discourteously squelched. You don't like that, but, on the other hand, you've sort of agreed to live by majority rule. It's a dilemma, but a solvable one. Think of your own happiness and goals first, then of the environment in which they are being compromised. If you are being stifled in a corporation, is quitting a risk? Of course not, it's a necessity. You don't have to swallow your pride and stay where you are; other options exist.

Assume that you are good at what you do, and that, even if you are fired—or feel that you have to quit—or are squeezed out or shunted aside in a merger—you have enough talent to land an excellent job elsewhere. Have confidence in yourself!

Assume that you'll be able to bear the interim costs of joblessness, if it comes to that.

Assume that the calculated risks you take will be appreciated by astute, fast-track managers and executives above you in any corporation, and that they won't wish to get rid of an employee whose aggressive tactics pay off more often than not. (Some companies are better than others in this regard; homework on the corporate culture will give you a handle on the situation in yours.)

Then, having made all of these assumptions—acknowledgments of the realities of the situation—make decisions about your future in any given company or particular post. Now, your fears calmed down to a reasonable level—maybe a slight ache, but not a continual nagging one—and with your long-term goals and objectives identified, let's get to the mechanics of managing your own fast track career.

PICKING YOUR SPOTS

Having conquered the fear of losing a job, you're ready to manage your own rise within the corporate world. As you progress, the key is finding the right assignments and maximizing what you can do with each one.

Now, many assignments created within a corporation aren't completely within your control. Cadres develop, attached to one mentor or another. Some people advance because they are part of a bunch, or because they have a cohort with whom they're always associated. In every company, at every level, there are hangers-on; it frequently amazes me how high some of them can go. You, too, can climb in these ways—but what happens if there's a power struggle and your mentor loses? Or if your bunch is understood by new management to be mediocre? Try to keep control of your own future.

A safe assignment will not bring you to the notice of senior management. Look for places where you can make an impact. Seek out the challenges, the places where your hard work can turn around a project, department, or a segment of the company that has previously been an underachiever.

Let's say you've been in a corporation for a couple of years. You've become acquainted with its corporate culture and have gotten a sense of the path that might lie ahead of you. You're ready to move, and, since you've done well where you are, you believe that the company is inclined to give you a new assignment. Three principles should guide your choice of new assignments:

1. *take jobs in which your actions can make a difference,*
2. *take jobs that are in the mainstream of the company's business, and*
3. *take jobs that continually broaden your mix of skills.*

Find a place where your competence and drive will bring results noticeable to higher management. Look for areas where you have a chance of bettering the market share, or where a key factor is missing—say, a distribution channel isn't being developed well enough, or the sales force needs new tools or techniques to obtain better results, and you can open the channel or provide the leadership. Many people believe that if they enter an area of a company in which results have been poor for some time, and they are unable to change the situation quickly, they'll become tarred by the results. That's only partially true.

One way of assessing whether it's possible to make an impact is to know the relationship to the overall business of the piece you're being asked to manage. Think of what place microchips occupy in the computer industry. Chips are small parts, but without them, new computers can't be built—so if your computer company's chip needs are holding up production, and you can unclog that bottleneck, you'll be a hero. Your hero status will last only until the problem is solved. Then you may find that you are in a backwater, an unnoticed or secondary part of the business. Chips are not truly in the mainstream of business for a company that makes and sells computers. They are components often purchased from outside vendors, even by the largest companies. Realize that you can't stay in chips too long.

> To get to the top in management, you need to excel in the mainstream of the business, not in any subsidiary or overly specialized area.

How do you distinguish a backwater from a main tributary? By studying your company intensively. Do you know what makes your company tick? What percentage of the total sales, and profits, your division contributes? What are the main product lines; what are the subsidiaries? Has anyone who's worked in your division ever become an elected officer of the company? If so, through what career path? One of the best reasons to profitably study these topics is because most people in a company's management *don't* know this data, even though the information is readily available from talking to colleagues, as well as from published materials such as annual reports, 10K, 10Q, and proxy statements. Your knowledge will be a plus.

It's all logical. When Ford goes to choose a new president or CEO, that person is likely to come from having been head of one of the automobile divisions at some stage in their career, rather than having led the division that makes batteries or sells financing to car buyers. It's likely that the candidate will have had experience with many parts of the company—but it's deemed essential that he have plenty of experience with the core of the business, the main product lines and markets on which upper management invariably spends its time. Your $50 million division may be doing rather well, but it won't get the sort of attention the upper executives pay to the $500 million mainstream entity. Size alone is not the issue; being in the mainstream is. If you're in an electronic gadgets company (computers, radios, and the like) and 20 percent of the company's business is defense, climbing the ladder in defense won't get you to the top of that company; eventually, if you want to continue your progress, you're going to have to go to a company whose main business is defense—or transfer back into that 80 percent of the company whose business is in its main strength, electronic gadgets.

The same *caveat emptor* approach should guide your thoughts about taking sabbaticals such as becoming a Sloan Fellow in Management at MIT, or accepting foreign assignments. In many companies, acceptance of such a position is the kiss of death for a career. The principle is, out of sight, out of mind. It's unlikely that after one successful year at the Sloan School or two years in Portugal you'll come back to headquarters and be offered a better job. This is true even though American companies increasingly like to have executives with international experience; it seems that the companies would still prefer that you obtain that experience before you join them.

I happen to think that foreign assignments, top-level management fellowships and positions in secondary businesses out of the mainstream are important for an upward-bound executive. Some companies agree, and handle them well. Ford, Procter & Gamble, and a few others understand the problem of being out of touch with headquarters while at school or on foreign posting and take care to work their people back into key management assignments. Most companies don't do as well—and, therefore, ambitious managers in them must evaluate and accept such posts and assignments only after understanding what may be involved. For instance, if you take a foreign post, you'll know that in two to three years, if you want to continue upward progress, you will most likely have to leave that company and return to your home country in a job with another company. As I've pointed out above, that's not so terrible a fate. Furthermore, I'm a great believer in foreign assignments as a way to broaden yourself; in them, you often learn a great deal. In addition, in a foreign assignment you'll likely have more autonomy than you'd have in a domestic post, and you'll probably have more fun, test and broaden your skills, generally have higher income, and greater perks. It's ironic, though, that in all likelihood when you get through with the assignment, your broader résumé will look better to another company than it will to the present employer who sent you overseas in the first place. Sad! "The Chief Executives In Year 2000 Will Be Experienced Abroad," trumpets a recent headline in *The Wall Street Journal* (February 27, 1989), reporting that in the future all big companies will have to have a global outlook to do business.

It's just for that reason I find it rather incredible that during my tenure at companies such as DuPont, IBM, Braun/Gillette, Burroughs, and Unisys, there were only two or three senior executives other than myself out of a hundred (twenty at each corporation) who actually had hands-on international management experience.

More had managed overseas divisions from corporate headquarters in their home country, but only this small number had actually operated a subsidiary or important business unit while living abroad. When one considers that companies such as IBM and Unisys derive 50 percent of their income from sales outside of the United States, this lack of international experience seems terribly shortsighted. Unfortunately, this myopia characterizes the attitude of most U.S. multinationals.

Reentry to the mainstream of a company's business from a foreign assignment or secondary business is usually difficult. But anything that broadens you in terms of experience is helpful to your career. Beyond the foreign stints, there are other ways to gain more experience within a company. If you've always been in finance or in another staff function, and want to have operating experience, you may seek a lateral transfer to a secondary business of your company because in it you'll get a chance to do what most companies consider essential for a top executive, and that is to manage an operating division. Sometimes making such a shift may cost you in terms of current dollars and managerial level, but it makes long-term sense in that it enhances your mix of skills. (By the way, there are companies that fill top positions with people who have never had any experience in operating units; they are a puzzle to me, because usually the move doesn't work out very well, especially insofar as shareholders are concerned.)

To become a businessman you have to have experience with at least two of the three legs of business: marketing, finance, and product operations.

One of the turning points in my career came after I'd been at IBM for several years and I'd gone up the ladder in the product divisions, specifically in development and manufacturing IBM's new products. I wanted to be what is called a businessman or general manager in the real sense of being a generalist, someone who is a senior executive and who daily deals with the overall business of the corporation, rather than just a functional part of it. I had already understood that, at IBM—and, I believed, at any big corporation— if you had knowledge of two of the three legs, you could hire line managers and staff to help you with the third. But if your entire career was in only one of the three disciplines, your upward progress could be impeded to the point where you'd be forever stuck in one of those functional areas. I knew that most top executives who reached the pinnacle early in their careers generally had experience in all three areas. For a CEO or a board of directors to hire a key executive into general management who has had experience in only one of the areas is risky for the company, and therefore unlikely. You have to have had experience in at least two of the areas to be considered a viable candidate for one of the top positions.

The opportunity for me to do something about broadening myself came when one of my former bosses at IBM jumped to another big company that was one of our largest suppliers; I'll call it XYZ, Inc. I then received a few calls from XYZ, feelers to see if I'd be interested in going there. I told the callers that I wasn't interested in leaving IBM—and, in truth, at that moment, I wasn't thinking about doing so. The XYZ callers didn't believe me. Eventually, because the two companies' business dealings were so intertwined, one of the top executives of XYZ felt compelled to call the head of my IBM division (who was three levels above me) and say they were talking to me. I had figured out that this could happen, and took advantage of the situation by going down the hall to our personnel department and telling the director there that I'd had feelers from XYZ, but wasn't interested; I also told the personnel director that I felt I wasn't being recognized enough at IBM for the work I'd been doing, and I expressed my disappointment at the lack of opportunities within IBM to broaden my career into general management. I swore the personnel man to silence, knowing all the while that the moment I left his office, he would have to call my immediate boss, tell him that I was being recruited and that I wasn't entirely happy with the future career opportunities I was being limited to at IBM.

Shortly thereafter, I was called in and asked if I were going to XYZ. I told everyone that I wanted to stay with IBM; but by then, upper management and the personnel department were worried that they'd lose me. A week later, I was asked by the division president what could be done to make me happier and keep me at IBM. That was my moment.

Forcing the issue, I told my superiors that I was feeling stuck in technical operations and wanted to gain experience in either finance or marketing as well as be exposed to corporate headquarters. Since the company wanted to keep me, my boss, personnel, and others worked hard to arrange for me to become the administrative assistant to the CFO, the chief financial officer and head of finance for IBM. Fortunately for me, he was one of the finest executives I've ever met, and a good tutor as well. I was able to learn a great deal from him, and particularly from his people, about finance in a relatively short period of time. He got me interested in finance, and I pestered everyone to teach me. I studied the hundreds of reports that were available, and, even when I didn't understand them all, would invariably return to work with dozens of questions about my reading. Seeing my interest quicken, and my efforts to comprehend their area, many people were willing to assist me in my learning, and were patient with me. I developed a fascination with all aspects of finance and accounting that is still with me today, almost twenty years later.

As a result of pushing into a new area, I gained experience with a second leg. Thereafter I was considered a more valuable executive—both by IBM and by other companies who wished to hire me away. Not only was my résumé enhanced, but after leaving finance I was able to secure in different parts of IBM a whole series of new assignments with lofty titles that helped broaden me still further.

A few additional thoughts about taking new assignments: When you're wanted or needed, or the assignment is known to be in a troublesome area, you can *extract a commitment from higher-ups for your involvement.* Before going to the new task, discuss with your superiors what can be expected to happen after you've unplugged that critical bottleneck, or restructured marketing, or beefed up sales in a troubled subsidiary. Here I must tell you that I didn't do this as much as I should have at IBM. In fact, I became typecast as a Mr. Fix-it, and was given too many assignments to go in and rescue something that was in dire straits. After a while, I felt straightjacketed by this role, and I had to consider leaving the company. So, the lesson is: always tell upper management what you expect as a reward for taking care of the problem or accepting the transfer; spell out that you want to get experience in finance, receive higher incentive compensation which is more directly related to your results and contributions, move to headquarters, or whatever is beneficial to your career.

Don't be shy about your career plans, and get whatever commitments you can in writing, even if only as a note to the files. "It's not that I don't trust you, sir; it's just that in a year or eighteen months, many things could change. You're such a good manager —that's why I want to work with you—that you could be promoted or transferred—probably both. That's why I would appreciate it in writing. It'll just be a memo. Can I draft it for you?"

On the other hand, *be open to what sorts of assignments you'll consider;* don't say no to everything, or else you'll be labeled as uncooperative and unwilling to act in the best interests of the company. Remember that all sorts of things are negotiable when it comes to new jobs—moving expenses, perks, cost of living adjustments, mortgage loans which are forgiven if you remain with the company for an agreed-upon number of years, and so forth. Some executives don't like to signal to other employees by the giving of visible perks such as a company car that one individual is being treated better than others. As an employee, be sensitive to such matters, and take your rewards in packages that aren't always open to inspection by your colleagues. How much are you worth to them? Why do they need you? Is time on your side, or on theirs? The answers to such questions will allow you to gauge the leverage you have in the negotiations. At times, certain good performers don't get the little extras because they don't negotiate hard enough to obtain them. In my career, I sometimes agreed to better packages for employees who asked for them than for those who didn't.

Find out as much as you can about that next job. Speak to people who've worked in that area. Size up your new superior-to-be. Is he or she the type of aggressive performer you'd like to emulate? In general, you don't want to work for someone who's not also on the way up. There are times, though, when it may be better to work for a superior who's on the way out, so you can take his or her job; at such a moment, you'll need to gauge how long you'll have to be established in the area before you can become eligible to succeed your present superior.

Encourage your potential boss to tell you about those who'll be reporting to you. Find out how much autonomy you'll have, and what the propensity of your new superior might be toward going by the book or making his or her own rules. *The main thing is to be always planning and driving for that next job*—but not in such a way that you become obstreperous, or are perceived as a person who is *only* negotiating upward and not working for the good of the company. Vary the style of your prompting; ask about pay once in a while; the next time, talk about "personnel matters"; the third time, tell your superior that you've been working too hard and are going to take a vacation. They'll get the message.

One final note on this process: once you've negotiated a new assignment and its criteria, go to work and perform to the utmost of your abilities. Keep a fine balance between pushing ahead and doing your job superbly. Remember always that hard work alone doesn't count—and make it your task to produce superior results.

GO WHEN IT'S GOOD

When you're looking around for a new job, you may let your current bosses know, by one means or another, that you're looking. This may provoke counteroffers from your current company. You ought to consider such offers—but, in my view, *once you've decided to leave, you shouldn't allow yourself to be talked out of it,* because whatever you squeeze out of the company at that transition point is probably all you'll ever get there. You'll probably have more opportunities at the next company.

And when you resign one job to take another, even if you've been unhappy at your former job, *leave cleanly.* Don't make a mess, or take the opportunity to tell off that awful person who's stifled you for years. That might satisfy you emotionally for the present, but why burn all your bridges? Invariably there will be times in the future when you'll need a reference from your former employer. I recently had a telephone call asking me to comment upon the character of a man I had known at IBM twenty years ago, and whom I hadn't seen much in the intervening years. I frequently get calls about people I've known or met in the course of being a manager at six major corporations; the corporate world can sometimes be like a small town, and reputations in it can be easily made or broken. Maintaining good relations with everyone on the job is an important aspect of creating and nurturing a good reputation.

It's often a good idea to offer as much help in the transition as you can give. If you can arrange it, *don't leave in the middle of a project.* Stay for a respectable period of time while your replacement gets his or her feet wet in the new pond. When you're going from one job in a company to another, try to leave behind you a management structure that has no gaping holes, a clean organization that has no hidden problems or secret agendas.

One helpful tool is to prepare a report for the edification of your successor, a sort of self-audit with your views of the healthy as well as the troubled areas in your organization, an appraisal of key individuals on the management team and recommendations that you have about them. This sort of evaluation is not what you'd put in an employee's annual performance appraisal, but, rather, deals with more personal characteristics: this one is good with figures, that one's strength is long-term planning, a third isn't good at dealing with young geniuses, a fourth has great potential as yet untapped. Also evaluate in the same, candid way all the programs for which you've been responsible. Write about trends that aren't showing up in the numbers yet; write about the aspects of the job and the territory that are not easily ascertainable and that would take your successor six months to learn for himself or herself. Such a document can be very helpful, both to your successor and to yourself, in evaluating how you've done in the job. It behooves you to be excruciatingly honest in evaluating your own strengths and weaknesses, successes and failures. Circulate copies of the report to several levels of management above you; it will be a good ambassador, for such reports are seldom made and will be greatly appreciated.

6

How to Manage
Your Boss

*M*ANAGING up" is considered a Machiavellian thing to do. But all career-ambitious managers do it, to some degree. What's important is to make such an action conscious, part of your ongoing plan for tackling your job. Machiavelli saw politics and government as sciences, fields of endeavor that could be assessed and quantified; in them, actions and principles of effective behavior could be described by rules. The managing of your own career needs to be similarly assessed and described. In career terms, then, a crucial task, and the one that separates the upwardly mobile manager from the docile employee who "goes along to get along" is *managing your superior so that you are able to advance rapidly*.

IN PRAISE OF SUPERIOR RELATIONSHIPS

The first stumbling block to managing someone above you is the feeling, common to many upwardly driven people, of being unable to accept the idea they have a boss. Let me assure you that nearly everyone in a corporation, except for that rare CEO who has been given a free hand by a board of directors whom he has handpicked and controls, reports to and is accountable to somebody. *Most aggressive managers fail to correctly assess and to praise the competence of their superiors.* Actually, all of us who try to climb the ladder have a tendency to underestimate those above us. But holding such a notion is incompatible with developing the good working relationship with your superior that is often the key to advancement.

> One of your primary tasks is to get along with the boss, and to manage him or her as much as he or she is managing you.

It's important to admit to yourself that now and then (and sometimes more often than that) you're going to be told precisely what to do. A smart manager will be able to make you feel that the direction of your work has been arrived at jointly, but there are times when you'll be told to do something even though you disagree with the order. If you've chosen your superior, such instructions may be easier to live with, but generally you won't be so lucky as to be able to choose the person to whom you report. Even so you must operate in the continuing context of being a team player, being supportive of your leader's decisions while refusing to become one who simply parrots what the boss says. Only rarely should your managing up be visible to anyone but yourself.

Managing your superior may be your most important challenge. You can perform brilliantly all the tasks set for you by the corporation and still not get noticed. But if you work properly with your superiors, the hard work will be more likely to pay off in advancement.

As stated above, the proper relationship between you and the next level of management is one of fine balance. You must do superb work, so good that if you were to leave, your departure would be felt and talked about in circles beyond the immediate area in which you work. Your task is to keep your superiors always on edge, wondering whether or not you'll leave your current position for a better one elsewhere. However, you mustn't act in such a manner that your manager decides that your head is already out the door, and must find a substitute for you. In other words, avoid being replaced at your superior's initiative, rather than at your own. Keep the upper echelons guessing at what you'll do, but make sure they believe that as long as they provide you with opportunities, challenges, recognition, and proper remuneration, you are here to stay. As a junior manager, this sort of understanding between your superior and you is a two-way, oral agreement; at more senior levels, it is often codified into a contract between company and executive. Though companies don't like to admit it, such contracts are invariably written in the manager's favor.

Here are some essential strategies for managing upward:

1. *Get to know your superior.* To have a good working relationship, get to know your boss's personality, quirks, habits, expectations. At the end of the day, when it's a little less formal, you can walk into his or her office and ask how things are going, what the quarter looks like—anything, to show that you're interested in the overall business and the superior's function in it. This is also a good time to raise your profile on essential issues. "I have this little blip on the horizon that might become a problem." "I'm doing okay managing that supplier, but it doesn't take up all my time. Anything else I can handle for you?" Be sympathetic to his or her problems. Try to understand them, so that there are no hidden agendas that might impact on your relationship. Is this someone who likes to have subordinates that are standouts? Or someone who doesn't like to be upstaged? Tailor your behavior in reporting accomplishments according to your estimate of your manager's character. For another instance, is your superior's progress blocked by his or her superior? Are there personal considerations you ought to be aware of? You need to know such things, both to be helpful to your manager, and to effectively communicate with him or her.

2. *Be supportive of the person to whom you report.* Avoid personality clashes by whatever means possible. Don't undermine or speak ill of a person in any way while you are reporting to him or her. If you disagree with the boss on an issue, be sure to say so, but in an environment where it is clear that the focus is on the task, not on the individual. Part of being a valuable manager is expressing your ideas, even if they are contrary to those of your superior. Don't be a yes-man. Followers who always agree with the boss are not wanted by aggressive managers. But once you've said your piece, and have been overruled, be supportive of your superior's wishes; once the decision is made, work to implement it.

3. *Be a team player.* The best employee is one who always acts in the best interests of the company. This invariably means subordinating individual agendas to the overall task of the team of which

you are a member. To some people, team-playing means going along with the crowd. To others, playing on the team means being submerged in the virtual religion of togetherness that characterizes most American business back-thumping. I define a team player as one who acts as part of a team all of whose members are bent on achieving the same corporate objective. Working with others for the good of the company is a principle that applies to the tasks of the vice-president in charge of a division as well as to those of the manager of the motor pool.

Recognize that in the lower ranks, most of those immediately above and around you will be relatively junior, inexperienced managers who need your support. At lower levels, no one has a true picture of the overall task, or of how your small unit is integrated into the whole, so you must assume that the interdependence of all these small management units is great, and must be maintained. All of your boss's direct reports need to pull together, or the whole team will look bad—not just the manager in charge.

4. *Do more than what's been assigned to you.* Even while trying hard not to make others look bad, your need is to outperform those around you. To do so, you need to know first what is expected of you—the objectives of your job, as stated in the annual appraisal and as you can elucidate your day-to-day tasks in conversations with your immediate superior. Once those are clear, you can lay out plans to outperform the goals.

If you do a job, even an ordinary job, in a superior way, you'll outperform expectations, and get noticed.

Suppose you were a man who has been put in charge of a motor pool, a terribly ordinary task in most companies. *How would an ambitious manager shine in such a job? Through imagining an innovative way to quantify and evaluate his performance.* He could do a customer survey, asking all the people who use the motor pool to rate its services. Which are adequate? Good? What areas need improvement? A survey in hand, he could write a report analyzing its findings, identifying what areas need work and his plan for improving them in the next quarter or next year.

This will also reflect credit to his boss. And, by the way, never take all the credit for such an innovation as a motor-pool customer survey; be sure to insist to higher management that your immediate manager share the credit with you, for giving you the latitude and permission to conduct the survey, for encouraging you. (Often, you won't even get the chance to take credit for your work; higher management grabs it all.)

5. *Run your piece of the company as if it were your business and your money.* Always keep in mind the relationship of what you're doing to the structure and main business of the company. Figure out what the bottom line is in your area of responsibility—unit sales, a schedule to be met, a service to be rendered, a staff function to be conducted—and strive to better the performance on it. Also, make it your personal objective to do something innovative, clever, or constructive on the job. This may involve thinking like an entrepreneur and conceiving a new service for that motor pool, or a new use for an already-existing product, or a way to speed up production, or shorten the development cycle for a product—but try to find some way to excel in the job, and to differentiate what you do from what everyone else does and how they do it.

Now we come to a pair of don'ts. As a manager and executive at various stages of my career, I let my people know that there were two cardinal sins they must not commit. Here they are:

6. *Don't ever surprise the boss.* Keep your superior apprised of all significant issues such as product problems; expected shortfalls in sales, say, due to orders being lost to the competition; or employee difficulties. Good news also should be no surprise to the boss. If you have good news, though, you need to be calculating as to when, where, and how to present it; do so at a time and place, and in a venue, that will reflect well on you. Will that be in a private meeting? In front of colleagues? Or would it be best to leak it out? And what about the flip side? Any aggressive manager, especially one who takes risks to achieve bigger results, is going to have areas that go wrong now and then. *If you keep your boss apprised continually about your area, he or she becomes your partner in all the problems.* The corollary of this maxim is even more important: never, ever surprise your manager in front of his or her superior. You'll gain nothing but anger and recriminations for doing that. It won't impress the next-level manager at all; if it does, the impression will only be temporary or negative.

7. *Don't make a mess of a personnel matter.* I've made mistakes in business, and tried to learn from them; mistakes are almost in-

evitable for a hard-charging manager, and most of them aren't fatal to a career. Bad forecasts can be corrected; monkey wrenches thrown in by outside factors such as governmental decisions or the lack of a crucial supply line can be understood. *The best managers are those who sometimes make mistakes but who recognize them and correct them as they occur.* Mistakes made on the basis of imperfect information, or because of factors that are beyond control, aren't really mistakes. When I became a more senior manager, my actions were often based on my belief that *mistakes in forecasting, scheduling, or other aspects of the business were forgivable (as long as there weren't too many of them), but that mistakes in handling people were inexcusable.*

Mistakes in dealing with people generally come out of not knowing your people very well, or out of being insensitive to them, neither of which has a place in management at any level.

> Bad Example #5: I Care for My People, but . . .
> Some top executives say publicly that they care for their people, but don't advance the interests of their subordinates who show promise, don't back them up; instead, they view their subordinates as interchangeable units, like commodities to be bought, sold, or traded. They treat underlings badly, but often pay obsequious court to their superiors. Eventually, if not sooner, their best people leave. And when they do, this manager blames them for being disloyal.

I can't countenance such behavior, and won't stand for it in those who report to me. A manager must relate to people in such a manner that they want to continue to work for him or her. I put a bad mark on that manager's record who fails at the task of working well with subordinates. I hasten to add that having a good relationship with one's direct reports does not mean you must foster an environment of instant forgiveness for mistakes, lots of hugging, and endless chatting about outside interests during business hours. I was famous—infamous?—for my oft-repeated line, "We're not here for a love-in, but to get the job done."

8. *Don't be a transparent manager.* This is the business school term for someone who administers and doesn't lead, who simply relays decisions downward or upward. Typically, transparents don't stand up for their people; they procrastinate; and they become known eventually as communicators or administrators of decisions, rather than the makers of decisions.

Bad Example #6: There's Nothing I Can Do . . .
An edict comes down from above: cut 10 percent of the expense budget. The transparent manager wrings his hands, simply tells his several direct reports that each one must cut 10 percent from his or her expenses, and that there's nothing he can do about the situation. Such an across-the-board cut requires no thought, and reflects no understanding of the specialized situations beneath the manager.

It may be the case that Department A could stand a 15 percent cut, while Department B needs a 5 percent increase; the true (that is, nontransparent) manager would allocate the cuts (and increases) according to a more detailed knowledge of the situation and sensitivity to it, and would make the total add up to the required 10 percent. Similarly, when his or her departments fail to perform up to forecast, the transparent manager typically blames the insufficiency on the supplier, whether internal or external, or on the inadequacy of his or her employees, and so on.

It's important for a manager to take responsibility in both directions, up and down, for what goes on in his or her area. Transparent managers may get by, but their tactics soon become known, and they don't progress rapidly, if at all.

9. Last, *get decisions made by your superior* in a timely, helpful manner.

HOW TO GET DECISIONS MADE BY YOUR BOSS

This topic deserves more lengthy consideration, since it's the essential ingredient in working with your boss.

Business proceeds on decisions. Managers at all levels need judgments made. Some they can make themselves; others are beyond their sphere of responsibility or authority and must be discussed with their colleagues and superiors.

Though the ability to make decisions—judgment—is the mark of a manager, many avoid making decisions altogether, and some only make them when forced to do so. The transparent manager described above is one type that avoids decisions, or insists on passing the problems upward or downward for solution. Another type is the manager who always seems to seek a second opinion: "The financial officer ought to look at this." "Let's set up a task force to examine this problem." (Task forces and consultants make recommendations but have no accountability for their decisions, because others must implement them. More about these corporate bugaboos in Chapter Eight.) A third type usually says he or she "needs more time to think" about a matter—but doesn't say how long—and hopes to avoid the inevitable by prolonging the process of making the decision. A fourth type is one whose own boss has difficulty making decisions, which renders decision-making painful for everyone down the line.

Why do people avoid making decisions? Every decision involves a choice among alternatives; each alternative may have unpleasant consequences, or may—in the cowardly manager's mind—open him or her to charges of bad judgment. Some people who like to avoid unpleasantness altogether often refuse to make real decisions; for example, they know that a particular allocation of resources will make one group happy and the other unhappy, so they don't make a decision on the basis of business needs, but, rather, allocate the resources half to one and half to the other. But that only spreads unhappiness and sidesteps the necessity for judgment.

What if you need a decision and the manager above you won't give it to you? Here are a series of strategies for dealing with that situation:

1. *Make the decision yourself, implement it, and tell your boss later.* Overspend your budget; fire an unproductive employee; lower the price on a product to try to gain a larger market share. Many managers want their subordinates to appear to take these sort of actions independently, so they can disavow the actions if they later turn out to be disastrous, and jump in to take the credit for judicious management if the actions pay off properly. As the subordinate, you shouldn't mind this too much, for you are willing to take the risks, and believe that management up the line of the hierarchy will understand to whom real credit for success is due. Be prepared to live with the consequences if your decision backfires. And be careful about letting the superior take all the credit. As John L. Lewis, leader of the coal miners' union, used to say, "Whosoever tooteth not his own horn, that horn will not be tooted."

I see now in retrospect that the biggest mistake I made at Burroughs and Unisys was to let the chairman take all the credit publicly for the company's success. He alone talked to the press, or represented us at important meetings in Washington. But we in senior management didn't do much to counter this notion of a single leader who functioned without any assistance. For example, my colleagues and I allowed the chairman to have annual reports issued with only his picture shown. Few other major corporations project this one-executive-only look.

2. *Ask for a meeting with your superior, and the person to whom he or she reports, for the purposes of obtaining a decision.* "Boss, I know that you have a problem on this issue because you can't seem to get your management to listen to you. But I need a decision on this. Let's go jointly to upper management and discuss the problem. Or, if you don't want to go, I'd be willing to go alone if you'd give me permission."

3. *Write a memo that is an ultimatum.* After several unsuccessful attempts to get the decision made, put it in writing: "I won't make my quota this quarter unless you permit me to reduce the price on the product. I recognize the risk inherent in this action, but because of factors one, two, and three I believe that dropping the price will pay off." A copy of this memo could be sent to your superior's manager. Your own boss then has the option of stopping you from implementing the decision—but, if he or she doesn't, then your boss has tacitly approved your actions, and will have to answer to them with you to higher management anyway. Another, even stronger version: "As you know from our many previous discussions, we've been having trouble making money from our subsidiary in Paraguay for three years, and I've asked before to be allowed to close it. Now, if I don't hear from you by the fifteenth of this month, I'm going to start the phase-out myself. A copy of this memo is going to the vice-president."

GOING AROUND THE BOSS, AND THE ART OF CONFRONTATION

When the above tactics don't work, it may be time to consider going around your boss. It's *always* risky to do this. You'll undoubtedly upset your superior, and the lower he or she is in the hierarchy, the higher his or her upset level. Your action may turn that heretofore meek animal, your immediate boss, into a ferocious cornered beast. Another possible disaster: imagine the scene when you present two levels up, identify a problem that needs a decision—and then have your superior deny having heard of the problem's existence before this. You could get pilloried! Remember, both you and your superior can play this dangerous game.

Then, too, going around your boss invariably sends tremors through the entire management structure, which is based on a keenly observed chain of command. Your actions will likely provoke a confrontation between your superior and his or her boss; also, word will spread that you've gone around, and this can make things difficult for you with your peers.

Those downside notions having been understood, there are times when the risk must be taken.

Now, I'm a person who doesn't run away from confronting issues or people head on; I'm not naturally argumentative, nor do I always seek out confrontational situations, but I do recognize that all too often in business, important issues go unresolved because they are not confronted at the proper time or in the proper way. There are moments when head-to-head confrontations are the only mechanisms that can lead to a resolution of an overwhelming problem.

Some people avoid confrontation at all costs; I don't see the point in that, especially if you want to advance rapidly in business. It's a game of percentages. At times I've lost a round; I remember particularly that during a meeting of top management I championed trying to find a solution to a problem that our CEO had purposefully been ignoring. In this instance, though I was correct, I was perceived as disobeying protocol, and my relationship with the CEO deteriorated. In many other instances, because it was clearly constructive, my confrontational posture paid off.

The time and place at which you go around the boss are critical. If your superior is weak, and you're suffering because of that, either because the weakness is blocking your climb up the ladder or preventing you from making important decisions; or if you want your superior's job and think you've earned it, ask for an audience with the next higher level person. It's often best to make this request outside of the normal daily routine. Approach that higher-level person at a quasisocial event and say that you want to talk privately —not just then, of course, but at an appropriate time; later, you call for an appointment. (Recognize the fact that your own manager will quickly find out about this potential meeting; don't have any illusions that it will be kept quiet. Nor should it.)

Having set up the meeting, you'd better do a lot of homework for it, because the going around meeting will be a crucial one. Your grounds for discontent will have to be meaningful and consequential for the business. For example, that every decision you need from your own superior must be forced; that the two of you aren't getting along and there are no prospects for improving the situation; or that the company's business is suffering in your department because of your manager's actions or nonactions. You'll have chapter and verse ready to back up your allegations. As a result of these blockages, you want your superior's job, or an equivalent one, or if that isn't possible, you want a transfer out of the department, or you may have to consider resigning from the company altogether. Make it clear that you have discussed these views with your immediate manager openly on several occasions and nothing has changed.

Most managers do, indeed, dislike their subordinates going around them to their superior. But it doesn't have to be that way. When I was a low-level, middle-level, or senior manager, I didn't mind my subordinates going around me. I even encouraged it. Why? First of all, there were no secrets between my manager and me; I always kept my boss fully informed about what was going on in my area of responsibility, so that nothing said to my superior by any of my subordinates could ever come as a surprise. Second, I was not one to shy away from decisions, and would not let a situation get to the point where anyone could ever complain to upper management that there was a lack of decisiveness in my area. Third, because I was an inveterate champion of my own people, I would frequently importune my bosses to meet privately with my people so their chances of advancement would be bettered, and similarly urged my direct reports to have that occasional breakfast or lunch with my boss without my being present so they could develop a better personal relationship with the executives up the line.

There are only two possible results of such a going around meeting with your boss's superior. You win in some way, or you lose—perhaps even lose big. Winning means that you get your superior's job or a significant promotion, get a transfer, or you extract from the hierarchy a promise of future reward if you'll stay where you are and try to make it work. You also must be prepared to lose. Sometimes you win the battle and lose the war. You get your decision from the vice-president, or you obtain that promotion, but from then on you're ignored by the hierarchy. In that case, ask for a transfer, or leave for another job. It's also possible to lose the struggle for reasons that are tangential to the problem at hand, for example, the second-level superior decides against you because, even though he or she knows that your manager is not effective, the chain of command must be preserved. Many such decisions are made to maintain control, not to advance the company's business. If that happens in your case, you can rest assured that even if you've lost, you've perhaps woken up your superior. Now you have to find a way to make it work with your immediate boss—or leave.

The amount of risk you are willing to take in going around your boss depends on your assessment of the situation and what the rewards are for success and the punishments for failure.

Is it essential for you to move ahead now, on your schedule? In going around the boss, how much in terms of salary, position, and new experience do you stand to gain? To lose? If you lose, could you be blocked for three months? Six months? Years? Is it an opportune moment to take such a serious step—say, during a reorganization, or when there have been some disastrous bottom line results? If you lose, are you prepared for the possibility of having to leave? If you fear that, you're probably not ready to take the risk of going around your boss. During my entire career in large corporations, I was usually willing to take that risk, because I was almost always willing to leave the particular company for which I was then working, firm in my belief that I'd be highly employable elsewhere. My tolerance for mediocrity is low, and spilled over into a refusal to go along with companies that allowed the continued employment of superiors who were indecisive or who contributed nothing to the company's progress. I was always prepared to go around such managers, or to take the consequences of losing a round and having to leave companies that valued them more highly than I did. Fortunately, I never had to leave. Those were risky stances to take, but no risk, no gain. And, for me, if there was no gain it wasn't a worthwhile game.

7

What Will My Family Say?

DEALING WITH THE PRESSURES

If there is such a thing as a natural home life, the situation of an ambitious manager in a large corporation often creates an unnatural one, or, at the very least, puts considerable strains on a manager's home life. Because I want to be entirely honest and frank about what is required for a manager to have a swiftly rising career, it is important to consider the strains on the family that come as a consequence of pursuing such a career.

No one sets out to have a family that is not close, but an ambitious corporate path can bring with it pressures that pull a family apart. One often sees among managerial families divorces and other problems at home: children going astray, personal breakdowns, alcohol and drug abuse. Of course these sad events are endemic, and not exclusive to upwardly mobile managers, but still, it is a fact that managerial families have more than their share of these difficulties. The largest single health care expense of big corporations is the amount spent to repair alcohol and drug abuse among their employees and families, and for psychiatric counseling.

My wife and I have been married since we were both graduate students, and our children seem to be turning out well and are involved in college and postgraduate work—but I consider us to have been lucky to survive as a unit and as individuals.

A fast-track corporate career entails long hours in the office and even more work at home; frequent moves, often to locations that the family may not like; a fair amount of stress that can't be left at the office at the close of business hours; and quite a bit of travel, which makes it difficult for the traveling parent to participate in parent-teacher conferences, to see a child take part in a stage play or in athletic contests, and so on. We moved on the average of once every two years; children are more resilient than parents, and it got to the point that my children were amazed when we stayed in one place for four years. I had the suspicion that they might even have come to prefer the excitement of a move on a regular basis. Similarly, they got a bit restless when I wasn't whisked away on a business trip at least once a week. Perhaps that's because when I was home for extended periods I brought the intense scrutiny I habitually used at work to bear on their schoolwork and young lives. Our children matured faster than those who stayed in one place throughout their childhood, for ours had to adapt constantly. Also, all five of us shared some important things that brought us closer together: enduring the moves, having joint adventures traveling. I did miss parts of their childhood, and I believe they lost something by not having Dad around more of the time.

Too many times I've heard of strains occurring as a tired executive goes home, perhaps just in time to pack to catch a late evening plane, and in no mood to listen to his wife's tales of triumphs and difficulties with the children at home. (I refer to the wife as homemaker because this is statistically the more common situation, not to be sexist.) I had such moments myself, but tried to exert control over my traveling so that I was mostly home for weekends, and would deliberately take very late flights so that I could first have dinner at home with my family before going out of town.

As one goes up the ladder in a large corporation, many things get left behind, such as hobbies and the ability to devote sufficient time to family life, other interests, even one's personal financial management. Your time is not controlled by your own needs, but, rather, by the needs of the corporation. Compensation rises apace with responsibility, and can help in ameliorating some of the difficulties, but others cannot be helped. As one's career progresses, the executive is constantly challenged to broaden his horizon, to think about far-reaching issues that affect his company: the federal budget deficit, the coming amalgamation of Europe in 1992, the education of the next generation of factory workers. Meanwhile, if your wife is at home or in a job of lesser station, she may not be challenged in the same ways, and so separation between the spouses on an intellectual level is added to the mix.

THE ROLE OF THE CORPORATE SPOUSE

The role of the corporate spouse is important as an element that can contribute to a manager's career, or detract from it. Very often, there is corporate entertaining to be done such as taking customers and their wives out for an evening, or attending an employee recognition dinner or a sporting or cultural event which the company is sponsoring and for which it has taken a block of tickets. One is expected to be present at dinner parties which an executive hosts at his home for business associates or board members, and even for more casual occasions at which most of the guests come from the corporation. At such events, the corporate manager is expected to bring his or her—usually his—spouse, since the entertaining is two-by-two.

What if you're single? *The single man or woman is tolerated, though usually with some trepidation.* There are three categories of "single" people. The first—and a frequent instance in large corporations where people are moved often and regularly—is a married man whose wife and family have not yet moved to the area where he is working. This is a problem at social events that couples are to attend. This sort of man can't bring a date to these events, nor can his wife be expected to commute to them regularly. Also, it's hard for this executive to play the host. The second category includes those who are separated from their spouses but are not yet divorced; again, the social mores of most corporations frown upon this sort of person showing up at a corporate event with a date. When the divorce is final, dates are fine. The third category is the genuinely unattached man or woman. Of course, single people can generally show up with other singles, though the acceptance of this practice varies with each corporate culture.

The higher you reach in a corporation, the more scrutiny is applied to you, and the lack of a proper spouse can be a problem.

A spouse plays a role in how you are perceived by others in management, especially when you are in the process of changing companies. Some corporations look askance at a newly divorced man or woman. They wonder if he or she is stable. And they raise eyebrows at men whose family difficulties have reached the level of being a problem obvious to others. Can a man or woman who apparently can't handle his or her own household—a child's wildness or involvement with drugs, a spouse's dissatisfaction—be a viable candidate to manage a business? Often, the conclusion is that a person who seems unable to control his home environment is not a good bet for a big job. If the manager is a woman, these sorts of questions are raised and considered with even greater emphasis than if the manager is a man. That may be unfair—but it's what happens, and an upwardly bound manager, male or female, must be aware of such matters.

A spouse must not be a hindrance to a manager's career progression, and preferably should be an understanding and participative partner.

I've seen corporate households run into the following difficulty more times than I would have liked: A young couple starts out together, fairly equal in terms of education, interests, and, while they are both working, even approximately equal in income. Children come along, and the wife remains at home caring for them; meanwhile, the man is shooting ahead in terms of intellectual challenge, responsibilities, income, and level of sophistication, while his wife, at home, becomes mired in the innumerable tasks of bringing up the children and managing the household. As the years go on, there is an increasing gap in interests and sophistication between the husband and wife. At the corporate dinner parties, she talks of children while the executive seated next to her quickly exhausts his supply of small talk on this subject and pines for escape. After a few such outings, high company officials become less eager to include this couple in entertainment plans—and the husband's career suffers. The solution for such difficulties is corporate wives who keep pace with their husbands' development in some way, either through their own careers or by developing and pursuing other interests that go beyond the home, in charitable or civic affairs, continuing education, and the like.

Other problems that arise have to do with the character of the corporate wife. Her behavior must stay within certain boundaries to be deemed acceptable. If you were the host at a corporate dinner, would you want to seat an important customer executive next to a corporate wife known to make *faux pas* or to be overly flamboyant or an outrageous flirt? Of course not. As was said long ago, Caesar's wife must be above reproach—more so than the ordinary spouse.

Then there are the corporate wives who derive satisfaction from manipulation based on their husband's position in the company. In a corporation where this is the case, the hierarchy of the wives follows the power structure of the husbands' organization, sometimes with deleterious effects. Middle managers' wives are supposed to be constrained to maintaining friendships only with wives of men who are on the same level. That's not good for anyone; my wife and I disagreed with such strictures and never followed them.

Some corporate wives meddle in the business by giving advice to their husbands. The fundamental problem here doesn't necessarily begin with the wife, but, more likely, with the husband who tells his wife what's happening in the office in sufficient detail for her to offer suggestions. Of course, one talks at home about how the day went at the office, and speaks of this or that friend or acquaintance known to one's spouse. But the details of business, especially insofar as they have to do with major business decisions, ought to be kept secret by the manager from everyone—including one's spouse. There's always the chance of information going astray. A wife who catches a hint of a reorganization from her husband's dinner table conversation, and who rather innocently passes that hint along to a friend who is the wife of another executive in that corporation—perhaps even an executive who would be affected by the change—can create problems. So although when I was at home I discussed in general how things went at work, I usually kept the details to myself. If no one else knew them, then the secrets were no one's responsibility but mine.

When wives begin to offer advice on business problems, the difficulty is not that they aren't smart enough to have an opinion —of course they have the intelligence to do so—but that they are acting on incomplete information, and are making suggestions without the years of experience that the manager has. Once in my business career I had a boss who not only listened to but championed

his wife's advice on issues such as product strategy, personnel matters, and reorganizations. I knew of this because he would tell me
his wife's grievances and views, as if she were in possession of
enough of the facts for her opinion to have a great deal of weight.
Frequently, when we traveled to business meetings away from home
base, his wife would accompany us; once, when we were in his
hotel room discussing a proposed new organization and candidates
for various executive jobs—a subject of great sensitivity and with a
need for confidentiality—he invited his wife to join the discussion.
I refused to continue the meeting, which astounded both of them.
It cost me plenty, I'm sure, in terms of my relationship with my
boss, but I couldn't acquiesce to that way of doing things.

I've done myself similar harm in other corporations: there were
times at dinner parties, sporting events, and other functions when
I knew that it would benefit my career to make points with the
senior executive's spouse, so she could go home and tell him what
a wonderful person I was. I couldn't treat the spouse as royalty to
be flattered; that was a game I wouldn't play, and, frankly, a game
I should not have had to play. At times, though, not playing this
particular game hurt my chances for advancement.

In the world of big corporations a good spouse—that is to say,
one who is an excellent complement to the manager—may not be
a plus in terms of aiding the manager's career, but a bad spouse
will always be a negative. Of course people and personalities
shouldn't be assessed in this way, but they are.

THE TWO-CAREER FAMILY

During my career in management, the upper levels of a corporation
were almost exclusively dominated by men, men whose spouses,
for the most part, were homemakers who bore the prime responsibility for managing the household and raising the family's children.
Today, middle management at many of the large corporations has
a healthy percentage of women executives, and I am convinced that
in the future, the upper levels of these corporations will contain
more and more women. Analyzing the work force of the year 2000,
the Hudson Institute estimates that native-born white American
males will account for only 15 percent of the net increase in that

work force, while 55 percent of the increase will be white females; the remaining increase will come from foreign-born people and minorities. Certainly the women that I have encountered in corporations are extremely capable; it's only a matter of time before they take on some of the top jobs.

As a result of the countrywide trend toward more and more women in the workplace, many women who work in large corporations have to deal with the problems of a two-career family. In the most usual case, one member of the family works for the corporation, and the other works elsewhere. There are instances, though, where both spouses work for the same corporation. Some companies like this; more have specific policies about the working and reporting relationships of spouses, as well as other family members.

It's important to recognize that for upwardly bound managers, the existence of two careers almost inevitably produces situations which present difficulties for the manager and family.

> The two-career family needs more planning, not less, than the traditional one wherein the man works and the woman raises the children and runs the home. Each partner must know what the long-term goals are for the family and for the individuals within it.

Suppose the manager gets a promotion and has to change work hours and travel schedule. How does the spouse adjust? Or the manager? Or suppose that the manager is asked to move to another location. Will the spouse give up his or her job and move, too? Or will the spouse commute? Or will the manager have to commute?

People whose lives come to crisis points when confronted with these situations are suffering because they haven't thought things out in advance. They have avoided such nearly inevitable issues. Virtually no career in management within large corporations is made without moves from city to city (and, at times, from country to country), and an upwardly bound manager will know this. Decide what's really important to you, and what you are willing to give up. You need to game out situations on a "what if" basis.

Very often, though, the moves you gamed out seem inadequate to the task of coping with the ramifications of the real job offer when it comes along. Let's take as an example a middle manager in a large corporation in a northeastern American city, a man with a wife who also works, and school age children, who is asked to take a promotion and a bigger job in the corporation's operations in Phoenix, starting within the month. How does this two-career family adjust?

If they have thought out such situations in advance, the husband and wife may have decided that such a promotion, when offered, would be accepted, even if that meant difficulties for the wife's career. Let's face this issue squarely: having dual careers is almost inevitably going to limit the rapid advancement of one or both partners, because somewhere along the line, one or the other of the partners is going to have to give something up, or to compromise when he or she may not want to. Whose career is more important at the moment? For the long run? Is it a matter of money? Opportunities? What do we really want in life? How are we going to accomplish those things? All these questions need to be addressed by both spouses in all managers' families, but especially in the two-career families.

To get back to the example: the manager may well begin negotiations for his new job by setting conditions for his acceptance of the assignment; for instance, he may ask that the company try to find a position for his wife in Phoenix. Many companies have policies of not hiring both spouses (though some do not), but the large companies do maintain generally good relationships with other large corporations and may be able to help in this regard. But, then again, they may not; or, the manager's superiors may resent the conditions which the manager is placing on accepting the job offer. As an upwardly bound manager, you don't want to appear uncooperative; to refuse such a promotion and move may put future promotions in jeopardy. You must be flexible.

Some of the problems can be alleviated by a bit of *trailblazing*. Now, every move is difficult. We moved eleven times in twenty-two years, and got it down to a science, but there are always sources of stress. To deal with the extra problems thrown your way by the need to move, I'd suggest two strategies: making the transition quickly, and loosening the purse strings.

For instance: even though a job hasn't yet been found for his spouse, the manager may pick up and go to Phoenix, taking up residence in a hotel or in other quarters provided by the company.

Being on the site will allow him more latitude to research a job for his wife. Then, too, she can make arrangements in order to accelerate her job search or moving plans to shorten the period of commuting, which is always stressful for all the members of the family. Extra money can be spent on child care and other ancillary expenses not usually covered by the company's willingness to pay during the move.

Here's another idea for easing the pain of transitions that most people seldom consider: if you are a family that has one member making a career in the big corporations, don't build a dream house! Why? Because building a house for your family takes a lot of time and energy (and expense) and you'll hate to leave it; therefore, you may well end up refusing a transfer or promotion to see through the building process or to stay in your castle. Usually, a family buys a house when moving to another location. This can become a long, drawn-out process, but it doesn't have to be that way. When we had to move, we always bought houses very quickly and moved the household from one city to another as rapidly as we could. This action helps to stabilize the home front and gains time and energy for the manager to focus on the new assignment. When my family and I were about to move from Detroit to the Philadelphia area, my wife and I spent two weekends looking at houses, but found nothing we liked; on the third weekend, when I was alone, I found one that I thought would suit us, and called to ask her to fly in and take a look. Because we knew one another's tastes, she told me to go ahead and buy it. I did—with the stipulation to the broker and seller that we had to be able to move in within the month. "It can't be done that quickly," they squawked, but soon managed to do the impossible and we were able to move in on schedule. We bought on September 16 and moved in October 7. This fast turnaround enabled me to concentrate on my work, rather than on the drawn-out process of choosing and moving to a new home.

The question here—as always—is, "What's your priority?" If the most important thing is to get ahead fast, then many other aspects of your life must be subsumed to that. Compromising on such matters as when and where to move, what sort of a home to live in, and other such questions is essential. Compromise on matters which are not central to your focus. After all, if you're an upwardly bound manager, the chances are you and your family will have to move a handful of times before you get a position far enough up on the management ladder to stay situated at a corporate head-quarters—so why tie yourself down to a particular house or location?

Although it is unlikely that the careers of both partners will succeed fully if both of you are managers in big corporations, if only one partner is in a big corporation, and the other has a different sort of job—a profession that travels with you, for instance, like real estate, medicine, teaching, graphic arts—the couple has an enhanced ability to move from city to city, and to roll with the changes often necessitated by having one partner's life intertwined with that of a large corporation. Contrasting yet complementary careers often offer more flexibility to families that are involved with corporations than two that are very similar. With both adults employed, each can take greater risks within his or her own sphere. If the husband is blocked in his career, for instance, he can feel more comfortable about quitting his job because the wife is employed, and therefore medical coverage and some income will continue while he looks for a position which offers greater opportunities. The dual career family actually affords a couple greater security of income and independence than that obtained by the more traditional, one-income for-two household.

PART TWO

Tactics for Coping with Today's Corporations

8

Pyramids and How to Climb Them

IS THEIRS NARROW OR BROAD?

All large business organizations have management structures that resemble pyramids: there are many first-line managers who report to fewer second-line managers who, in turn, report to still fewer third-line managers—and so on, up the management ladder until at the top of the structure there is a chief executive officer who reports to the board of directors who are supposed to represent the interests of the shareholders, the owners of the corporation.

> For a manager, when considering a job at another corporation or trying to maneuver within his present one, it is essential to understand what sort of organizational structure he is operating within.

This is not as simple as it sounds, because corporations frequently reorganize their structures. Often newly appointed senior executives reorganize to fit their own management styles. At other times reorganizations occur as a result of mergers or acquisitions, or to accommodate certain marketplace pressures such as rapid growth or changes in technology. SBUs—strategic business units—are created or destroyed. Centralization of decision-making is instituted or scrapped in favor of decentralized decision-making. Even if a manager takes a job in a particular structure, chances are that it will be altered within a few years at the most. That difficulty notwithstanding, a manager considering a new job still needs information about the company's structure, and the organizational alterations that have taken place in recent years. This can be a guide to what may happen in the near future, particularly if the people in the top positions are those who have implemented the recent changes.

Most large corporations have anywhere from seven to twelve levels of management between workers and CEO. Typically, each middle manager in such structures has from two to sixteen direct reports. More layers and fewer direct reports makes for a rather tall, steep, and narrow pyramid; the structure is theoretically sound, but, in practice, the many layers become an impediment to the management process. *Show me a steep or narrow organization chart covering a great many layers of management, and I'll show you a company that isn't working efficiently.* In such corporations, senior management is invariably out of touch with the employees, and, as a consequence, is poorly informed. In such companies one observes:

1. slow or often garbled communications up and down the line;
2. many approval or concurrence signatures are required before action can be taken on even moderately important matters;
3. lots of time-wasting meetings at all levels of management;
4. the prevalence of many committees whose tasks are to substitute for the poor or turgid communications;
5. an atmosphere wherein groupthink prevails, accountability is diffused, and a good deal of time gets lost before ideas are translated into actions.

A company with a broad or flattened structure is more likely to be efficient. In a broader, flatter, lower pyramid, there will be fewer layers between workers and the CEO, and each manger is likely to have a greater number of direct reports than his counterpart in a narrow structure. In a broad pyramid, one observes:

1. fewer committees;
2. enhanced communications;
3. speedier decision-making;
4. a reduced amount of bureaucratic procedures; and,
5. the most important factor: management at all levels that is forced to have greater personal knowledge of the business and of their key employees.

For an ambitious young manager, this last point is essential: in a broad, low pyramid he or she is more likely to come quickly to the attention of senior managers who can foster a career.

Now, organizational charts are usually proprietary documents, not the least because they are a headhunter's dream, but as a job applicant you should ask to see one while on the company's premises. You can probably get enough of a glance at one to tell you what you need to know. Count the levels between workers and CEO. See what the divisions and groups are, and the titles of various managers. You're not interested in the names of the managers, and the titles are only of marginal importance. The titles are noteworthy only if they are not liberally given out. Some organizations—banks are the foremost perpetrators—habitually bestow a lot of grandiose titles such as vice-president, group or division president, and so on; there are so many of these in such organizations that the titles are meaningless insofar as evaluating their power in the corporate structure. Such a profusion of titles is made to impress the outside world, and often in lieu of pay. They can, however, be useful in a résumé; after all, "president of division X" sounds better than "manager of division X," though the job's responsibilities may be precisely the same.

The main item for your edification is the number of levels. If there are too many, then the probability is high that on accepting a middle management position with that company, you'll get caught in a bureaucratic jumble that will undoubtedly slow your progress to the top. The number of levels is also a good indicator of the management style of the company because it is a reflection of the proclivities of your potential new CEO and COO. If faced with a narrow pyramid, you may well have reason to wonder if you'll ever get to meet either of those two officers. Some people argue that it's not important for a middle manager to meet the top people until he has moved further along. I disagree. The CEO and COO need to be approachable and visible to middle managers, and the reasons go beyond the symbolic importance of having the troops know who the leaders are. If they are distant figures, it will be hard for a middle manager to challenge the bureaucracy in any meaningful way—and challenging it is just what an ambitious person needs to do.

As a manager in an organization, you can do certain things to help yourself within any kind of structure. Lead by example: *start flattening the organization beneath you;* other managers may well pick up on the style, and the company will benefit in two ways—by improving its efficiency and by saving money. In two companies in which I worked, by routinely reviewing our structure we were able to eliminate literally thousands of middle management jobs and to save millions of dollars in expenses. By flattening your own structure, too, you can raise your own visibility, not the least by demonstrating how you've saved the company some expenses, and probably improved both the productivity and the happiness of your employees.

Speaking of getting rid of excess management, I must point out that one component of most pyramids that tends to perpetuate itself is the staff. Every once in a while, when there's a drive within an organization to reduce expenses through the elimination of layers of management or even through straight layoffs, a favorite target is the staff, and particularly the staff at corporate headquarters. When the dust clears away, though, I usually find that the staff function and their people have survived. Somehow they've made their way into operating units so that their presence is no longer visible at headquarters, or otherwise hidden themselves in the woodwork. But they're still on the payroll, and the likelihood is that when the cost-cutting frenzy eases, they'll find their way back to headquarters.

When looking at a prospective new employer's organizational chart, then, *evaluate the size of the various staffs and try to get a sense of the power they carry in the bureaucracy*—another good mirror in which to read top management's style and philosophy. Some staff people have titles that are so obscure as to render impossible the task of discerning what they do. Can you tell me precisely what is done by the vice-president in charge of corporate development? VP of special programs? VP of strategy? Someone in charge of these areas could be doing a great deal—or nothing at all. Examine the staffs attached to marketing, engineering, manufacturing, program and product management, as well as those in the regular staff areas such as legal, accounting, finance, and human resources. I am a supporter of a lean, highly professional staff, each member of which adds value to the corporation beyond controlling and policing the organization. Some executives prefer to manage through the use of larger staffs. Staffs generate work that feeds on itself, and, further, that results in extra loads for line operations which are asked to turn out volumes of often meaningless paperwork in answer to staff queries. When line operators take the time to respond to staff inquiries, their own decision-making process gets slowed down.

Push your interviewer (who may well be your next boss) about what the staff people on the chart do, and what certain ambiguous titles mean. If the answer contains the phrase "some things are difficult to explain," or the answer itself is so vague as to be without value, my advice to you is to forget this job.

Another alarm bell should ring when you see a structure that shows complete symmetry throughout all the organizational entities of the company. Why? Isn't such a structure clear, simple, and logical? It may appear so, but look closer: in that structure if the general manager of the subsidiary in Uruguay, with $10 million in sales, has the same complement of subordinates and staff as do the $100 million each subsidiaries in France or Japan, symmetry can be an indication of trouble. It will mean that the organizational structure has been centrally imposed, that the general managers are given very little latitude in managing their business affairs, and—even worse—that all of the subsidiaries, even the smallest ones, are expected to report operating details to corporate headquarters in the same format, degree, and frequency. Such reporting, in turn, means the existence of many gnomes to process the materials at division, group, subsidiary, and corporate headquarters—and added expense—that a small or a growing company cannot afford. Does every subsidiary require a human resources office? Of course not; in some small entities, the general manager and a secretary can handle the paperwork. If every small unit within a large one has its own HR, legal, accounting, and other such staffs—for the sake of symmetry—trouble lies ahead for an ambitious manager who wants to run a lean unit within such an organization.

How are the organizational chart's reporting lines drawn? Are they dotted or solid lines? This matter comes up only in reference to staff functions, and frequently in regard to the financial and legal organizations. There is debate in the business world as to whether all financial people (accountants, analysts, controllers) should report directly to others in finance above them and eventually to the CFO, or whether divisional controllers and their minions should report to their respective division presidents and only take functional guidance—that's why their lines are dotted—from the CFO's office. The debate carries over into how controllers at remote locations such as a factory or sales office should report to divisional controllers. And how about the legal or HR staffs in those locations?

As a senior executive in several corporations, I never found much difference in efficacy of people holding financial jobs who reported by means of solid as opposed to dotted lines—except to be subjected to a lot of dickering about the rival approaches, and to conclude that such dickering took away from getting the job done. Invariably, people in these functions end up having two bosses, one at their site and another at headquarters; it's bad enough having one boss, but two is enough to make anyone's life miserable. In a company where such debates are prevalent, what you're likely to see are turf battles, the CFO and his organization battling divisional presidents for the right to decide to whom the financial officers report, and to whom they owe their allegiance and their next jobs. *Middle managers often get caught in the crossfire of solid and dotted lines, and seldom emerge unscathed.*

HOW MANY SIGNATURES DANCE ON THE HEAD OF A MEMO?

The number of approval or sign-off levels required before an idea is translated into action is another indicator of potential career progress or lack thereof. Ask to see the distribution and approval lists on internal correspondence. Are they lengthy? Long lists indicate sand in the gears of the bureaucratic machinery.

When considering joining an organization, you seek a sense of whether your presence will make a difference. How can you know that before you sign up? Basically, you are looking for opportunities to advance, and there are less of these in an organization whose processes are encumbered. *A manager's cutting edge rests on his ability to get things done, which depends not only on his ability to make decisions, but his effectiveness in getting his own decisions ratified.* The ratification process is a reflection of senior management's willingness to delegate authority. Are the senior managers willing to trust your judgment, and to what degree?

Partly, of course, their willingness to delegate will depend upon your own ability to *sell* your ideas upward. Every good manager must be a good salesman and champion for his own ideas; if not, rapid progress is almost impossible. Many approvals can be obtained on perception and image—the way it is presented—rather than on the substance of an idea. Still, even if you're a good salesman, those above you need the authority to ratify your ideas if you are to be able to execute them in a timely fashion.

Delegation of authority begins with the board of directors' degree of willingness to allow the CEO latitude in running the company. Once this has been established, the CEO will define how much authority is to be given downward throughout the organization to the lowest-level manager. The ways in which authority is delegated will determine the amount of time it takes to execute decisions, that is, to turn ideas into action; it will also affect the quality of managers the company is likely to attract and retain. An ambitious, hard-driving manager, if he is to act as a valuable asset to the company, needs the elbowroom to operate with the minimum amount of constraint. Where a large number of management reviews and signatures on memos are common before decisions are made, companies will either lose good managers or will cause those who stay to become risk-averse, slow-moving bureaucrats.

Good delegation of authority starts at the top. Management can foster it by hiring and promoting decisive managers, trusting them, and letting them do their jobs. This will not mean an abdication of responsibility by management, for there are many ways to keep track of what's going on and even to correct decisions made by poor managers. The occasional price that a few-signatures company pays for having some management errors is less than the price paid every day by a many-signatures company whose processes are bureaucratized and whose initiative has been dampened by overreview. I worked for one large company that used a complex and lengthy standard document to justify and obtain approval for capital improvements, research and development projects, and product-pricing strategies, even those which had been initiated at low levels of the organization. The top page had a list of six to twelve signatures from ascending management levels, all of whom had to approve the investment before it could be made. You can imagine how slowly such a document passed through the bureaucracy. Sometimes, to test whether certain people below me had actually read and understood a particular request document, I'd telephone one of the managers or executives who had signed it and pretend to require clarification from them about issues in it that I didn't understand. From their answers, or, as often, their lack of answers, it was apparent to me that many who had signed and approved the request either hadn't read it at all, or hadn't understood it if they had. The culprits were not all bad or irresponsible managers, they were simply overwhelmed by the work load and the paper that the bureaucratic process was generating. Since they knew that additional signatures would have to follow theirs, they assumed (1) that the manager who initiated the request was a responsible person and had good reason for putting in the request, and (2) that if there was a problem one of the many following signers would stop the request from proceeding. Thus the very process that was supposed to help the system be a controlled one was hindering it. Nobody was accepting authority. Instead of being based on trust, the process was based on mistrust—and it still wasn't working. I tried hard to change it, arguing with my own superior that my phone calls had proved the system's ill worth, but was not able to alter it, and by the time I left the company the number of signatures required on certain documents had actually increased! That was because it had become prestigious to be on the distribution list.

Of course it is important to have your colleagues, your superiors, and certain support functions review important decisions such as large capital and engineering investments, the alteration of product schedules or costs, the proposed changes in organizational structures, those expenses which may be outside previously approved annual budgets, and so on. In functionally organized companies, where interdependency among various entities is great, a fair number of lateral management signatures may well be needed, because a decision taken by, say, the manufacturing organization will certainly have an impact on sales, and vice versa. Circulating a document about such a decision is, in fact, a good way to inform everyone and to ascertain whether there are any objections before going ahead. But if there are too many memos of this sort, or if too many signatures are required on each one, corporate gridlock is the result.

In another company for which I worked, there was a program for recognizing employees for outstanding performance. One part carried a cash award of up to $1,500, and another the novelty of a company-paid dinner for two at high-quality restaurants. If, for example, a secretary had come in over the weekend to help ready a report for an important Monday meeting, and to do so had left her family at home to fend for themselves, it was good for the manager to be able to call her in on Monday and suggest that as a token of his and the company's appreciation she take her husband out to dinner, and to hand her a chit for one of the restaurants in the plan. Thus, as thank-you's for special efforts, these awards caught on quickly and were well received. Then the bureaucracy got into the act; soon, to give out such an award began to require budgetary approval from the personnel department, the finance department, the divisional manager, and so on. Shortly thereafter, what started out as a good program was bogged down. The secretary who should have been rewarded immediately on a Monday had to wait weeks, sometimes even months, for her award, and the effectiveness of it was vitiated. Fewer and fewer managers chose to use the program. When confronted with the slowdown imposed on it by the bureaucracy, I continued to reward people instantly with dinners and such, paid for out of my own pocket, or by inviting people out to dinner with my wife and me, or to come to our house for an evening. I never asked the company for reimbursement. The saying of thank you in some form to colleagues who have worked hard should never have to wait for twelve signatures.

Often, managers who want to break the bureaucratic impasses are told there is no hope for doing so, that someone—presumably the man at the top—has created the system and so it can't be changed. I don't accept that premise. *The fault lies not only with the "someone" who instigated the bureaucratic impasses, but with ourselves, all of us who perpetuate the system by cooperating with it and acquiescing to those elements of it that slow down and emasculate the decision-making process.*

BEWARE OF COMMITTEES AND CONSULTANTS

As I've pointed out, companies with steep pyramids are invariably loaded down with committees. This is not to say that broader pyramids are not also encumbered, just that they are less likely to have lots of committees. *When interviewing for a job, find out how many standing committees or task forces or study groups are in existence in the company as a whole, and in your area in particular.* What is their makeup? How often do they meet? What important decisions have they made lately? Committees can also slow the management process and hamper an individual manager's ability to make his mark. The more committees, the more meetings a manager must attend and the greater the amount of paperwork to be read and generated; most decisions arrived at by committees are consensus positions, compromises that are never as radical or as innovative as decisions reached by individuals. And, of course, when a decision is made by a group, accountability for it is diffused. No single person gets the blame for a bad decision—but no single person can take the credit for a good one either.

The least useful committees are the permanent, so-called standing ones. (If the members actually stood up at the meetings, their sessions would be shorter!) Standing committees are generally composed of senior members of management who review jointly the various parts of the business for which they are responsible. Members are urged to speak their minds, but most don't; they are cautious and unwilling to offend their colleagues, and fear the consequences of candor that they would feel when it is their "turn in the barrel." Having been a member of high-level standing committees at three corporations, I can categorically state that they are not worth the time spent on them. Occasionally, some of these meetings serve to convey information to uninformed senior executives, people who could easily obtain the same information if they were more involved in the day-to-day business of the company. Incredible though it may sound, many senior executives have neither the experience nor the knowledge of the business to evaluate the information presented to them. I've seen many who sit in these meetings and say nothing, out of fear of their ignorance being discovered. Others are silent because the chairman of the committee—usually the most senior executive of the group—has made it plain by his earlier actions that those who question or, God forbid, criticize what is being presented will later be crucified.

I know that there are many executives who profess to like management by consensus—what has been billed as Japanese-style management—but I don't think the style is applicable to the mentality, needs, and financial performance expectations of U.S. corporations. For instance, the Japanese take a long-term approach to a company's profitability and growth; American companies are forced by the pressures that we collectively call Wall Street to focus on the short term. In our companies, managers are paid to make decisions, and those who want to advance itch to make decisions. *My preference is for open discussions in which everyone is encouraged to air his or her view, after which the executive in charge makes an informed choice among the options presented.* If the open discussion metamorphoses into a permanent debate, the few positive aspects of a group meeting are usually lost. Some other positive things: certain operating committees can accelerate the approval process, say, on capital expenditures or other key investment areas, by meeting regularly and issuing prompt decisions on matters that would otherwise have to go through the twelve-signatures dance. Most useful are those committees that are really temporary task forces to analyze and recommend how to solve specific business problems whose solutions require the diverse skills that the various members bring to the task. Such a task force makes its recommendation and then self-destructs; the negative thing is that once the task force has reported, and unless one of the members is put in charge of implementing the recommendation, the good idea is often shelved or derailed by the bureaucracy. The main reason for such disregard: all too often the recommendations run counter to the wishes of the executives who commissioned the task force. *A good commissioning executive guides a committee so that it will come up with recommendations he can live with.* Occasionally, though, even with the surest of guidance, an internal committee delivers recommendations counter to the commissioner's expectations.

That rarely happens with the recommendations of those outside committees called consultants.

My antipathy to consultants is rooted in the fact that virtually none of them have to stick around to implement their recommendations or findings, nor are they held accountable for them. Consultants come, they see, they critique, they write and present a report—and then they vanish. Or, just as often, they phrase their recommendations in such a way that the matter is said to require further study by, guess who, themselves.

Now, a certain kind of consultant is occasionally needed to solve highly specialized problems for which the company doesn't possess the skills and doesn't need the expertise on a recurring basis. For example, I recall a serious problem at a textile company— corrosion around ball bearings in certain looms—that required the services of a consultant. Downtime in looms is bad news for a textile company, and so this one called in a professor of metallurgy to analyze the problem. He determined that the factory's environment was hostile, meaning that the air in the factory contained certain corrosive elements. The airflow was filtered, and the looms worked happily ever after. The professor was sent on his way. Had the problem been endemic, that is, had rust been occurring regularly throughout the system, I would argue that the company should put on staff someone with the necessary expertise to take care of the problem—but not to continuously rehire the consultant.

Most consultants don't fit into the highly specialized, one-time-only category. I feel confident about saying so, because, since leaving Unisys at the end of 1987, I have myself occasionally been a consultant to several companies. I took on the consulting work because it could be done in short bursts, and therefore would not cut too deeply into the time I wanted to spend on my own personal affairs, and also because it offered me the opportunity to keep my hand in.

I'm happy to report that I found the work pleasant, containable, and adequately paid. I'm even happier to say that I was actually able to help in a few instances; some of my recommendations were implemented, though not as many as I thought should have been. Further, some of my recommendations were badly compromised when implemented. I think I was a good consultant; I gave my best advice, based on hands-on experience with a half-dozen multinational corporations over twenty-plus years, and I didn't care whether or not the companies for whom I was consulting ever hired me again.

Also, I should confess that during my career in management I occasionally hired consultants for specific tasks. I remember two cases, at two different companies, where the circumstances were remarkably similar. I had been in each company less than a year and had found, to my dismay, that a couple of highly specialized areas lacked the proper management. In each instance I brought in an experienced executive who didn't want to be employed on a permanent basis but who agreed to take on the job full-time for a limited period during which he would manage the area and help me find permanent replacements. Both instances worked out well; in one, we decided to get out of the specific product line, and I had in charge a consultant who wasn't concerned with working himself out of a job. In the second situation, the consultant succeeded in recruiting a top-notch executive to replace himself, which was just what I'd wanted.

They came, they worked, and they left—or, in the case of the second man, accepted an even more responsible job with our corporation. But these were executives with years of experience; as I have frequently been astounded to discover, *most consultants are sorely lacking in hands-on experience with the areas in which they are giving advice.* Often they have sharpened their skills in academia; more than a few are professors whose sum total of experience has come from textbooks or from the consulting they've done for other companies. That's okay when it comes to solving such specific problems as the rust on the ball bearings, but not very good when the issues are broader and more vague. In regard to important business problems—how to best organize the company, where in the world to site key facilities (including corporate headquarters), the development of strategic plans, the formulating of programs for uplifting the morale of the employees—consultants are of no help to the companies that hire them. *I cannot think of a single instance where a broad-based consultant helped solve a real problem for a big corporation; more often than not, for their healthy fee consultants just participate in the decision process or are used as political tools by the managers who hire them.*

Consultants are supposed to come into a situation with two important givens: their own expertise, and their independent, unbiased viewpoint. On that first point, as I have described, most of them flunk. And on the second—well, let me state categorically that *consultants are frequently biased toward the views of the executive who has hired them.* I'll give you a personal example. During my work as a consultant in 1988 I was asked by a senior executive in a company to look at one of his business units and assess its viability. It was an area in which I had previously had extensive business experience; I investigated and concluded that there was no future in that area for my client's company. This was not the conclusion my client expected or wanted to hear. He asked me to look again, and debated the matter with me in an effort to have me change my mind. The facts were still the same, so my conclusion remained the same. I suspect that executive won't call me again to get my opinion on other problems. But had I been in the consulting business as a serious and long-term endeavor, I would not have ventured to suggest, and certainly not to push, a conclusion contrary to the commissioning executive's predilections, for that would dry up future business.

Many inexperienced young MBAs join consulting firms that are hired by large corporations at exorbitant fees, and are soon offering advice based on nothing but classwork. This is a puzzle to me.

Here is a scenario that shows how most consulting work comes into being. A CEO who is considering a major reorganization of his company thinks it might be reasonable to form it along business unit, rather than functional lines. To give him advice on what needs to be done, and the options open to him, he hires a consulting firm. After he has briefed the firm's partner, who will head up the project team, the firm's team will arrive on the company's premises and spend several months or even longer educating themselves and asking a lot of questions, during which time the company's rumor mills will be going at full blast. Then they will labor and produce a report that will characteristically run to several weighty volumes. Invariably, these reports will come to the following conclusions:

1. The concept of the CEO or the manager who hired them will be proven correct.
2. The volumes will give inordinate detail on how the problem should be solved, with some mildly innovative suggestions for improvement.
3. It will be stated that there are more problems inherent in implementing the change than the company has heretofore realized, and that these problems are of even greater complexity than had been envisioned. The consultants document these problems to the degree that senior management's eyebrows rise in consternation. However, the consultants point out, these are "managable risks," and. . . .
4. The consultants will recommend their own rehiring to help management cope with the next phase of the problem and the execution of the solution. (I call this the flypaper factor. Once consultants arrive, they stick to you like flypaper.)

Whether the problem is a reorganization, an acquisition, an office site relocation, or some other business issue, the four cardinal points of consultants' work remain the same. Sometimes they will juggle numbers or redefine geographical areas to reach the proper conclusion—that is, the one the CEO or commissioning executive had in mind. When Burroughs acquired Sperry and senior management wanted to move our headquarters, consultants were hired to assess the availability and cost of housing in the Philadelphia area. Now anyone who picked up the Sunday newspapers in Philadelphia and in Detroit and compared real estate prices would soon have concluded that, in general, housing in the Philadelphia area was significantly more expensive than in Detroit, where Burroughs had been located. But our consultants defined the metropolitan area very loosely and included districts far from downtown Philadelphia and beyond the proposed headquarters site in Bluebell—sites so far west that they were beyond reasonable commuting distance and out of reach of airports—in order to come up with numbers that showed it would cost only about 20 percent more to live in the Philadelphia area than in comparable suburbs of Detroit.

In this instance, as in so many others, the consultants were principally useful to the commissioning executives as a *selling tool*. Senior management was going to move one of the dual headquarters to Bluebell anyway and was using the consultants' study to justify the move to the board of directors and to pacify employees like myself who would be forced to relocate. *It is often the case that a decision reached by an executive may not sit well with senior managers, or with the board, or with any other constituency within the company, and having the conclusion come from the "independent, unbiased" consultants seems to make it more palatable to the target audience.*

When faced with a company that has gotten into the habit of frequently using consultants and committees, an ambitious manager may want to change employers; but, these days, it's hard to find a company that is not besotted with committees and consultants. Therefore, it behooves the ambitious manager to learn how to maneuver in an environment influenced by these twin evils.

In most companies, committees tend to be multidisciplinary, and in their work they favor people who are committee members, or who present to the committees; this, in turn, usually means people whose verbal and written communications skills serve them well. In most cases, the people who are the best at such things are not the engineers, technical people, or financial experts, but, rather, those whose backgrounds are in marketing and sales, since it is by communications skills that these latter individuals make their living. Looking back on my own career, I can see that when I began in management, as with most engineers and scientists I was deficient in communications skills; my written and verbal reports were not the best. And, in front of committees, I had to counter the silver tongues of my colleagues from sales and marketing by my own absolute mastery of facts, my hard work, and good results—and to balance my own not so well delivered and oftimes abrasive presentations. I am convinced that my career would have moved along even more quickly had I mastered the art of communication earlier than I did. I now know what the skills are: they include an understanding of the audience and of the environment in which the meeting is taking place, the use of proper presentation format, a well-paced and clear verbal delivery (you'd be amazed how many people drop their voices to an unintelligible whisper or talk too fast during a presentation), good command of the language, a sense of humor, and good use of hands and gestures. Just as actors learn all these skills, managers can master them, too.

Good communications skills are absolutely essential to getting things done when working with committees.

Now, which committees to work with? Choose them carefully. You can't, and shouldn't, avoid them all. If these groups play a pivotal role in the company, you should be part of them. You can gain good visibiltiy by heading a key task force, which I define as one whose findings are of importance to senior management; that's especially helpful if the findings can lead to a new job for you implementing the recommendations. Even if you haven't been asked to be the committee chairman, you might well participate if you can see that most of those on the committee will not work as hard as you will; in that case, through hard work you can assume a leadership position. When in charge, even of a subgroup, you have a position of power because you can control:

—*the final conclusions and recommendations of the group;*
—*the presentation format (choosing one that is to your best advantage);*
—*the content of what is being presented; and*
—*the distribution list (so that the information will go to those who you think ought to have it, rather than only to those whom your colleagues and superiors want to keep informed).*

As far as working with consultants who have been retained by your bosses, *if you as a manager agree with the obviously preconceived conclusions of the consultants, then embrace these and assist the inquiry.* Remember, the consultants are looking for all the help they can get in order to justify their final recommendations. If, on the other hand, you disagree with the conclusions you expect them to hand in, try to guide the consultants to include in their recommendations the options that reflect your own thought—while still appearing to be supportive of their work. Often, in this manner, you can use the consultants to send a strong message to senior management, a message that would be unpalatable if it were delivered by you in person. Remember, too, that consultants are often asked informally by the commissioning executives to give their views on the quality, reputation, and other aspects of the individual managers they've encountered in the company. Their "independent, unbiased" opinion may carry a good deal of weight with upper management, and can often make or break a career.

9

Keeping in Touch with Your Allies

*T*HERE ARE many allies whom an upwardly bound manager will want to nurture. There are *networks within a company*, associations of *professionals through professional organizations and acquaintances at other corporations*, and, third, *community allies* who operate, for the most part, entirely out of the workplace.

NETWORKS WITHIN THE COMPANY

In any company, there are cadres of people. Some are associated with a single leader, others form groups that tend to stick together. While I advocate never tying yourself exclusively to one mentor or group, it is useful to belong to a network within a company. A network consists of people with whom you trade information, a commodity essential in business. Information in the corporate world means power and control.

A network of trading partners is the key to gaining knowledge of what's going on in your company, and can be crucial to your advancement.

Don't be like . . .

Bad Example # 7: Stingy the Nonsharer
When it comes to sharing information, this person keeps the cards close to the vest; he or she also doesn't know how to ask for help from others. This dunce thinks it's weak to ask for assistance or to share information. That's definitely not true. In many large companies, certain essential work will not get done if you follow all the rules. When you live by the rules, you can die by them. Say, for instance, you're in marketing, and you develop a friend in the manufacturing or engineering side; you may learn from that person well in advance about potential shortages of products coming down the line. Such knowledge may allow you to make the most timely shift in your sales emphasis onto products you had previously not expected to sell as well as those that had been foremost in your forecast, and thus achieve your targets. Network information can often make the difference between your being a winner or a loser.

It behooves you to *cultivate people in other parts of the corporation*, those lateral to you, as well as those a level or two above and below you in other divisions—and some who are at lower levels but by the nature of their assignments happen to be privy to important information. It's equally as imperative to pay attention to the flip side of the equation, and not to blame other divisions for problems in your own area of responsibility. If products are in short supply, don't automatically blame the product-supplying divisions (manufacturing); rather, work with them to solve the common difficulty—and always be sure, if it gets solved, to share with the other division the credit for success. Often the information is given to you in strictest confidence, and you must realize that it can compromise the one who gave it to you; respect the trust by finding uses for it that won't reveal its probable source. Be clear on what sort of information is being passed. Most of the time, it's hunches, things that haven't yet reached the status of fact, or even trends;

it's preliminary, early information, the sense of which way things are going. One friend involved in procurement tells you there *might* be a shortage of chips. Another hints that a position *could* open up in another division in the near future. A third, over coffee, suggests there *will probably be* more leeway to adjust margins in the selling price of the winches than in the price of the screwdrivers.

It's nice that you can develop friendships through such networks, but the vital thing is that from them you obtain and share information. *If you have more information about what's going on, you will be ahead of the pack.* Having more information will allow you to:

1. not be surprised by new developments;
2. be able to pick projects to work on within the company that are likely to have the greatest impact; and
3. be well informed at meetings crucial to the department, division, or company.

In order to obtain information that is both vital and helpful, you have to offer some of your own. Think about what you might provide, and dig to get a tidbit you can pass on to a friend—don't be a taker without also being a giver, because your sources will soon dry up. The amount and quality of the information you receive varies with the degree of trust that you share with the other participants, and the amount of information (or assistance) you can provide them.

Recognize that *it takes work to set up and maintain a good network.* If people are transferred, keep in touch with them. When you transfer your subordinates out to take jobs elsewhere, keep in touch, for a trust, once established, can be a wonder if it is reinforced regularly. Here's an area where your own self-interest, the part of you that seeks to advance, has a complete commonality of interest with the part that wants to keep faith with friends. Make mental notes to yourself to call your previous colleagues frequently, even if one is now in Tuscaloosa instead of at headquarters in Chicago.

I've noticed that when you ask people how things are going, they give you the best answers when the state of affairs in their corner of the world is either very good or very bad. When you get bland answers to your questions, you can assume that not much of interest is happening, or, at least, that your network partner doesn't know much about it.

Networks are also vital in obtaining for yourself points of view other than the ones you are exposed to in your own, usually narrow, area of responsibility. The view in marketing differs from that in sales, or in engineering, and so forth. The wider your perspective, the broader your potential understanding of the way the company as a whole is operating. Those with the broad views are the most likely to find things to do that most directly impact the company's business, and consequently be more promotable.

You can also obtain good information by talking to people who work in unpopular departments or organizations. The prime examples here are the company's internal auditors. The main mission of any company's internal audit department is to ascertain whether or not employees are complying with the company's policies, practices, and procedures. At the beginning of each year, the auditors pick topics on which to concentrate; it's impossible to audit every area of the company every year, and so they are done in rotation. Generally, good audit departmental assessments go beyond deciding whether organizations are in compliance, and offer suggestions for procedural or operational improvement to areas and people that don't have access to ideas already current in other parts of the company. For example, they might audit a subsidiary in Brazil, find that most aspects of it are going along fine, but that the subsidiary could use more stringent inventory controls. Sometimes the auditors make recommendations for management changes, disciplinary actions, and the like. Most people in large corporations view the auditors as a police force, or, at best, an unwanted bunch of interlopers. As a consequence, many auditors feel left out of the normal camaraderie of the workplace—which means you can befriend them a bit more easily than you can other employees. Usually, such auditors have excellent information on many aspects of the company's business. As you go up the ladder, if you've kept faith with the auditors, you may ask to be placed on the internal distribution list of their reports, which are a sure source of information on the company. Audit reports are not always trouble reports; some are routine, but they are still excellent descriptions of how various sections of the company operate.

As you ascend the management ladder, networking becomes more necessary than ever, and more perilous. For instance, there are risks associated with being too personally close to those who work directly for you. *It's important to separate the friendship aspect from the work—though it's not always possible.* Also, there are often times when you may be torn between doing what's right for the company, and doing what's good for your friends; this, too, argues for keeping a proper distance from your subordinates, lest you be caught deciding matters on the wrong basis. What do you do in a situation where you and a subordinate are friends, and your wives are friends, and there comes a time when the man isn't pulling his weight and should be separated or transferred to a less desirable job? Sadly, I've been in this situation more times than I would have liked, but it hasn't stopped me from being friends. Some of those who remain my best friends have worked for me at one time or another.

WHAT DO YOU HEAR IN KOKOMO?

Upwardly mobile managers will want to participate in professional associations and other groups that draw their membership from many different companies. Information is the key in these networks as it is in an internal network. At the conventions and meetings of the professional associations, of which there are many, one can learn details of everything from management to marketing to engineering; there also are opportunities in such organizations to interact with your peers. Out of these meetings often come tips on jobs, on the way competitors run similar businesses or departments, and so on. Membership in associations also looks good on your résumé, but only in the prestigious ones; most members attend very few meetings, and, frankly, aren't expected to attend them all. For the upwardly bound manager, attendance at a meeting every now and then is enough.

Another aspect of your external networks is having good relations with the various executive recruiting firms—the headhunters. Often, reference to them will come initially from an outside professional association. By talking to the headhunters when they call, and by making referrals to them, you establish helpful allies for your own career moves.

For the most part, the professional associations are useful to lower- and middle-level managers, but not to higher-ranking executives who no longer need the sorts of information provided at the meetings, or the jobs the external buddy system can suggest. People at a higher level will join other associations, such as the Conference Board, which has hundreds of member companies, or the National Chamber of Commerce. At the highest levels, there are certain industry-wide clubs which are the key to networking, and can be interesting and fun to belong to. Most of the public, and, indeed, many people within large companies, including many senior executives, don't know of the existence of the Electrical Manufacturers Club or the Conquistadores del Cielo, to name just two important organizations in electrical equipment manufacturing and the aerospace industry.

The EMC was founded in 1908, and the eighty or so members are all invited to join. They are mostly presidents or chairmen of companies which have electrical equipment or electronics as a major component of their business; they hail from such companies as IBM, Westinghouse, AT&T, Northern Telecom, Zenith, Xerox, and Motorola. The EMC holds two meetings a year for members and spouses, always at resorts and scheduled for weekends. On Friday there is a business session of an hour or so, but from then on through a brunch on Sunday, it's entirely social, with plenty of time for golf, tennis, lawn bowls, shooting, swimming, and other recreation. Friday night's dinner is informal, Saturday's black tie, and at the dinners seating is assigned by pulling numbers out of a hat, so no cliques will form. If you miss several meetings in a row, you are asked to resign. Members refrain from talking about business except in the most general terms—the state of the economy, the health of the industry. The ideal is for the senior executives in the industry to establish relationships with one another, and they do. It's one of the most pleasant groups I've ever had the privilege of joining.

YOUR COMMUNITY OF FRIENDS

Other organizations with which an executive can become involved are more specifically based in the local and national communities. Because of the economic clout of the large companies, high-level executives from them are always in demand for chambers of commerce, the boards of hospitals, universities, and museum or other cultural committees. These organizations hope that the executives will involve their companies and obtain donations from them, but they also expect to benefit from the senior executive's experience in management. On the other side, the companies are helped by increased access to the institutions. For instance, when I was on the board of Henry Ford Hospital in Detroit, and a colleague of mine developed what he thought was a cancer, I was able to make a phone call to the hospital's chief of staff which helped my colleague obtain a quick and thankfully negative diagnosis. The hospital was glad to have me on the board, too, because that helped seal our company's arrangement to send many of our employees to their facilities for their medical needs.

The intermingling of business executives with leaders from other sectors of society on such boards often has serendipitous consequences:

—A person who serves on the same hospital board as you do happens also to be a board member of one of your company's major suppliers; you will now have an unofficial but very important channel to that supplier.

—You become involved with the local symphony; a banker on the financial committee of the symphony has been trying to get your company involved as a contributor for a long time—and it so happens that your company is in the process of seeking favorable banking arrangements; in such a situation, you have a lot of room for trading.

Then, too, when you are on one company board, you invariably receive invitations to join other company boards, which leads to higher visibility for you within the industrial community as a whole, as well as providing perspective on other industries than your own. Such community and company board memberships burnish and broaden your image; you gain the reputation of being an individual of wide interests, and are invited to participate in other select circles—say, for instance, a White House committee, a gubernatorial task force, or a multi-industry national group.

10

Targets and Opportunities

*Y*OU are a competent, even a very competent manager or junior executive, and are determined to advance further. Looking around, however, you get a sense that just doing your job is not the key to getting ahead quickly. You see some people making great strides while others, who seem equally as competent, aren't getting the breaks. What's the difference between those who progress rapidly and those who stagnate? Most people ascribe it to being lucky enough to have good timing. But timing is not ephemeral or beyond your control. *Timing is a matter of targets, opportunities, and how you take advantage of them.* By picking the right targets and finding opportunities you create your own good timing.

How can you know which targets are important? For that matter, how can you decide on the real importance of anything in a corporation?

WHAT'S YOUR OBJECTIVE?

To get at the answers to the questions just posed, let's begin by taking an insider's look at some corporate ground rules. Most large corporations use some form of what are most generally called MBOs—Management by Objectives assessments—to judge how their people are performing. At least once a year, a manager sits down with his or her immediate superior and they work out objectives for the employee to meet in the next twelve months. Employees are told that their performance will be evaluated on the basis of these goals.

Most employees, and not a few executives, think that developing MBOs is just another of those endless bureaucratic procedures that mean so little but generate so much paper. While I'm a paper-hater myself, and I prefer setting quarterly goals that are tougher and more realistic, I find that annual MBOs are necessary, though not for the usual reasons given. For the rising star, *MBOs are a road map to understanding what's really important in your job; they are a way of assessing your targets.*

MBO lists are weighted toward the top; that is, the first objective may count for 30 percent of your annual evaluation, the second for 20 percent, and so on down the page in order of diminishing importance. If your prime MBO is achieving a sales quota, and the second is making sure the orders are delivered, these are the major tasks. That item down near the bottom—the hiring of an assistant manager—is of much less concern. If you spend too much time hiring that assistant, and if in the process you let your sales slide (on the mistaken assumption that all the objectives are equally weighted), your boss may well have grounds for evaluating you badly. Study your MBOs as a guide to where to put your energy and time, and understand that to excel means to surpass all the goals.

This is another way of saying what I've advocated earlier in this book: that you must be keenly aware of what the bottom line is for your area of responsibility, and apply yourself to it as your foremost task.

But what if the bottom line isn't adequately reflected in your MBOs? For instance, your top priority has been listed in terms of sales, but the boss keeps harping on containment of expenses. What's going on here? If what your immediate superior expects of you differs from the objectives listed in your MBOs, you need to revise your understanding of your own bottom line. In this instance, making the sales quota is important, but keeping a lid on your area's expenses seems to be more important.

Your objective is to learn what things your immediate supervisor and other senior managers see as truly important, and to act on those.

As an example: an interesting but not central project has been included in your MBOs; in conversation with your superior, though, you learn that he or she isn't truly interested in that project, so you can make a personal decision to deemphasize it, even though it's on your list. Actually, if circumstances permit, you'll be better off pinning down these changed priorities/objectives in a written memo to your boss. That way, you're covered if at a later date management up the line questions why you haven't completed that particular project.

Now we're at the heart of the matter: the key for a manager is to *get a sense of what impact the manager's own tasks will have on the boss's success*. On what objectives will your superior be evaluated by his boss? What are his MBOs? How does what you're doing relate to those items? If your manager's main concern this year is sales, and your area is service, then determine the best connection between your service and sales, so your efforts can assist your superior in achieving his goals.

At higher levels, senior management's MBOs are usually clear—they relate directly to the company's order, sales growth, profit, and the quality of the balance sheet. But at middle and lower levels of management, the objectives may not be so obvious; nonetheless, it behooves you to find out your boss's MBOs or else you'll be doing your work in the dark. *You want your superior to succeed, since his or her success reflects positively on all who are his or her subordinates,* especially on those who helped make the success happen.

If your manager's objectives are not apparent from research, ask directly, "What constitutes success for you in the company's eyes?" Such conversation may be a bit delicate, as you don't want to seem presumptuous, but you can certainly ask what the sum of his or her goals are, and how you can contribute to them. Generally, if you put the question in the proper way, your manager will be happy and will want to share his objectives with you. These can be of great assistance. By identifying your superior's goals and relating them to your own, you'll increase your chances of doing work that is meaningful in his eyes and that will increase your chances for recognition.

THE TARGET DOWN THE HALL

To broaden yourself, expand your knowledge of the business, and gain a perspective similar to what you presume is held by the highest executives in the company, try aiming at a target that, when hit, can lead upward.

It's often right down the hall.

I've frequently been chagrined to see managers whose noses are so close to their own work that they have no understanding of what their colleagues are doing, nor how their own or their colleagues' tasks fit into the objectives of their group. "My job is components, not packaging," says one. "I'm an analyst, not a marketer," says another. Such attitudes are narrow; they also constrict those who hold them.

Think larger. What is the aim of the big project of which you are working on only one part? What is your neighbor down the hall doing on it? What's being done by your opposite number in a lateral division? How do all the disparate pieces fit together? To find the answers to these questions, and to develop fields for action, *spend some time thinking about your colleagues' jobs.* How would you attack their tasks? What are their goals? How are they applying their resources? After studying your colleagues' work, you may well come up with ideas about how some aspect of their work could be better done. Utilizing those ideas is a matter requiring subtlety. First, try making some suggestions on the work to your colleague. If these are accepted, fine. If they are brushed off, don't bury them—rather, *make your suggestions known to those who will care about them.* For instance, write a white paper that encompasses your ideas for improvements, and circulate it for comments by your co-workers before formally issuing it. This action will clearly signal what you're about to do, and may lead to quicker adoption of your suggestions. It might work so well that you needn't publish the paper at all.

If that fails, air your suggestions during the weekly or monthly meetings in which your boss's direct reports provide updates on their respective projects. Your group is sitting around a table, and after you've reported on your own province, make your suggestion. *Always put such notions in the rhetoric of teamwork,* since the idea that all of the company's employees are members of a team is one of the controlling fixations of today's management. (In fact, the belief in teamwork has become almost religious, and by couching your suggestion in terms of working together, the suggestions become difficult to refute.)

Here are a few ways to phrase your suggestions:

—"My group is ahead of schedule, but I think Jim could use more technical support, and I'm willing to loan him several of my people."

—"Our goal is to get this new software package onto the market promptly, and we're falling behind; I'm willing to participate in or lead a task force that will assess where we've failed and how to improve our performance."

—"My group sells typewriters and Jill's sells computers, but we've developed advertising techniques that have boosted our sales and might help computers; I'd be glad to share them, even if that dilutes the effectiveness of the advertising for typewriters, because I know that computer sales make more of an impact on the company's profit."

You do take a risk in making such suggestions, but the danger is slight and the potential rewards are great. In fact, such suggestions, if made courteously and within the framework of team play, are irresistible. They demonstrate to your superior that:

1. you're aggressive and willing to stick your neck out in the interest of the team and of the company;
2. you're willing to do more than just your job;
3. you take a realistic, bottom line view of the whole department, division, group, or company's goals; and
4. you're willing to give up part of your turf (resources) in pursuit of the company's objectives.

But what if your colleagues don't like your notions?

Bad Example # 8: I Object to the Plan . . .

"I don't need any help," one says. Another snarls, "Mind your own business." A third: "You haven't understood our situation." A fourth: "We've already thought of that idea, and rejected it." And the last, groaning, cries "All we need is another task force." *If such objections are raised by colleagues, whether smoothly or angrily—you've won.* The colleague who objects will be judged as refusing help on an obvious problem, or as being not amenable to new ideas or not attuned to the larger company goals. In contrast, you will be viewed as the offerer of help, the one with the new ideas, and with the broader company's interests ever present on your mind.

This adds to the image you are trying to create—of being an achiever, a spectacular performer, a broad businessman. You hope that later, when all the men and women on your level are being evaluated for promotion, management will remember your broad perspective, and that it will give you the edge over other candidates. Making key suggestions, when coupled with other demonstrations of your superior skills, could persuade your boss to allow you to assume broader responsibilities, or even to recommend you as his likely successor should he be transferred or promoted to a higher job.

ONE-ON-ONE WITH THE BOSS

Maybe it'll happen when you stay after hours and walk in for a chat, or when you go to a monthly breakfast meeting and while everyone else is stuffing in doughnuts, you ask for a private meeting. There are many occasions you can create to go one-on-one. If the boss is the type who discourages informal approaches, call the secretary and ask directly for a one-on-one meeting with him. If the secretary stiff-arms you or delays your request, say, "It's about a personnel matter," or, "It's personal." Both subjects are guaranteed to open a door that might otherwise be closed. (Further up the ladder, the surefire door-opener is, "I want to discuss the outlook for the quarter." Saying such things signals that you need immediate attention.)

A sure subject for a one-on-one meeting is a general evaluation of your team, discussed in terms of their attributes and potential. Show your detailed knowledge of them, your concern for their careers. "At that meeting next week, I'm going to ask Jeff to present the department's report; this man's a comer." By championing your people in this manner, you achieve good public relations for them —and for yourself. You can also do the same thing with the programs in your area, that is, lay them out so that your manager is informed about everything under your command. Your candor and detail help achieve another important objective—*making your supervisor feel like a boss* by offering insightful, concise reports to him or her.

Such one-on-one meetings, or the trip you take with your manager, can also be the moment to voice certain personal confidences. "I didn't do too well in that meeting with the divisional president last week; I think it was because I was worried about some family problems, which have now been resolved. I want you to know that I'm aware of my shortcomings and that I'll do better next time." "I know that you and I agreed on my goal of a hundred units to be sold this quarter by my group, but I set that number conservatively to offset risks in other areas; now I'd like you to know that my own goal is 120 units, and you can hold me to that."

By telling your superior about such matters in confidence— matters that if widely known could hurt you—you are taking a risk. But that risk is dared in the cause of *developing greater trust* between you and the manager, and that's an essential element in building a relationship.

Is it too conniving to use your personal concerns in this way? I don't think so. First of all, the concerns are legitimate; don't manufacture personal crises in order to have something to say to your manager. Second, you do seek his or her trust, and the matters under discussion are important to you both. You are perhaps being a bit more calculating in your timing than many others might be, but such control on your part is in pursuit of your primary goal, rapid advancement up the ladder. And you know that your rise depends in large measure on the opinion your bosses hold about you and the trust they have in you.

MEETING WITH HIGHER-UPS

Every so often, you have a chance to participate in a meeting with someone above the level of your immediate superior. At least quarterly, for instance, the person to whom your immediate superior reports will probably want a full area review from everyone on your level in his division. Such opportunities are extremely important, because they contain more potential for your advancement than almost any other moments at the corporation. Most managers simply view these report-giving sessions as times when they will sit through hours of drudgery and then only be allowed to give presentations of things which could as easily be passed to the management on a sheet of paper.

The manager determined to rise, though, will understand that such meetings are targets of opportunity.

> The upwardly bound manager must view a meeting with his or her superiors as moments of opportunity to create a favorable impression on the audience, to make an impact.

Centuries ago, in the times of Molière, a gentleman was asked what he wanted to have happen when in the theater. "Astonish me," was his answer. The same applies to the corporate world today. This requires devoting a lot of thought to the kind of impression you want to make and how to make it. At the very least, it will involve doing a considerable amount of homework.

1. When you are in charge of a small area, by diligent study you will know more about its operation than anyone else in the company. Those who are senior to you won't comprehend its details, and those junior to you won't have the perspective. Use the opportunity of a meeting to *impress higher-ups with your total command of your area.* Dazzle them, for example, with your analysis of numbers. Show them that you understand financial terms as well or better than the financial experts; cite important figures and percentages and ratios having to do with overhead and expenses, gross margins, the details of the balance sheet. A related idea: talk in terms of details that are important to your customers. A third: use technical jargon to show your understanding of complex technical matters. A fourth: use pictures and graphs to make your presentation memorable. Show them that you not only know your people and your product, you know the relationship of what you're doing to the department's goals, and to the company's; demonstrate, for example, your thorough understanding of the interdependencies in

the company. Your area is not only under control—you're in perfect command of its every detail. Make your superiors see you as supercompetent, and, therefore, capable of managing more than what you now do.

2. After summarizing your area's progress and problems, seize the moment to discuss an aspect of the company's overall business that is clearly beyond your present responsibilities. If you are in sales, you might mention a competitor's recent announcement of a new product line and present your analysis of how this may affect your own company's market share. If you're in marketing, you could make your own analysis of the way the company sees its profits, and discourse on a subject like gross margins, which are usually the province of the financial experts and more senior line executives. Act the complete businessman. *Suggest your competence in a discipline which the bosses didn't know you had—and which you were not expected to know.*

How do you obtain such arcane knowledge? In a large company, there are many resources you can tap—the controllers themselves, for instance. I've always found such people eager to assist, say, someone who is managing the technical production of a new product and who wants to learn how it will be priced for the marketplace, or how plant overhead expenses are allocated in calculating the gross margin. Let your intellectual curiosity push the whole process, as it must do with your entire career. Hard work is necessary to prepare for these meetings, but in the process of doing it you will learn things that will stand you in good stead throughout your career. Know your brief well, and leave little to chance.

By astonishing higher-ups with your new (and broad) knowledge, you once again *exceed the expectations* of your superiors. And you do so not only in terms of quantity—more sales, faster delivery of product, better service—but also in what sorts of competence they expect from you. In discoursing about gross margins or market share analyses you're also doing something else considered extraordinary: in most large companies which have quite a bit of support staff, managers are expected to manage, but are conditioned to leave to "experts" such arcane but important matters as setting prices, working out accounting procedures, and developing the employee benefits structure. To me, that's the lazy way of management, and *wherever a point exists where the usual way of doing things is lazy, you have an opportunity to direct your intensity and to go beyond the ordinary.* Here, the usual way of management provides an opening for the man or woman determined to advance, to dazzle superiors with demonstrations of competence in critical areas. As important, by learning about aspects of the business you haven't been expected to master, you have upgraded your skills and demonstrated knowledge that will serve you well as you are given increased responsibilities.

At all times, *your task is to convey to your management the notion that you are the sort of manager who won't be satisfied with less than full knowledge about the company, about the art and science of its management, the infinite details of its operations.* This image of competence should strike a responsive chord in the audience of your management superiors. You've shown them that you have invested your time and energy in learning the business beyond the small piece you presently manage, and have seized an opportunity to demonstrate to them both your aggressiveness and your capacity for business leadership.

11

Presenting:
The Career Crucible

I *HATE* meetings.

I'm not sure how many years of my life I've spent in conference rooms, but it's quite a few, and most of those hours have been less than productive or fascinating. A survey reported in *The Wall Street Journal* in 1988 suggests that I'm not alone. The average top executive spends seventeen or more hours per week in meetings; 58 percent of senior managers surveyed felt that the meetings were productive—but that means that a large percentage also believed them to be unproductive. In fact, 22 percent of the high executives felt that the business of most meetings could have been handled over the phone or with a memo. During my career in six large corporations, I worked in two companies where meetings and committees consumed far more than seventeen hours each week.

The reason a manager must bear these meetings is also provided in the *Journal* article: "Meetings can't be missed," it says. "Even when there's no clear agenda, corporate powwows are power arenas where careers are made and broken. It's here, in the conference room, that chief executives reveal their strengths and weaknesses and middle managers fight turf battles." That's the point: we must all accept the notion that meetings are a fact of corporate life. No one is going to be able to stamp out meetings; therefore, an upwardly bound manager must learn to deal with meetings—and leverage them to his or her advantage.

WHAT KIND OF A MEETING IS IT, ANYWAY?

The first task of a manager confronted with going to meetings is to determine what sort of meeting he or she is about to attend, and to decide how to act in it. Some meetings are for the purpose of a group coming to a decision; others are more specifically for the presentation of information and the analysis of it. A third type of meeting really has to do with reinforcing the corporate culture—cheering on people who've met or exceeded their goals, or ratifying decisions that have been previously made by individuals but which need to appear as if they are made by consensus.

The meetings at which *you* can make a difference are many. Foremost among these, though, are the ones in which you are presenting. It could be an informational meeting, or a meeting held for the purpose of coming to a decision; it could even be one called to ratify a previously taken position. As I suggested in the last chapter, the act of presenting is a critical task for a manager determined to control his or her own destiny. Now let's examine presenting in greater detail, and from some diverse perspectives.

KNOWING YOUR AUDIENCE

As a presenter at a meeting, your first task is to know your audience. Who will be there? What positions do they hold? How many of them will there be? ("The more who attend a meeting, the slimmer the chances any work will get done," reports the *Journal*.) Are the audience members company insiders, or are there also outsiders who will watch and listen to you? What is the knowledge level of these people? Do they, for instance, know a lot about technical matters, or are they not concerned with such things? Will they be tired when you get to present to them at four in the afternoon, or will they be fresh and alert at nine in the morning? Will they have had lunch, or will they be impatient to take a break and eat, and not give you the proper sort of attention? *Put yourself in the mind of the audience, and ask yourself: what do they need to know and what do they want to know?*

One of the most difficult presentations I ever had to make turned on just this point about what the audience needed to know. I had been asked to give the board of directors of a large company at which I was then employed a presentation of our work in the defense industry, which made up about 25 percent of our total sales. Since other sorts of products and services made up the bulk of our business, a good deal more time had usually been spent on those aspects, and few of the board members had more than a fleeting grasp on our defense work. Working with a colleague, I tried to figure out what the board members needed to know about the defense industry as a whole, and our part in it. We kept the necessity of achieving good communication with our audience uppermost in our minds as we prepared a two-hour presentation. In essence, we designed a tutorial. The board was led through the maze of doing business with the Pentagon. Defense work is crowded with acronyms; our military customers had dozens of them. I had the acronyms all spelled out and explained, so it didn't appear as if we were talking in an unknown tongue. I applied the same principle—*don't be afraid to explain that which differs from the norm*—to other unique aspects of the defense business. For example, accounting procedures on government contracts differ from those that apply to jobs for commercial customers. Allowable margins also differ, as do such things as time schedules. You'd read in a newspaper that a defense contractor got a $100 million contract, but you might not understand that the contract was for a term of ten years, that payments would only be made upon delivery of the systems under contract, that the first anticipated delivery was several years into the future, and that the contract which appeared so lucrative on first sight wasn't quite so attractive when all these other factors were taken into account. The board members had expected this presentation to be a bore; afterward they were appreciative of this long and detailed presentation, and several told me that because of it they understood our defense business better than they had before. That was a satisfactory presentation! Of course, I was surprised that some of them had sat on that board for years and had little or no understanding of the defense business, but at least we'd enlightened them a bit.

I've also made similar presentations on subjects such as plant consolidations and facilities closings, which are difficult to manage. The audience must be brought to understand the intricacies of assuring smooth transitions in production while moving the work to what are often distant locations. People seldom realize that this must be done while the company is simultaneously dealing with employee transfers and the numerous personal problems that arise when jobs have been eliminated. In this, as in other effective presentations, we tailored our language, exhibits, and charts to the level of the audience's knowledge. By customizing your presentations in this manner, you pay attention to the needs of the people who are to form its audience. Both the audience and the presenter benefit from that.

Those presentations just described were difficult to prepare because of the preparations that had to go into making them, but they were easy on another count: I knew without a doubt their purpose—to give information to each member of the audience. But that's not always the case.

To make meetings work for you, ask yourself before preparing your presentation: "Am I there to give information, or to obtain a decision?" If you can find the answer to this simple question, you'll be well ahead of the game.

Generally, it's not that difficult to figure out.

INFORMATION AND WHAT IT CAN DO FOR YOU

If it's information that you're to dispense, you can and should research it, and shape it in the most exciting manner. Take pains to make it absolutely clear. I like charts and graphic materials as aids for presenters; it's always good to be able to dim the lights and throw a slide up on the screen. If you're talking about the necessity of erecting a building in a remote location, let's see the location, or a proposed design—almost anything—to give people an image on which to focus. However, it won't help you to rely exclusively on such visual aids. At IBM many years ago, the corporate culture had become so used to flip charts that no one dared to present without them, even if the material being presented didn't require such charts. For audiences who are not completely familiar with the subject material, I suggest spelling out all acronyms or other forms of business shorthand. A chart-maker can just as easily write out "Cost Per Thousand" above a line on a graph rather than abbreviate it "CPM"; the short form runs the unnecessary risk of confusing some member of the audience who may not be familiar with the abbreviation, and thereby causing them to lose interest. Also, never assume that your graphics or charts will do all the work for you; you have to do the real work of interpreting these for your audience.

> Bad Example # 9: Squinting at Squiggles
> The lights are low, except at the presenter's lectern. There's a slide or chart on the screen, and instead of explaining its significance, the presenter is squinting down at his or her copy of the chart. You in the audience can tell that the presenter is trying to read squiggles or crib notes—probably written by someone else—to help explain the chart. This is a sure sign that the presenter doesn't know his or her subject. If you want to appear to be in command of your information, don't squint at squiggles. And do away with "crib sheets" altogether.

Another tip: if you're forced to hand out copies of the presentation ahead of time, or even after the fact, just put in the charts and leave out the interpretation; the audience will have to be there to understand it—in your terms.

Whether you are there to present information or obtain a decision, it's important to let your audience know your purpose, and to briefly outline at the outset of the presentation what you plan to accomplish. Many good presenters have as their first chart something that lists the topic, the objective of the meeting, and, if they are there for a decision, what decision is required. If it's a decision you're seeking, you probably have a recommendation as to which course you think should be chosen. Don't be coy about it. State your recommendation up front. Don't keep people guessing. (Many people disagree with me on this subject; more about that below.) Be specific as you begin: we're here to discuss Product X, not the whole product line; we're looking for a marketing strategy for introducing the product; the decision must be made by the beginning of the next quarter. Very often, to ratify a decision, the signatures of people in higher management are required. If the potential signers are in your audience, and you want to expedite that decision, you might even be so bold as to bring along a form on which the responsible parties in the audience can sign off on the project (and your recommendation) right then and there. I've done it. You can do it, too.

GOING FOR THE DECISION

Now let's talk in more detail about those meetings in which your objective is to get a decision from a group which probably includes your superiors and their staff support people. When you're going for a decision, it's vitally important to try out your recommendations and logic ahead of time on people who will be in the audience at the presentation. Meet in advance with the potential decision makers—individually, if possible—and try to influence them or at least understand their views. If those views are not in line with your own, you will have that much more time to prepare counterarguments.

Many managers, when presenting a subject to such a group, withhold their own conclusions or recommendations until the end of their presentation. They seem to believe that the logic of their case will sway everyone; or, perhaps, they may be thinking that since the meeting is a long one, the participants will be worn down by the time they finish their presentation, and so they'll get the desired decision by having outlasted any opposition. As a senior executive, I've sat through many such presentations—wondering all the while what the presenter was up to, and annoyed at being kept in the dark about his or her conclusions. I haven't been worn down, and neither have other executives, because we'd all been to lots and lots of meetings during our careers and had developed stamina for them.

That's why I recommend that a presenter *put the recommendation up at the top of the presentation.* "I think we ought to close that plant in West Africa, and I'm going to give you the reasons why I've come to that conclusion as well as the alternatives we face if we don't close it." Having said that, you can proceed logically, and let the audience follow your thoughts without being distracted by the side business of trying to figure out where you are heading. You're being both courteous and are taking into account the intellect of your audience by allowing them the proper grounds on which to evaluate the information you're presenting and the decision you seek.

Have you rehearsed the presentation? Most junior managers should do so; most senior managers will have been through enough presentations that they probably won't need to rehearse. You do have to be prepared, but how that preparation is achieved is really up to you.

Tell the audience how long your presentation will be (as short as possible!) and what you'll cover. State the problem in definite terms. Do your homework so that you can allude to all the personnel, plant, and supply resources the company can bring to bear on the problem. Give the reasons for your decision, and discuss as many realistic alternatives as you can.

In such meetings, some people, especially harried bosses, will want you to give them hard copies of the material you are presenting. Some will want such documents before the meeting, or ask to see them while you're up at the podium or the blackboard. While I'm working hard to make my points, nothing is more disruptive than to have an executive leafing through the pages of a presentation. That means he or she is tuned out, is getting ahead of me in my brief, or is going back to concentrate on something that I've already covered. And if I've been forced to hand out the information the day before the meeting, I'm stuck either with people who didn't bother to read what I worked up, or those who've already glanced at it and come to conclusions that might not agree with mine. To avoid these distractions, I tried never to hand out hard copies before the performance. If I had hard copies—and I always did—I'd "forget" to send them ahead of time to the conference participants. I might bring them to the meeting, but I'd try almost anything to avoid giving them out. "Stern, don't you have that on hard copy? I want a copy now." "I'll have them by the end of the meeting." I would previously have asked my secretary to bring them to the conference room at an agreed-upon time. I knew that if I had copies available earlier, people would insist on reading them and not listen properly to what I had to say. Retaining the hard copy was part of my continual attempt to *control information flow and timing, and thereby to control the meeting.*

ANY QUESTIONS?

If there is any part of presenting that you should definitely rehearse—or at least research—it's what happens after you ask, "Any questions?" Often you won't even get to the point of asking this, because the questions will start coming while you're in the middle of your presentation. Either way, you have to be ready for them.

Try *rehearsing your main points with colleagues,* both inside your department and out, so you can anticipate many potential questions at a time when you can consider your answers in a situation less pressured than that of the big meeting. The President of the United States fields likely questions from his own colleagues and rehearses the direction of his answers before press conferences; it's a legitimate exercise. Give a trial presentation to people who haven't been invited to the meeting, and see what queries they bring up; often, they'll be able to help you learn in advance not only what questions might be asked, but how your presentation may be perceived—in time for you to change those aspects of it which might produce reactions which don't help your cause and which might make trouble for you.

Now let's examine what to do in meetings where someone else is presenting, and *you* are the questioner.

BEING A PARTICIPANT

There are many things you can do to prepare for a meeting in which you will be in the audience rather than, or in addition to, being a presenter. Some of the ways to prepare involve the flip side of suggestions made earlier in the chapter. For instance, you can *find out the subject of the meeting, and research it so that you know something about it.* If a meeting has to do with sales projections, read up on the past results as compared to past forecasts; if someone is to talk about how things are going in the field, you, too, can get on the phone and find out some of that information for yourself. (You might even learn that the facts are contrary to the conclusions the presenter is going to advocate.)

You can learn *who else will participate in the meeting,* and spend time with them before the meeting. "What do you think we can expect out of this meeting, Jim?" Are they going to be as well prepared as you are? Will they express their views on the subject, or let the presenter go on without voicing them? Through your discussions, and through observing your fellow participants' behavior at the meetings, you'll be able to get a lot of potentially useful knowledge about their personalities, work habits, and management styles. Someday, you may work for one of these fellow meeting participants, or he or she may work for you.

Beyond doing your homework—another word for research—you can also *prepare questions in advance of the presentation.* Remember that, as an upwardly bound person, you want to use the meeting to your own advantage, and, if you're not presenting, you can make almost as much of an impact by the quality and incisiveness of the questions you pose. Your target is not so much the presenter, but, rather, everyone else at the meeting, to whom you will demonstrate your greater grasp of the business. At times you'll add constructively to the presentation of the topic and thereby make the presenter look good; doing this will help you develop an ally even while it establishes your credentials with the audience. At times, your comments may be those that see through inadequate or inept presentations.

Again, as an audience member, you can bring in notions that are out of your own usual area of expertise. If, in answer to your question, the presenter from marketing says he or she doesn't know anything about how overhead costs are allocated against the product—and you do—then you'll shine.

Ask questions which try to understand the assumptions on which the presenter's conclusions are based. Sometimes, the best questions are the simplest ones. "Why do you think sales will jump when this improved product is introduced?" "What do you mean by 'according to LIFO procedures?' " If you get a hostile response to your question, don't buckle under; rather, suggest that you'll later approach the presenter for tutelage and clarification on this matter. If the presenter responds to a question of yours by saying that the subject is too complex to explain, keep pressing, because often those who say such phrases don't really know the subject themselves. The maxim is, to truly understand something, you should be able to explain it; if you can't, chances are that you really don't understand it yourself.

12

Decisions, Decisions

NOT MAKING DECISIONS IS HAZARDOUS
TO COMPANY HEALTH

Decision-making is the essence of managing. Despite the obvious nature
of this statement, for years I have heard aggressive managers complain that they can't get anything acted upon within their companies.
Though willing to make certain decisions themselves, they have
been "forced" by company rules to go to their superiors for the
decisions—and couldn't readily obtain them. Most middle-level
managers have trouble understanding why their superiors seem unable to make decisions. Having been in the upper echelons, I can
pinpoint several reasons for the lack of decision-making.

The first is, simply, *the weight of the bureaucracy.* Often you'll
have a plan of action, but to put it into practice you need to obtain
the consent by signature of eight or ten senior executives. Getting
that many people to sign off is not only a time-consuming process,
it's also an exercise in sapping and making meaningless the decision-
making mechanism of the company. The first and second signers

are the ones who actually know the area of responsibility in which the decision is to be made—but the half-dozen above them don't, and their cursory consent on the document is not helpful. If I were in a position of power, if a signer didn't know what he or she was signing, I'd make every effort to remove them from the sign-off sheet on similar decisions in order to speed up the process. Or if the process required signatures and I learned that a signer hadn't understood the document and signed it nevertheless, I'd institute disciplinary action. Usually, all I could do was discipline, because real reform would have to come from the chairman's office, since it was invariably the CEO who set the limits on delegation of authority and, therefore, the number of approvals necessary on a document.

Needing ten signatures on a document is, to me, a visible indication of the *lack of delegation of authority* within a company—another big problem which is, of course, interrelated with the existence of a cumbersome bureaucracy. If authority is being properly delegated, a middle manager can make many decisions and implement them without having to clear it with people several levels above who are not in realistic touch with the situation on the manager's level. As a senior executive, wherever possible I'd try to have as many decisions as possible made by those below me; after all, the company was paying managers to be decisive, not just to be administrators. A major consequence of refusing to delegate decisions is that senior management's desks get piled up with matters that are minor and which really ought to have been decided by more junior people. For instance, why should a senior executive have to concern himself or herself with the problem of precisely how many people in the company ought to be allowed to hold the title of group vice-president? Or how many people should have offices in the executive wing? Or what perks particular executives should get? What clubs the company should pay for them to belong to? The need for such decisions can be obviated by having clear rules for these situations, and having them strictly adhered to. Senior management needs to concern itself with key short-term and long-range decisions that require an understanding of how such decisions will impact on the company as a whole, and on its various component parts; top executives should not have to waste their time or concern on secondary issues far better handled by managers familiar with those specific issues.

The third failure of senior management in the decision-making process comes *when all matters of importance have to be referred to a committee* which considers the options and makes the decisions. Committees are the scourge of the competent and aggressive manager. Some committees only make recommendations, which then go to the decision-makers. Others actually vote on many matters. As I've described earlier, in Germany, by law public companies beyond a certain size must have a *vorstand* (theoretically, the management committee that runs the company) to which the management reports; when I was at Braun, we had to have such a committee, and I worked with it. But to insist on committees when they aren't necessary seems to me a sign that something in a company is seriously deficient. Does the proliferation of committees come out of a lack of talent in management? Or a lack of leadership? Both, possibly. Committees divide and diffuse responsibility on the part of individuals—one can always say that it was the committee that made the unpopular (or even wrong) decision, not a particular executive. Moreover, committees tend to be conservative and eschew taking those bold moves which often make the crucial difference between a stagnating company and a steadily rising one. Let me state categorically that *most decisions should be made by individuals, not by committees or task forces.*

When decisions are *not* made—and it's surprising and disturbing how many matters are let slide in big companies—the issues sometimes go away or are resolved in some other fashion. For instance:

Bad Example #10: Let's Study This Matter . . .
Someone in sales asked for a decision to be made to cut the price of one of the company's product lines at the moment that a problem first appeared in its marketplace acceptance. Some executive decided to refer the decision to a committee for study. The committee took the matter under consideration for several months. While it was still being studied, a competitor's products overtook the first company's product line, and the line was eventually phased out. The issue was resolved, but not in the best way.

Despite such scenarios, some senior managers continue to feel comfortable with a decision-making process that is overly lengthy or devoid of real responsibility. The basic problem with this approach is that when decisions are not made, eventually the middle managers stop championing issues such as a timely price cut, a new product idea, or an innovative market opportunity—with the result that the managerial environment itself deteriorates to the point where people stop trying to win, and instead accept the status quo.

There are, of course, some decisions that need study. For instance, the company may have to decide at which plant to manufacture a new product. With such a decision, the likelihood is great that the executive in charge of the company's plants will not have all the information necessary to make such a decision by himself or herself. There may be factors which the executive would not be likely to take into account at first. For example, it might not seem economical to keep open a factory in Australia, when the cost to produce a small volume of your product there is high; however, the Australian government may insist on having one of your plants there or else the government may consider a prohibitive tariff on goods that you manufacture elsewhere and sell within Australia's borders, or will make it less likely that you will be able to compete for government-controlled contracts. Even in such a case, though, the executive in charge, by working with the marketing executive for Australia, should be able to gather all the information necessary to make a decision. A committee won't be able to do it better than the person who is most knowledgeable about that area of responsibility. Similar formulations can be made to explain why other important decisions, such as whether to bid on a contract, ought to be made by individuals. If a bid doesn't have an internal champion in the organization, it's often better not to make it.

One of the more complex decisions is that on an internal reorganization. In many large companies, such decisions are often deliberately delayed; for instance, the decision about a reorganization in management that will surely offend some people in the organization. The rationalization is that by delaying, rumors will play themselves out, and because the move will have been discussed to death before it happens, the reorganization, when announced, will be a nonevent. To me, that's an inconsiderate way of doing things. If a necessary decision is going to hurt people, why not be kind to them and get over quickly both the drama and the trauma? I liked to move fast, especially when there was going to be some pain involved for other people.

THE DECISION-MAKER AS RISK-TAKER

The decision-maker is a risk-taker. *Most decisions involve weighing the pros and cons of a situation, choosing a path, and then implementing or, as some would say, executing the decision. In this process, there is always some risk involved.* To make a fast-track career, you need to take significant risks and to make many decisions. If you always go to your superior to concur in the decision, you may spread the risk by associating him or her with the decision—but since that demonstrates you are avoiding the decision, it will not help to get you ahead. So you must make decisions by yourself and take risks.

> It doesn't usually matter if your decision is right or wrong. What matters more than being right or wrong is being decisive.

Many decisions taken in corporations turn out to be wrong—and are then corrected in mid-course. By making decisions yourself—quickly—you encourage decisiveness in the people under your command, and that decisiveness translates into a vigorous environment for business. Making a decision, any decision, is usually better than not making the decision, or referring it to someone else.

But what if a decision appears to be a puzzle? What if it involves breaking the company's written and unwritten rules? How do you weigh the risks in making certain decisions? Most people in corporations don't realize that *many decisions that have to be made are relatively risk free.*

Many supposedly problematic decisions involve bending the rules of the corporation that say you need your superior's approval for hiring people, making certain bids, or capital investments. It's important not to break rules cavalierly, for that won't be tolerated; and if you do bend them, you'd better be right. For example, you have been told not to hire without the boss's approval, yet you have a good candidate who may be lost to the company if he's not hired right away—and the boss is out of town and can't be reached. You can make the decision to hire, but you'd better be ready to explain the special circumstances and to say that it's not your normal way of doing business. That's because such individual actions, if replicated by all the managers in a corporation, can have a cumulative effect far beyond your own decision. For instance, if a hiring freeze was in effect and every middle manager in the company decided anyway to hire just one person, there would be chaos.

You have to choose carefully your moments and evaluate the risks in beating the system. Weigh all breaking-rules decisions with regard to the percent of your budget they represent, whether they be capital equipment decisions, bids, or anything else. Bids are tricky, since the making of them has consequences beyond the dollar amount, and often gets into the area of overall company policy. But in other instances, if the monetary impact is small, you can move with confidence. For instance, you've been told to hold down expenses, but want to reward a manager for good work by a one-time travel upgrade from coach to first class, a difference of a few hundred dollars. Surely you can absorb that small amount in your budget by tight scrutiny of other expenses, and bending the rules of the company in such minor matters is one of the ways available to you to reward one of your people. If your superior objects, you must be willing to take sole responsibility for these actions and for the impact they will have on your particular bottom line. A superior who echoes the corporate culture in saying publicly that he or she wants decisive managers under them cannot object to your decisiveness if you are willing to be responsible for the results.

Make decisions—lots of them. Make them quickly. Establish your reputation as a decision-maker, as one who sets a fast pace because you are responsive to the need to make decisions. Insist that those under you also make decisions; also make them understand that if they bring something to you, you'll decide on it, and the decision may not be one they'll like—so that they're better off making it themselves and taking responsibility for it. Bend and break the rules (but not company policy) when to do so is, in your judgment, in the best interests of the company. Understand, though, that your judgment may sometimes be wrong, or that you may misjudge, and be willing to weigh the consequences of each rule-bending. Take actions and explain them afterward. *Decision-making is the essence of management.*

13

The Art of Hiring and Firing

*H*IRING and firing are two essential tasks for a manager. To build a good unit, and work with it effectively, you must have competent people who are willing to conform to your own way of doing business. The unit will be shaped by judicious hiring and firing. Of course you can't just walk in and fire everyone who doesn't see the world your way, nor should you; people already in place must be allowed time to change, and it is part of your task to help them change. Realistically speaking, the unit can often be more quickly shaped through new hiring.

You can hire from within the company or from without. Often you are asked first to search inside for new people before recruiting outsiders.

Hiring from within has built-in pluses and minuses. Some companies continue to believe that they have a data base on promotable people within the organization. The keepers of this treasure trove are the personnel executives. In a few companies, the files are worthwhile because a lot of thought has gone into them; at IBM, for instance, line management evaluated people regularly and took pains to make the information in the files accurate and helpful. Even at IBM, though, one had to rely on appraisals performed by other managers who tended to write more positive reports than were warranted; their reliability was questionable, and, in some cases, even misleading. In short, most companies don't appreciate or properly administer the annual performance appraisals which form the basis of company files on employees. Yet these are the key tool for managing people. Let's take a moment to examine the appraisal process.

APPRAISALS: HOW DO YOU RATE?

In a performance appraisal, a manager rates his or her employee on a scale that ranges from unsatisfactory to outstanding, and writes a few paragraphs describing the employee's virtues and shortcomings. The employee usually gets a chance to respond to the ranking and the comments, in writing, on the same document. The appraisal is usually tied to the employee's agreed-to objectives, and is supposed to be used as a basis for salary increases and promotions.

In the ideal company that pays strict attention to its appraisals, promotes and administers compensation on the basis of them, and punishes or severs employees who don't measure up, such appraisals are worthwhile tools that help in hiring. Unfortunately, *most performance appraisals are less than accurate reflections of an employee's work and capabilities* because the system puts constraints on the appraisals' accuracy. For instance, if as a manager you have several employees whose appraisals are well below average, and the situation doesn't change for a lengthy period of time, upper management will raise questions as to why you as the manager haven't gotten rid of the underachievers. To avoid such entirely reasonable questions, many managers and their employees equivocate on the appraisal documents. Joe is "average"; Jane is "trying harder"; and Fred "met the objectives" (which, the manager does not say, were set purposefully low so that Fred would have no trouble coping with them). Most managers don't like to be critical of their people face-to-face, and therefore take the easy route of writing an appraisal and keeping out of it any negative phrases that would expose them to the employee's anger. It would be far better for the company if they would confront the underachiever, and if he or she continues not performing up to standard, to separate them. Still another problem: the manager who writes unrealistic appraisal documents is usually the manager who'd prefer to transfer a problem employee (and often does) rather than deal with the real difficulty.

Use the appraisals as a rough guideline, but, when contemplating hiring someone from within the company, talk to your own managerial colleagues and get more frank opinions on the potential new blood for your department or division. That will get you some information. On the whole, though, there is no substitute for a direct interview with a job applicant, whether from inside or outside the company. It behooves a manager to spend as much time as possible with an applicant before hiring, since your own success depends in large measure on the quality of people in your organization.

CONDUCTING AN INTERVIEW

In an interview with a prospective employee, you will not find out if the person is competent; only time on the job will tell about that. Don't rely too heavily on what outside recruiters say about a candidate; in general, headhunters want to close a deal, and are not necessarily going to do much extra work to select the most ideal person for the opening that you have. Also, headhunters never understand your requirements as well as you do, even if you spend considerable time explaining them. Personal references, too, may not be very reliable; it's unlikely that a candidate will give references that will say negative things about him or her. (Actually, if you get references that are all totally positive, you must conclude that the people giving them are being less than completely truthful.) Often, if you're working in a fairly narrow field, you can find your own references for a job applicant who will be more candid than the candidate's choices.

After an initial decision to put the candidate in the possible category, make an assumption that the interviewee has the basic professional skills you are seeking, and set up an interview. Here are a handful of areas about which you should ask probing questions:

1. *Is the person keeping up with his or her field?* When you are hiring a professional, or a low-ranking manager, find out whether he or she is reading the professional journals in, say, marketing or engineering. Is the candidate a member of the appropriate organizations, and what has he or she learned from their meetings recently?

Can the applicant give you additional references in the field who can attest to his or her competence and standing in it?

2. *Try to understand the interviewee's personality.* What are his or her ambitions? You hope they are unlimited; surprisingly enough, when asked in interviews, many people admit to limited goals. You want to know whether the person has potential—and knows it; whether he or she is reaching for the stars—or for the nearest easy chair. Look for external clues as to the personality: manners, style of dress, habits.

3. *Try to discern the thought processes the interviewee has gone through in order to come to this interview.* Why is he or she interested in leaving the current job? How badly does this person want this job? You'll prefer someone who is eager for this job, and is leaving the old one because he or she has accomplished certain goals and is restless for new challenges. How well does the interviewee know the company? Ask questions about this subject in order to ascertain how much the interviewee has prepared for the interview. Listen to the questions asked by the candidate about your company. Are they naive ones, or based on some research? Do they get to the heart of the matter, or are they just questions for the sake of appearance? If the interest is only surface deep, you may still want to proceed, but do so cautiously.

4. *Is he or she flexible?* Will the interviewee be willing to go out of town for the job? To work long hours on a specific project? What are the salary expectations? What are the candidate's expectations about future promotions and career path? What are the limitations on the candidate's mobility; for example, does he or she have a son or daughter in high school and not want to move right away? Sometimes an executive who commutes on weekends but who is available long into the night during the workweek is a good one to have around, because with no family to go home to, that executive can concentrate entirely on work, and get more done. However, such a commuter runs the risk of being overly demanding of subordinates who do have family obligations in the evenings.

In higher management echelons, and very often when the position available is in marketing or sales, interviewees are asked about their spouses, since a good deal of business entertaining is done by couples. Is the spouse available for such events? If not, will it matter or have an adverse impact on the job?

5. *Ask the interviewee to describe his or her management style.* This

question can be put in a number of ways. Ask the person to describe a typical day or week. Try to learn, for example, whether he travels only when there's a customer complaint or inquiry, or whether he makes a proactive effort. Is he used to long hours? Or a management style that will fit in well with your own? What does he or she think about working in committees or task forces? How does the interviewee go about making a decision? (Incidentally, when *you* are going for a job interview, have answers ready for this sort of question. You'll need to have thought about issues such as management style and your major career accomplishments.)

When I reached the ranks of senior management, and one of my tasks was to reinterview other people's potential hires, I found that lower rank interviewers were spending too much time selling our company, and not enough finding out about the potential employee. In these interviews especially, I tried hard to listen more than I talked. Let the person ramble, if necessary; you'll find out a great deal more that way than if you work hard to make the interviewee like you or your company. Of course, you must be judicious here, because even if you're not going to hire the candidate, you want him or her to leave the interview with a favorable impression of both you and your company. Because I conducted so many interviews, I came to understand that not everyone knows how to market himself. Some people are better at it than others; some are so good, in fact, that they are able to conceal their inadequacies, and talk themselves into jobs for which they aren't specifically qualified.

Never hire someone out of desperation, even if there is an urgent need to fill a position, and even if the person is qualified.

It's not a good idea to hire the first qualified person who arrives on the doorstep. You are being more fair to yourself and to your potential employee if you take the time to be certain as to the match between the applicant and the position. The hiring process is a courtship dance, and in it everyone tries to put their best foot forward. Take your time, make your steps courteous—and keep your fingers crossed!

EXTENDING THE OFFER

All too often, a manager has an interview with a prospective employee, wants to hire him or her, and then the process gets bogged down and somehow unravels. I prided myself on being able to successfully hire the people I wanted for my team, and for keeping them on that team for years. In a few instances, I wasn't able to hire a manager I wanted on the first go-around, but I did get that person a year or two later. Many other managers don't apply their own skills to this important task of hiring, and as a result lose opportunities to build a good team.

When you are ready to hire someone, work quickly and decisively. Learn by your questions in the interview what sort of an offer would be acceptable—before you make it. Part of the reason you try to get to know the person in the interview is so you can fashion a package that will appeal to him or her. Structure as many elements as you can: salary, moving expenses, special privileges, bonuses, stock options, and so on. I generally liked to have a firm offer ready within a week after the final interview. And I'd follow up the offer with phone calls asking if the prospective employee needed information on housing, schools, anything that might make the transition easier. As a manager, you need to recognize that changing jobs can be a difficult experience, and your ability to smooth the way may make the difference between an offer that is accepted and one that is turned down.

When you are trying to attract people for more senior positions, court them. After the initial interview, when interest has been mutually established on both sides, ask the potential employee to bring his or her spouse and children to your city to look around. When that person arrives, make sure that he or she knows that you are personally involved in the courting process, that it's important to you that this person come on board. See that every arrangement is perfectly done: the driver to pick them up at the airport, flowers in the room, a handwritten personal note from you giving your home phone in case they arrive after office hours and need assistance. Bring the couple to your home before dinner—there's nothing like a house full of children, bicycles in the driveway, dogs, and such to break down barriers between strangers and to emphasize the personal nature of the recruiting manager's actions.

I once went so far as to interview a man that my company wanted to hire while I was on vacation. I was then president of Burroughs, and the man, who was currently employed by Xerox, would have to report two levels below me. That I would give up my time off to meet him, and that I would conduct the interview at my home was, I believe, an important factor in getting him to work with us. At the very least, he was able to learn that Detroit had some nice residential areas.

Because I habitually used such tactics, I was able to obtain a high percentage of acceptances to job offers that I made. Also, I was often able to lure into the fold people who were "just looking" and weren't initially interested in working with our company. I've also been fortunate that, over the years, a number of people I've hired have followed me within companies from one division to another, and, occasionally, from company to company.

Before going on to discuss other aspects of hiring and firing, let me suggest some hints for going into an interview when *you* are the one who is being interviewed for a job.

WHEN YOU ARE THE INTERVIEWEE

An interview is a game. To win it—to receive a job offer, or to learn as much about the new company or position as you need to know—you must play it well.

> The most important task facing an interviewee is to tailor his or her responses to the perceived needs of the interviewer.

If your interviewer seems to want to know if you are technically expert, sprinkle some technical jargon in your conversation; if he or she appears to be looking for someone with an international flair, find ways of making reference to your experience in that area, even if it's only a reference to places you've traveled.

Do your homework about the company; consult annual and

proxy reports, press clippings, Dun & Bradstreet rankings, what has been written about the company in such publications as *Value Line*. Obtain from the company's corporate secretary or office of shareholder relations copies of the proxy, 10K and 10Q forms. Proxy statements will reveal the salaries, bonuses and even the contract details of the company's elected officers. All public companies are required to file annually a 10K with the SEC, though they send such documents to shareholders only upon request. A 10K contains a great deal of information not given out in proxy statements or annual reports. For example, 10Ks usually detail the company's products, identify and assess its competitors, list the geographic distribution of sales and manufacturing facilities. A 10Q does the same, but with more current information since these reports are issued quarterly rather than annually.

With such information in hand, *prepare for your interview as if you were getting ready for an important presentation*; you'll think out in advance your questions, and your responses to the questions bound to be asked by the interviewer. Some of your questions must be deliberately interesting and provocative, even if you're not particularly keen to know the answers, because you recognize that what you're doing is racking up points with the interviewer, not merely gathering information.

Ask questions that will impress the interviewer with the scope of your knowledge. For example: "I see that at your last shareholders' meeting, one stockholder asked the chairman whether or not you had made environmental disaster contingency plans. The chairman ducked the question, but what is your position on that?"

You can ask the really tough questions: "How many managers have you lost in the last year? Why did you lose them? What are they doing now?" Show that you're not afraid to obtain the information you need to evaluate the new company or new position. Show them you're not there with your hat in hand, begging.

Within a few minutes of beginning the interview, by adroit listening and by gauging the reaction to your own responses, you will be able to know what impression you have to convey. If the person to whom you're talking is fixated on the bottom line, you don't want to sell yourself on how nice and easygoing you are; rather, you talk about plant consolidations in which you've been involved and experiences you have had with cutting expenses. On the other hand, if the interviewer seems concerned with people matters, you might talk about your successes in that area. If he or she speaks in the jargon of long-term planning, you can do the same.

Between your first and second interviews, send the first interviewer a note of appreciation. Then, turn up the heat, for example, with a telephone call: "I'd like to come for a follow-up interview, but I need a decision soon. There are some other offers I'm considering, and I'd hate to have to accept one of those because I didn't hear from you for several weeks." If they really want you, you'll have a response quickly. If not, you probably weren't going to get the job, and it's best to know that early. Then, too, if the company can't move fast, you probably don't want to work there anyway, because the molasses present in the hiring process is probably a symptom of the company's management style and other problems.

HOW TO FIRE AN EMPLOYEE

I'll never forget the first time I fired someone. It was a terrible experience; after it, for days I felt sick to my stomach. Firing is among the worst tasks that a manager has to do, but it is also among the most necessary and essential to the task of managing.

> Managers who are unable to fire nonperformers become hampered by their own direct reports' incompetence, and their careers often stall.

The result is stagnation, both for the manager and for his or her subordinates. Even so, some managers, faced with a nonperformer, hate to wield the axe. Many look for a way to help the employee transfer. In my view, *one should try never to transfer a problem*. Transferring should only be done in certain circumstances; for instance, if an employee is a "fish out of water," a talented person, but in the wrong place; or if he or she has certain skills but has been mistakenly promoted beyond his or her competence. Those employees constitute a minority of all the cases. Even in these cases, transfers or demotions don't generally work out well for the individuals or the company. The people may find the change hard to swallow, or they may swallow it temporarily because they have no alternative—but, sooner or later, their difficulties with the organization will again be manifest. In such instances, separation is better for both parties.

Then there are the difficulties that arise in *companies that have the reputation of not firing employees,* even if the employee has not performed up to expectations. Any private sector company can—and should—fire an employee for continual poor performance or shoddy work. Some companies tolerate the nonperformer far longer than others. Also, nonperformers are generally looked upon with more indulgence when a company is flying high—but not forever. Firings are a fact of life, and shouldn't be avoided.

Some managers believe that a career will be affected negatively by firing people for bad performance. It probably won't be. More likely, *your hiring and firing practices will become part of your reputation.* As a manager, you seek a reputation for fairness and openness in hiring and firing. People in the company ought to recognize you as someone who fights for promotions for your good people, but who also fires nonperformers. *Ideally, you should be known for sensitively but firmly and fairly dealing with people issues.* Remember: as I've said earlier, many mistakes made by managers are forgivable, but not people mistakes.

Such companies as Procter & Gamble, DuPont, and IBM, which have gained the public image of being long-term successes, are invariably the companies that have truly realized that "people are the most important asset." These companies believe the adage, and handle all matters pertaining to employees as if they were dealing with the crown jewels. They do the same with the people aspects of relating to suppliers and customers, which, of course, reinforces their successful and sensitive image. That image connotes a corporate environment of integrity, and I suspect that if companies deal well with their people, they have integrity and not just the image of it.

But all too often, we hear in the speeches of high executives in many large companies—and, for that matter, we read in their annual reports to shareholders—a reiteration of the line that this company's prime asset is its people. The notion has become a cliché, an idea that has been dissected in academic circles, written up in countless articles and books. Being good with people is viewed as an important element for management to address. I'm suspicious of companies who preach respect for the individual yet have high turnover rates for employees and management. What most companies don't realize is that inhabiting the image of dealing properly with people takes large amounts of management time, effort, and extra money. Until very recently, IBM has been reluctant to break its no-layoffs policy during bad economic times, and this, obviously, has cost them money, but has bought them goodwill from their employees and the communities in which IBM operates.

Most companies won't take such steps; they are good with their people only when it's convenient or economically feasible to treat them well. The crunch comes when hard times or difficult problems arise. Even the best of companies has to occasionally face unpleasant realities. The key indicator of a company's commitment to its people is how well it behaves in such situations. IBM showed its true colors by offering employees early retirement rather than laying them off, and by making available retraining for technical people who would otherwise be terminated. The best companies face difficulties in a classy way. And they find that doing so pays rewards in terms of employee loyalty and morale, ease of recruitment, and public image.

The individual manager must have the same attitude toward people. There are right and wrong ways of dealing with unpleasant matters, and one must choose the right way. Employee illnesses, drug or alcohol problems, difficulties at home: all require sensitive handling. So do matters that affect large groups of people at once. I'm troubled when I hear of an instance in which a plant employing a substantial number of people is closed, and the senior management has not made an appearance at the facility or in the community to explain the reasons for the shutdown. Often the decision to shutter a plant is made at a lower level, and a senior executive ratifies it because he has confidence in the judgment of his subordinates. However, if you have a work force of 100,000 and for unfortunate reasons must close a facility that employs hundreds of them, you owe it to the work force and to the community to do so properly, and that entails going to the site, explaining the reasons for the closure, perhaps even negotiating a more magnanimous settlement than agreed to by your immediate subordinates. To do less is to avoid "doing the right thing," or, in the German term, is not *korrekt*.

As an individual manager you must always handle employees better than anyone around you—and by better I mean in a more equable and even-handed way. That includes hiring good employees and firing incompetents as well as setting standards for your own people that are consistently higher than those rival managers maintain for their own subordinates. For example, your standards will mandate that those of your direct reports who are in the lower 5 to 10 percent of your annual employee rankings for more than a few quarters in a row ought to go.

If an employee's work is substandard, tell him or her one way or another that this is the case—as soon as you can. All of your employees ought to know, at all times, how they stand with you. If a warning isn't heeded, repeat it, and make certain that the employee understands the probable consequences of not improving his or her work. When it comes down to doing the difficult job, do it in person. Never fire someone over the telephone, or through an intermediary. It's your decision, and you must have the courage to communicate, explain, negotiate, and implement it.

Some managers fire people and expect them to clear out their desks and leave immediately. Others give several weeks' notice, and some allow severed employees to stay on for many months and gradually fade away. I have no set rule for separations except to suggest that the good manager should adjust the circumstances of the firing to the individual affected. One sensitive way is to call the person in and have him understand that he will have to go—but don't set a date. A few days later, after the shock has worn off a bit, work out the precise details.

Always consider the employee's seniority, his or her family, the reasons for the firing. If the person wasn't performing up to your standards but that was really only because he or she was unsuited to the job—or just because you refuse to be needlessly harsh to another human being—you might allow the employee a few months to use the office during which he or she can look for a new position. On the other hand, if a severed employee would, in your opinion, prove disruptive during that grace period, you may be better off asking the person to leave immediately and paying him extra severance to stay away from the office.

One more guiding principle: an understanding that being fired is not the worst thing in the world that can happen to a person, though it may be a shock at first. After the initial trauma, some good people who have been fired discover that their dismissal has awakened them to their own behavior patterns which may have been the source of their difficulties; also, firing can force people to consider new directions for their lives.

Those managers who treat people properly, who are fair and even-handed, though they set high standards, are bound to succeed because their methods will generate respect and personal loyalty.

I've seen it happen dozens of times: when a manager works assid-uously to get and retain the best people, employees drift to him because they want to work with such a person, especially if the overall environment is not perceived as being good for people. As a matter of fact, when the environment is bad, this sort of good managerial behavior shines out even more than when, as at IBM, such behavior was expected of managers.

14

Working with People

WHAT IS A BOSS?

Most employees don't want a boss—they want a leader and a colleague.

Unfortunately, most companies and schools have trained us to fear those who are in charge, rather than to follow them because of our respect for their judgment. We pay more attention to the intimidation factor than to the element of respect that a good leader commands. This unfortunate aspect of things is reinforced by the way in which organizational hierarchies are most often represented, that is, by an organizational chart that shows who reports to whom. It is also reinforced by companies whose corporate culture permits managers to covet jobs for the power those jobs give them over other people in lower ranks. Generally, the companies who behave in this way are *not* those that are considered good with people, or good places to work.

Of course there are some managers, and some companies, which do have this enviable reputation. Analyzing them, one finds that these are the corporations that treat people with respect and foster an environment of equality among all their employees. These companies generally don't have chauffeured limousines for their executives, nor do they have executive dining rooms, parking slots reserved for the upper management, and paid country club memberships for the select few. By their actions they show that all their employees are valued, all the way from the lowest hourly paid or salaried employee to the person in the chairman's office. They pay attention to their employees' needs, treat people with respect, and value them as individuals. *In the best companies—the most effective ones—managers at all levels devote even more care and thought to their people than they do to other components of the corporation.* People are, indeed, the most valuable assets of a company, and although many chairmen and CEOs paraphrase this thought in the opening letters of their annual reports, in reality only a rare few manage their daily businesses as if this most important of assets were the most important concern of their managers.

As a manager, it is essential to create and foster an environment that is good for your subordinates, one in which you are able to care for them. This environment can be nurtured or destroyed according to even the most minute details of what a manager does.

Let me give you an example of a good company that could have done better in this respect. When I first joined DuPont in 1966, it was evident to people inside and out that the company cared for its people, and did so in a paternal way; many employees joined and stayed on until they retired. One of the company's many concerns was safety. At factory locations this was carried to the extreme of insisting that all employees wear safety shoes, which looked like regular shoes but had a steel cap on the inside that would protect you should a heavy object drop onto your feet. The shoes could be bought on the company's premises for a sharp discount; many of the styles were actually attractive, and the shoes were of good quality. When I bought my first pair, I put my hand inside and inadvertently scratched it on a protruding nail. I licked my finger and tried to decide what other pair of shoes I would buy. But at DuPoint, that wouldn't do. I had to stop buying shoes and fill out forms about the "industrial accident," and if I remember correctly, I even had to go and see the facility's nurse. This incident was a display of DuPont's deep concern for their people. However, it was at the same DuPont location that another side of the company's attitude was displayed. Each morning we had to come into the "campus" through a gated fence that surrounded the place and show our identification to security guards; this in itself was not unusual, for many companies have this kind of security. But at the end of the day, as we departed through the gates, we were obliged to open our briefcases to show the guards that we were not leaving the premises with any company drawings or secrets—in other words, to demonstrate that we had not stolen anything. The company that was so paternal didn't consider its employees trustworthy, nor would it treat the employees as adults. I found it offensive, and so did many others.

One of my reasons for telling this story is to point up my belief that *a manager ought not to act as a policeman toward his subordinates.* It is better to trust them, and not to promulgate orders which have as their basis the management's belief that employees are trying to get away with something. Most people want to do an honest job, to be proud of it, and to feel that their efforts make a difference; they also want to be recognized and appreciated for their endeavors. Many companies promise that this will be the case, and then undermine a new hire's enthusiasm by attitudes and strictures that prevent employees from feeling good about what they do.

CREATING A GOOD ENVIRONMENT

An aspiring manager must be aware of his employees' legitimate concerns—and of the company's attitudes toward them. Although such a manager should be realistic about the environment, it is my belief that he should do everything in his power to create a work environment that is good for his people, an environment that is based on integrity and trust.

At the time of coming into a new job, a manager has an opportunity to create this important, people-oriented environment. Some do it. Others—and there are far too many of them—see the moment as the time to politicize their areas of responsibility. Politicization is their way of introducing fear into the organization and using it to mold their people into those who become loyal followers and others who are permanently in disfavor or whom they try to sever.

Which brings to mind . . .

Bad Example #11: Let's You and Him Fight . . .
People who encourage politicized environments invariably view the office as a place to promote rivalries between employees in

such a way that the employees' competition leads to infighting and intrigue, rather than to a proper contest (based on merit) for the next promotion. They stir things up, never miss an opportunity to tell one of their subordinates how badly or how well a "rival" is doing. They play games that do not move the business forward, for instance, creating cliques or classes of employees in the office, usually divided into "them" and "us," the privileged in-group and those who are left out. In this environment, when someone loses their job, the separation is often cloaked in mystery, fostering the sense among the survivors that belonging to a select inner circle around the boss is more important to their jobs than doing what is right for the company. They learn to tell the boss what he or she wants to hear, and become yes-men—and the effectiveness of the organization deteriorates. Perceptive survivors learn not to offer suggestions that might be contrary to the boss's views, because that might get them fired. They know their work is not being judged on its merits, and that their future depends on where they stand with the boss.

Competition within a company can be healthy, even when there are power struggles for key jobs and promotions, so long as the struggles take place within an atmosphere of fairness, and so long as candidates do not undermine one another in order to get ahead. If promotions are based on merit, this can happen. When management leads by good example, internal competition can actually move the company forward. Remember that as a fast-track manager, you will have to compete with others, but make it your business to do so in a spirit of mutual respect.

And, especially while subordinate to many others, *the fast-track, ambitious manager must set fear aside.* When faced with an inadequate leader, remember that you don't have to become a puppet to get ahead; in fact, if you do become a puppet, your future is compromised. Others may be afraid to stand up and defend what you believe in. If you give in to fear, or to politicizing bosses, you lose your pride—and it is pride that you'll need and that will propel you to achieve many things in your career.

Politicizing behavior on the part of an executive turns my stomach, because what the politicizing manager does is dehumanize people by taking away the integrity of their work and their self-respect. Today most people don't work in corporate jobs only for the money; they're in a company because they've chosen the environment, and they give their companies the bulk of their waking hours. They view their own time as a precious commodity and, therefore, the company and the manager must view it similarly, and treat it—and them—in a judicious and respectful manner. Albert Camus, the French existentialist philosopher, once wrote that "Without work, all life goes rotten. But when work is soulless, life stifles and dies." The politicizing executive takes the soul out of work. An executive who cares for people must do everything to insure that the soul, the joy, the excitement, the rewards, are in the environment of the workplace. Friendliness and treating people with respect are essential in creating such an environment, but the core is something I've mentioned earlier (and often) in this book: *mutual trust*. Factors in achieving this trust include *being accessible* to people, the *honesty* of the manager's responses to inquiries, and the manager's willingness to *deliver on promises* and to *treat all employees equitably*. Let's take these one by one. An *accessible* manager is a person who most of the time doesn't operate behind closed doors, and who is known to be approachable when a subordinate has anything of importance to discuss. This sort of manager is willing to work hard to establish a relationship with subordinates which goes beyond the conventional; part and parcel of that notion includes being accessible to the point where the subordinate knows that if he or she has a personal problem which may affect doing the job, or even if they're just seeking advice, he or she will feel comfortable in discussing it with the manager. (Such managers won't betray confidences or spread gossip either.) Those subordinates will also know that when they ask a question, make a suggestion or a complaint, do especially good or bad work, the manager will give them honest and direct responses. "Yes, that's a fine idea," or "No, I won't promote you to that position until you've obtained experience in the following specific disciplines." Such a manager refuses to be evasive and won't equivocate on answers unless there are business secrets at stake.

People knew where they stood with me, knew my view that we were basically at work to get the job done—that we must *deliver on our promises*—and that I held performance toward our common goals to be more important than being buddies or having a comfortable environment in the office. I wanted my colleagues to be my friends, of course, but the job and our objectives came first. I may not have won a lot of awards as "Mr. Congeniality," but I was known as a good and fair man to work with and for.

Fairness. It's human nature to like some people better than others. In the office, you have to fight natural instincts to favor those people with whom you feel compatible, and to treat all subordinates with an even hand. If a manager is not one who is comfortable with women employees, for instance, he can't be too harsh—or too easy—on women subordinates; he must treat them just as he treats his subordinate men, and work to promote the notion that all employees are being judged equitably.

BEING "GOOD WITH PEOPLE"

I always had the reputation of being "good with people," which, in a way, is a bit curious. For instance, I'm not a very good socializer or mixer at, say, events where I don't know the people. My heart's not on my sleeve, and it takes a while to get to know me, but I am loyal to those who do know me, and I believe they are loyal to me. I never suffered from the illusion that all of my direct reports loved me; I knew my true friends as opposed to those who were simply smiling at me because I was in charge. I was often good to people whom I didn't personally wish to befriend, because I knew they were deserving. Maybe my caring for people has something to do with the frequent changes of situation I encountered in my childhood; even as a child, I was sensitive to people. I think such sensitivity is not a learned characteristic, but, rather, one that comes from the heart and the gut. Later, being concerned about the people who reported to me turned out to be good for my career.

Caring for your people enables you to get to know them well; this, in turn, brings in the information that allows you to sense alterations in mood and performance in your people, often before negative changes have reached the level of being intolerable. Knowing your people, you become more adept at understanding when to put pressure on and when to let up. And this helps you be a more effective manager. What many managers don't realize is that being good with people involves a lot of work.

In my car driving to the office, for instance, I'd think about my people. "Why does this individual have certain ideas and character traits?" "How can I develop trust with that employee who's been burned before by a bad manager?" "What's the best next job for this third person?" It takes both time and effort to build relationships with people that will stand you in good stead. But to help people and to lead them to successful careers is one of the most rewarding and pleasurable things a manager can do.

FEAR AND LOATHING: HERE COMES THE MANIPULATOR

Now, many managers get high performance out of their people through the use of fear. They are skilled at manipulating subordinates, rewarding personal fealty but often promising what they can't deliver. I've seen many instances where that sort of manager's employees bend their knees to him constantly, but yearn for the opportunity to get away from him, and, once away, stab him in the back if they can. At one company where I worked, the CEO, who was powerful because he had the general support of the board of directors and had been given a free hand, held many direct reports in place because he made promises to them, promises he had neither the ability nor the intention of delivering. He liked to be flattered, politicized the working environment of those below him, and often ostracized or punished those who didn't go along with his likes and dislikes. His character was well known among the top several dozen executives of the company. Many feared him and played up to him in order to keep their jobs and try to obtain promotions. But whenever groups of managers would gather, no one, not even a manager who benefited from obsequiously flattering the CEO, would have a good or positive word to say about him. Over time, nearly all of the company's most able managers left because they were unable to continue working in this environment. However, the CEO, because of the size of his ego, refused to acknowledge that his arrogance and the emptiness of his promises had anything to do with the steady stream of executives who were leaving his company. Such behavior was evidence that when managing people you can't build a Potëmkin village—a beautiful facade that masks emptiness behind—but nonetheless expect the true loyalty and trust of your subordinates. You really do have to give a damn.

SET A GOOD EXAMPLE

I've suggested earlier that *a good manager must set an example for his or her people to follow*, and I've described some principal components of that example. Beyond integrity and a good work ethic, another major factor of leadership is the pace set by the manager: an executive who drives himself hard can rightfully expect the same push and dedication on the part of his direct reports; and someone who makes decisions quickly can reasonably expect that his employees will do the same. Another important factor is the manager's comportment. It is your way of behaving toward the employees that engenders and supports trust and openness in dealings with the people who are in your area of responsibility.

REWARDS . . .

Trust, openness, and integrity are all essential to working well with people, but beyond these, a manager has recourse to a system of rewards and incentives which can be used to get the best performance out of subordinates. Rewards, of course, cannot be arbitrarily handed out. They must support the basic notion of direct dealings with the employee that the manager tries to establish from the first day on the job.

You want to have a reputation of being both demanding and fair; of being someone who fights to have your good people promoted, while at the same time you insist on the right to separate employees who are not able or eager to keep up with the brisk pace and standards of performance you set.

Your *willingness to go to bat for your own people*—to champion them within the organization—is the foremost reward that you can offer to them. I was always known as a winner who always delivered or exceeded the commitments I had made, a man who ran a successful organization, one with which people wanted to be affiliated. Those who were on my team were known to be in line for greater opportunities and more rewards from the company than those on other teams. I would back my good people for challenging assignments, raises, and promotions, and wouldn't take a no from higher management. Other managers might accept the usual arguments that "We can't give a raise to Joe unless others at his level get one," or "Why don't we wait awhile and review it when his twelve-month cycle is up?" but I knew these excuses were often illogical, without merit, or hollow, and I wouldn't sit still for them.

The other side of the equation was that I would demand quite a bit from my people, so that when they did well I could legitimately reward them and fight for them.

The process of challenging and championing your employees begins as you set up jointly with the employee some precise goals —schedules to be met, sales quotas, expense containment, factory output, and so on. These will go into the employee's MBOs, and are expected to be the major component of the annual or semiannual performance appraisal. Beyond the goals and appraisal process, the enterprising manager can establish within his or her area of responsibility a number of ways to recognize good performance. Some are for private consumption—between you and the employee—and others are for public recognition.

Showing personally that you care is essential. In business, all too often the interaction between a manager and his or her employees can become formal and impersonal. Writing personal, handwritten notes, or making that extra, unexpected phone call to say thanks for a great effort can mean a lot to an individual: it's an action that says that you, the manager, are keenly aware of the accomplishment, and that it's important to you that the recipient of the call or note is doing more than just a good job. People appreciate praise, and praise motivates them to do even better. I used to memorize or write down the birthdays of all my employees, and would send cards or sometimes even small presents to commemorate these occasions. When somebody from my division was sick or in the hospital, it was not unheard of for my wife or me to visit them.

I remember there was once a man working for me whom I thought had been toiling too hard and for too long without a vacaton, even though I'd asked him several times to take a couple of weeks off. He was of the type that keeps his nose to the grindstone and always finds excuses not to get away from it all. The results were showing up in his work—he was riding people too hard, becoming irritable. Finally, I decided that it was in the company's best interests for him to take a vacation, and so I arranged it. My secretary and I worked to get plane tickets and accommodations at a resort, to have his spouse be able to take time off from her job, and—the crowning touch—to have the couple's thirteen-year-old daughter cared for by one of her teachers while they were away. This last point was crucial; I knew that the girl was the apple of their eye, and that they worried constantly about her.

Then I called him into the office, handed him the tickets, told him of the arrangements, and insisted he go on a vacation for which the company would foot the bill. He was flabbergasted that we had put in the personal effort to make this happen for him, and when he got back, his efficiency zoomed.

I did get grilled by my superior for breaking the rules, but word of the feat got around the company, and eventually brought me a great deal of goodwill among the employees. And, in real terms, the cost to the company, even to my area, was insignificant, especially when measured against this man's contributions.

I like *recognition events*—specific achievement awards complete with plaques, perhaps given out at dinners or retreats and accompanied by write-ups in the company newsletter and/or membership listed on an honor roll. As a manager, you need to be creative in inventing awards, and in utilizing them in a reward structure. When necessary to encourage a particular kind of behavior, invent awards that haven't been given before—for quality, for leadership, for outstanding professionalism, for being the best in dealing with people. Don't only reward the salesman who exceeds his quota; also reward the support and staff people who make that accomplishment possible.

For some employees, the mere recognition of their achievement is enough satisfaction. For others, there must be a more tangible consideration. A star baseball player's contract often reads that if he makes the all-star team or wins the batting championship or certain other awards, he gets bonuses. In your business, you could write into an employee's MBOs that if he or she makes the "quality honor roll" or the "sales 500 club," he or she will be entitled to certain upgrades or additional income.

Money is not the only reward that can verify to an employee that he or she has done good work—but, as the saw goes, it's quite a bit ahead of whatever is in second place. *Money as a bonus*, in the form of achievement awards, or as a consequence of exceeding certain goals, is always a helpful tool for a manager to have and use. Without the ability to reward your people, you are hampered in getting the best from them. Making sure you have the discretionary funds and authority to reward your people is another aspect of standing up for them within the organization.

... AND PUNISHMENTS

Rewards are wonderful. But unfortunately, as a leader you must ride with your people not only when something good happens, but when something bad happens—and that means having to use discipline. The other part of the system of pushing people is punishments, which are never fun to administer but which are, for some employees, as necessary for motivation as rewards are to others. There are some managers who do not believe in punishing employees, and think, rather, that recognition and rewards are such motivators that merely the absence of receiving them is enough to spur employees onward. Certainly the preferred route is through rewards, but it has been my experience that a system of carrots only doesn't work, for two reasons. *First, some people only respond well to discipline. Second—and as important—employees who work hard and excel resent it when they see others not doing their share and the management not doing anything about such shirkers.*

Punishments should only be administered after clear indications that an employee's work, and, at times, their attitude, is below acceptable standards or disruptive to the organization. My belief is that if you tell an employee early enough about an inadequacy in his or her work, and help them to change, the person has an opportunity—and the motive—to improve. In fact, *it's unfair not to give people timely warnings that their work is below expectations. Employees should know at all times how their performance is viewed;* they should not be surprised with a negative report during an annual appraisal; such events should only serve to formalize the results of what should be a continuing process of evaluation. However, there are plenty of people who, when warned that their performance is inadequate, just filter out negative comments and resume, without alteration, their previous behavior. It is to these people that punishments must be meted out.

The first weapon that might be used in a carefully considered punishment structure could be to change your verbal warnings to written ones. Confronting the employee with inadequacies in the context of a departmental or divisional meeting is not my style—I prefer dressings-down to be done privately—but there are employees who only respond to a public expression of dissatisfaction. In my view, managers who never issue warnings in private first, and who habitually deal with employee problems by embarrassing the individual in front of others, don't belong in management.

After a certain amount of warnings—the number will vary with the individual and the task—have been ignored, you can begin to administer more harsh punishments on the same sliding scale as you'd use with rewards. *The visibility of a punishment (or of not receiving recognition) is a definite element in its efficacy.* Some people can brush off admonishments given in private, or that aren't very noticeable to fellow employees, but react as if stung when it comes to losing face with their co-workers.

Frankly, I'm not certain that taking away rewards is an effective motivator for most people. Such disincentives can backfire; soon, an employee may feel that nothing he or she does will have any positive effect on their tasks and goals.

Beyond small punishments looms the specter of dismissal or an unrequested transfer. As I've explained, my management philosophy has been never to transfer a problem. Some managers prefer to take an interim step—putting people on their own bad lists, or freezing them out of important meetings or decisions, or even giving them the silent treatment. I reject these sorts of punishments. They help no one—neither the employee, nor the manager, nor their colleagues. They are, in effect, forms of torture which demean the dignity and efficiency of both parties involved. Embarrassment and humiliation in front of others is highly dramatic, and thought by some to be effective, though I see it as also counterproductive. Managers employing these techniques do so in the belief that making an example of the nonperformer will keep the troops in line, but I believe that the negatives attached to the techniques far outweigh any supposed benefits. Leading by the example of your own hard work, rather than punishing others as examples, is the key to inspiring those who report to you.

As I've said earlier, I prefer to separate people who aren't doing a good job rather than subject them to repeated, long-term diminishment of their jobs, perks, humiliations, and so on. Under certain circumstances some managers believe that firing is not really merited, and transfer is a more equitable solution. For people once thought to be adequate performers who just aren't making it in a newer, more demanding environment, or for those who make a major mistake— that is, those who don't entirely deserve to be fired—employees can be shifted from positions of responsibility to lesser ones, say, sent to "exile" in a location remote from company headquarters, or transferred to a lateral line in a smaller division or given a staff job with ill-defined responsibilities and less impact on the company's bottom line and its future. These transfers are, in effect, demotions, though generally the employee's salary is not cut.

In general, I disagree with transfers and all that they imply—which is a lot. A company that habitually transfers problems soon sinks to a level of low performance standards, institutionalizes mediocrity, and loses its competitive edge.

But few companies realize this. Companies believe that an employee can recover from being put into the penalty box by demonstrating renewed vigor, upgraded performance, and so on. Some do well when transferred and grow into major jobs—this happens when the initial job loss comes not as a consequence of shoddy work but due to a merger in which many departments and jobs disappear—but, truth be known, most people sent into the penalty box do not come out. Usually they end up in permanent disfavor. I have known a few people who have come back from disfavor and have learned a lot in the process of returning to grace. Generally, though, the process is lengthy and will add unwanted years to an ambitious manager's career plan. I'd urge would-be rising stars to leave a company, rather than accept this sort of punishment. Starting over with a new company is much to be preferred, and is more likely to result in the manager's getting his career back on track more quickly.

IF YOU'RE ON THE RECEIVING END

I've never been placed in the penalty box, though I have received my share of criticism from various bosses, most of it communicated during annual performance appraisals and couched in terms of suggested improvements I should make to my style of management, or recommendations for skills I ought to acquire. No one likes to have their weaknesses pointed out, and it's particularly galling to an ambitious, upward-bound manager. When I first began to receive so-called constructive criticism I tended to debate the points with my manager; later I learned that at most companies the standard appraisal form has space to fill in under the headings of "strengths and weaknesses" and "recommended areas of improvements" which force the evaluating manager to write something appropriate to these subjects. Well, there's always room for improvement, and I learned to listen to the comments and suggestions. Those communicated to me by managers I respected I wrote down and carried them with me so I could refer to them with some regularity, as a way of placing pressure on myself to take action in the desired areas and to seek guidance from those who could provide it.

If you're the manager who has received an award which carries with it more than a plaque, perhaps in the form of a bonus or cash, what, besides saying thank you, should you do with it? As always, look for a way to recognize your people and show appreciation to them. It will mark you as a good leader and help develop the loyalty of your people. Why not use it for yourself? Generally, in the early stages of a career, the amount of a reward or bonus will be relatively small and won't make a noticeable impact on your lifestyle or savings account. But it can make a difference if used properly. Here's one idea that worked well for me. When I was still quite junior at IBM, I received a cash award, and used it for what I considered an investment in my career: a party at my house for those who had helped me in my achievement. Later I did the same with some other awards, and used the occasions to invite some colleagues whom I'd never had an opportunity to meet on an informal basis. These parties generally cemented relationships which later helped me in my work. As I rose in the organization, I no longer waited for awards in order to continue giving such parties, but bore the expense on my own, even when I could legitimately have requested reimbursement from the company. The parties became my own way of saying thank you to my fellow employees—part of my style of "being good with people," which has always been good for my career, and part of the way I always tried to develop an environment of camaraderie with my colleagues and employees. To me, business could be fun, and I wanted everyone around me to feel that way, too.

15

Other Ways to Enhance Your Progress

DO I WANT MORE TRAINING?

Training and managerial courses are important early on in a management career not only because of what can be learned in them but also because they enhance your résumé, which, early in a career, doesn't show much beyond formal education and limited job experience. Most companies offer managerial training, both internal and external, and make it seem important to professional advancement. For internal training, some offer sessions on their own premises, or hold seminars at outside facilities such as hotels or conference centers. While I was at IBM I went to several training courses offered for lower-level managers. Of course, most large companies have similar ones. The first was a real how-to course designed to teach us newcomers to the ranks of management the way to fill out forms for various administrative tasks, to suggest what was required of us in our duties as managers, and, most important, to familiarize us with company policies and procedures. These were followed by other courses whose emphasis was on the people aspect of being a manager, the personnel practices including hiring, dealing with poor performers, and administering employee appraisals. The Advanced Management School course lasted several weeks and was, as I have described earlier in the book, for high-potential managers.

Other than having learned the mechanics of doing necessary paperwork, I can't put my finger on anything taught in these courses that was useful or even revelatory to me as a manager. Much of it struck me as common sense, and I found them a waste of time, except insofar as they enhanced my résumé. The sessons were useful, perhaps, in terms of networking. I met people from other divisions of the company with whom I would later interact, and there was the excitement of working with those from other disciplines. In these short courses, we were always told to relax because we weren't going to be observed or graded and so could do and say whatever we wanted to. However, very often the training staff were asked, formally or informally, for their impressions of the students, and so it was always beneficial to leave a positive impression, even if, as often happened, one thought the specific course was valueless.

I also didn't learn much in the short courses at various business schools I was sent to, such as a summer course in Management of Human Resources at the Sloan School of Management at MIT to which I was sent by IBM. Other than meeting some interesting people from a variety of companies, I vaguely recollect only that the class discussed at some length the problem that a fellow student of mine, an executive from a film and camera company, said he was having with a female administrative employee who wore a miniskirt to work that was disrupting the males on a factory floor to the degree that it posed a safety problem. She claimed she couldn't afford two wardrobes, one for the world at large in which miniskirts were then the fashion, and the other for work. What was her manager to do? After twenty years, I recall the dilemma, but not even what conclusion was suggested for the perplexed manager.

Today, all the better universities offer courses for business executives over a whole range of topics, and lasting from a few days to several months; the fees charged to the corporations are high, and these executive-training facilities are profitable for the schools. The courses are sought after by rising managers at all levels, and are often willingly given to them by their companies. Having been to one of these courses is akin to receiving a gold star on your kindergarten report card.

Eventually, as you rise in management and are able to substitute solid achievements for good marks, the gold stars become irrelevant.

It is rare for a potential hirer of a senior manager to care how you became competent; he simply wants to know if you can do the job, and will only accept as evidence the fact that you have produced significant results in your former and current assignments.

Some companies will even give their middle managers fellowships to attend a school full-time at Stanford, MIT, the University of Pennsylvania, or many others. To be a Sloan Fellow takes a year, and is arduous for the student and expensive for his or her company. You must be under the age of thirty-five, and you get a master's degree at the successful completion of the program. Clearly, the students selected are highly thought of by their companies, and are sent to these programs to heighten their awareness of matters relevant to senior management. It's tough to turn down such an opportunity. As I've described earlier, however, the manager may earn an MBA in this way and then return to his company to find that upper management no longer knows what to do with him. Very few companies properly reintegrate their returning fellows into the management structure. You might want to take the fellowship with the understanding that if a significant assignment is not awaiting you on your return, you are prepared to leave the company. One certainty: if you attend such a program, or even one of the midlength courses at a good management institute, you'll be on the lists of headhunters that regularly track these classes looking for potential candidates for openings at other companies!

OTHER COURSES CAN BE VALUABLE

Now that I look back, some of the most effective and valuable courses I've encountered in corporate life were those that were offered by various companies, including Burroughs: practical instruction in how to use computers, finance for nonfinancial people, and similar expert and hands-on courses given by volunteer instructors who were company employees, on our premises, after hours and at no cost. The courses were well subscribed and helpful. They didn't enhance anyone's résumé, but, rather, were designed to give people knowledge and skills that they could use in the practical performance of their jobs.

Many managers take advantage of company policies that allow tuition reimbursement for courses taken at night. If you want to obtain extra sheepskins, do it early in your career, for at later periods managers simply don't have the time or the latitude in their schedules to regularly attend courses at night. Certainly, at lower levels of management, having more degrees is helpful; for instance, the starting salary for someone with a bachelor's degree in engineering today is around $28,000 per year, while the starting salary for an engineer with a master's degree is closer to $40,000. And a master's degree can be earned in one year of full-time attendance, or in two or so years through night and weekend courses. Many companies have great respect for degrees earned at night schools, for they know how hard an employee must work to successfully juggle full-time employment and school attendance. Despite their respect, it is a curious fact that the company that has paid for your advanced degree generally will not recognize your accomplishment in tangible ways on the job. It is like watching your own children grow, and not realizing how enormous are the changes that take place over a short period of time, changes that are more apparent to those outside the home who don't see the children as frequently as you do. By earning a new degree, you will have become a more valuable employee—but you may have to change employers to reap the benefits of your added education, knowledge, and degree.

APPRENTICESHIPS

When I was at IBM working in operations and wanted to learn finance, I was able to finesse an appointment that essentially apprenticed me to the CFO; in that position I think I learned more than in any other, and the credentials I obtained were key to my further advancement at IBM and, later on, in other businesses. In a sense, what I did by making this move was to transform myself into an executive assistant and take a healthy step on the road toward becoming a general manager. Today, many large companies have formal executive assistant programs designed to allow young managers to become assistants to senior executives for a year or two, after which it is expected they will be able to jump several job levels and assume more responsible management positions. The company considers this an investment in its own future. Depending upon the company, a formal or informal network or company-wide structure is established to identify promising individuals, and to assign them to senior executives who either need assistance or—as in my own case as a senior executive—are willing to have some junior manager apprentice with them.

During my career in business I was fortunate in often having bosses who took the time to tutor me in the finer points of management, and to allow me to get involved beyond the borders of my defined assignments. But not every young manager is so fortunate; many bosses do not have the time or the inclination to teach. That is why the executive assistant programs are so valuable: they make the teaching of the next generation a definite part of management. The results justify the time and expense of the effort. As I think about the companies with which I've been associated, and those whose structures I know, I cannot readily name many current senior managers who did not, earlier in their careers, spend time as executive assistants to someone considerably further up the corporate ladder, or in some other, less formal kind of apprenticeship to a senior man. Being an executive assistant can be the key to a fast-track career—or a swift ticket to oblivion. I believe it is a risk worth taking, but the outcome depends on how the prospective assistant manages the situation.

As a senior manager, I considered executive assistants somewhat of a burden. I could expect very little of them, and had no real way of measuring their output. They had no specific on-going work of their own to complete; typically, they tackled a series of projects, yet they took up a fair amount of my time. However, I recognized that helping to season an executive assistant was an obligation an executive has to his company, part of the training of the next generation of managers, and so I generally took one at a time, for a period of about a year each. I allowed that person to participate in nearly everything I did, with the exception of personnel matters and dealings with the board of directors. They would sit in on meetings, go on trips, and be my liaison to other executives. As I gained confidence in their abilities, I would sometimes assign to them specific projects that I needed done in support of my own job, and which I knew would broaden their horizons. In working with me, the assistants would learn:

1. *the game plan*—that is, how things were done at very senior levels in the corporation;

2. *how a senior executive works and communicates with even higher-ups*—something they would not be privy to at lower levels;

3. *what sorts of problems senior executives regularly face and how they deal with them;* and

4. *to develop a broad view of the corporation and how it operates.*

Because of their contiguity to me, the assistants had frequent contact with other senior managers, who would occasionally use them to send messages to me. An assistant's interaction with these managers was at the heart of the assistantship, because, after a year or so, if he was well thought of by the other executives, invariably one of them would offer him an important job.

The best of my executive assistants took the opportunity to learn everything they could about the company and the workings of higher management. Ones that were not so good abused the privileges of their position in a way that damaged their careers. It was a matter of tact and style; they had to learn to extract information without using the power of my office or conveying the impression that they were actually representing me.

For example, a shrewd assistant would call up the manager of a distant facility and say, "Paul is sending me to the West Coast on some other business, but I'm going to be near your facility. I would really enjoy the opportunity to tour your location with anyone whom you can spare for a few hours to take me around." If he phrased his request in that manner, the executive assistant would probably be able to learn a lot. However, if the assistant tried to swing the weight of my office on his own behalf, and said, "Paul is sending me to the West Coast and would like for me to tour your facility," he might get a very good tour indeed, with the manager himself doing the honors, but would probably significantly reduce his future chances for obtaining a position from that manager. Since every official visit to a facility entails considerable time, energy, and expense for the executives at it, they don't take kindly to their time being wasted by someone who has requested a private visit in the phraseology appropriate to an inspection by an official emissary from headquarters.

I would try to counsel my assistants on how to walk the fine line between gathering information on their own and acting on my behalf. Usually, for my own assistants—indeed, for most executive assistants—the position was a golden opportunity to interact with senior management and bring themselves to the attention of people who were able to substantially further their careers. During Burroughs' acquisition of a large California company, my assistant so impressed the CEO of that company that after the deal was finished, that CEO requested my assistant move to California to become his vice-president for planning. My assistant from another year, secretary to a task force, similarly made an impression on one of the task force members and was offered the opportunity to take a good position implementing the recommendations of the task force.

In sum, then, good executive assistants are able to make the company's system—and their own networking skills—pay off extremely well. In exchange for a year of listening, learning, asking good questions, and seizing opportunities to contribute, they are able to skip several job levels and assume responsibilities that are beyond what is usually available to most of their peers. It is an excellent career platform, and one that managers should make every effort to obtain while still early in their careers.

SUCCESSION PLANNING

Whether one likes it or not, in the world of big corporations, every one of us is replaceable. Those of us who try hard to make an impact wherever we go sometimes begin to believe that we are irreplaceable—but that's not so. I remember when I made my first change, I deluded myself that the institution I was leaving would soon miss me. My fantasy: *Après moi, le déluge,* as Louis XV said on the eve of the French Revolution. It didn't happen. As I was leaving and looked back, the lights didn't even flicker, and the company continued to prosper and grow.

Succession planning is every manager's responsibility. The problem is that most individuals, and most companies, don't do that very well. Most companies will admit that succession planning is logical, and a necessity, but they avoid making plans that have a chance of success. Interestingly, owners of small and even large businesses often understand the need to plan for their own exit; some train sons or other successors, others hire a professional manager and eventually retire, still others sell their businesses and then stay behind or keep in touch to help the buyer maintain a viable entity.

For individuals, another dynamic is at work. In the corporate world, many managers become afraid of being replaced. They don't trust their superiors, and they don't like to conceive of themselves as replaceable; their distrust translates into a fear that they could be shelved at any moment. As a consequence, instead of planning for their own succession, they entrench themselves and try to make those superiors feel that the unit couldn't function without them. They worry that if they plan their own succession, they may be maneuvering themselves out of a job, and that they will be laid off or retired once someone younger (and perhaps better and definitely able to command a lower salary) is ready for the job.

> The successful manager must plan his or her own succession. Managers need to realize that in order to be able to move up the ladder, they make it easy for top management to provide continuity; upper management needs to be reassured that a manager's slot will be adequately filled before he or she is promoted.

If your bosses don't know who they're going to replace you with, and have no clear or obvious choices—you may get stuck, and for a career-ambitious manager, that means delays and unhappiness. So it behooves managers to make it easy for senior management to offer them a promotion by assuring their own succession. In fact, a manager must consider finding a successor to be part of his or her job. One simply can't leave the task to the company, because, as noted above, most companies don't do it very well.

A good many large corporations have a management process that is supposedly designed to facilitate succession planning. In the typical process, a manager is asked to evaluate his direct reports and to make recommendations as to what each needs in terms of additional training or experience in order to be ready for promotion to the next highest management level. All of this information is usually presented to the manager's superior (in a conference with human resources representatives) biannually or annually, and is often codified into books. There is a lot of paper shuffling, and a lot of earnest talking about "growing" people. From such books, a senior manager ought to be able to tell which junior manager is ready or almost ready to step up into the current manager's position should the current manager be promoted. The problem is that once such books have been written and presented, they are usually put directly on a back shelf and are never looked at again. The recommendations for training and seasoning are usually not followed up, and if a diligent HR person tries to nudge the manager as to when one of his subordinates will have time to attend the recommended management school or get some other seasoning, he is told that things are currently at such a frenzied and critical phase that the manager can't release the subordinate at any moment in the near future. Then, at the time the manager is being promoted, there is panic at the senior level and flailing about to guess who would be the best replacement. No one consults the boks that have been compiled precisely to make that information available. Furthermore, since the recommended training has not been provided, the promising candidates among the manager's direct reports may be no more ready to take his job than they were at the time the succession plan was prepared. In such an environment, because the system permits and encourages it, the new manager is chosen not always on the basis of merit, but, more likely, on his political savvy. The final result may be a manager who cannot be promoted because there is no one to take his job, or, as likely, a situation wherein the manager is moved anyway and an outsider is brought in to replace him, with possible bad consequences in the form of excess resentment from the former manager's direct reports who expected one of their number to be promoted into that job.

Clearly, succession planning for a company works well only when it is assiduously practiced, and primarily when the example comes from top management and filters down through the ranks. Some boards of directors regularly review succession plans for the top two or three dozen positions in a corporation. If, similarly, the chairman is a strong believer in succession planning and works at it, less senior managers will do the same. In this regard, succession planning is like the spreading of the gospel of quality in a company. Once the chiefs pay attention to the matter, their followers learn that it is to their own benefit to do so as well, and as a consequence the company's strength in this area grows.

For individuals who wish to remain on a fast track, succession planning is essential, and must be done whether or not the company is good or bad at it. Your own successor—or, as likely, the several candidates for the job—must be identified and developed so that when you are ready to move on, they are ready to replace you.

How do you identify candidates? Some will come, of course, from your own organization, your own direct reports. At times, however, you may come into an area that has been badly managed, and there may be no stand-out candidates to replace you, or you may not have time to train them before you're ready to move on. In such instances, you can hire good people, either from within the company or from without, and train them. It is said that most managers hire in their own image; in my own instance, this meant people who were results-oriented, hardworking, and ambitious. I'm proud to say that many of the people I've hired with an eye toward having them replace me have done very well. But some managers avoid hiring really good potential replacements because they are afraid these people will outshine them! To me, that's a groundless supposition, because part of what characterizes a good manager is the group he puts together or shapes. Hiring an outstanding potential replacement will free you sooner to be promoted. Then, too, if you have no fear of losing your job, you will similarly not fear being nipped from behind by a brighter rising star.

If for some reason you are unable to recruit a possible successor, you can make it your business to identify and evaluate good candidates who are not directly in your organization but have the proper characteristics and have built a reputation in other parts of the company.

After candidates are hired, you need to develop them, and, as important, to let your own bosses and senior executives get to know them, so that they will feel comfortable with them. You need to help build a candidate's own network. To both train and expose candidates, you must:

1. *Give them a sense of how decisions are made.* As I also did to some degree with executive assistants, I spent many hours after the end of the normal business day discussing with potential successors why and how particular decisions were made and implemented. In explaining the decisions of upper management, the most instructive sessions were about decisions that seem to have been contrary to their own notions of what would have been best to do.

2. *Bring along candidates to sit in many of your own meetings,* as observers if not as direct contributors. They must participate in sessions that go far beyond their current

responsibilities. This contributes to understanding, too, and also allows your bosses to get to know them.

3. *Provide extra assignments* that go beyond the current scope of their work. Through these assignments, you can help them see that they can do more than they are presently doing; others will also be able to gain this same impression of the candidates.

4. *Sell your own candidates upward.* Expose your superiors to the good work of your people. This becomes more important the higher up you go, for at senior levels more people are involved in making a hiring decision than at junior levels.

5. *Delegate authority to your candidates.* Develop their self-confidence and allow them to make some mistakes.

Eventually, if this program is followed, your potential successors will begin to take your work away from you. This will free you to do many of the things I've suggested earlier in this book in regard to expanding your horizons and thus increasing your promotability. It will also demonstrate to your superiors that you are ready to move, that candidates are available to replace you since they're already doing some of your work, and that these candidates are people with whom they are already familiar and comfortable.

16

Beyond "Playing Games"

*P*LAYING corporate games will only get a manager so far; beyond game-savvy must always lie performance, the manager's ability to produce results for the corporation. In this chapter, I'll briefly outline three basic attitudes that are imperative for a manager to have or to develop. The first is the need for the manager always to act as an owner would; it is key to having the best interests of the company at heart.

ACT AS AN OWNER

> While in the ranks of corporate management, always act as if you are one of the principal owners of the firm.

This sounds easy to do, but many factors in corporate life conspire to make it difficult to act as an owner. The money one works with is not one's own, it belongs to the shareholders, but managers often handle it differently than they would if it were their own fortunes at stake. Many actions that a manager takes as an employee are not devoted to maximizing financial returns to the shareholders, they're concerned with furthering his own career. For example, managers spend a lot of time and energy making sure that they and their respective areas of responsibility look good to superiors; they show a predilection for taking interesting assignments that will help them get up the ladder; they make quick fixes that will allow them to shine, even when such fixes may not be in the long-term best interests of the company. As employees, they have to answer questions, fill out monthly reports, and work within a bureaucracy that they don't control and therefore can't change; frequently they are doing things that may have only questionable connections to the short- and long-term profitability of the company.

Recognizing this, most companies encourage management and other key employees to own stock, and this is done by giving them options. However, these options, while they could potentially net an employee a good deal of money, have very little risk associated with them. Let's say you had an option to buy your company's stock at 20. If it went up to 30, you "exercised the option," bought it at 20 and immediately sold it at 30, and realized a 10-point gain per share (on which you had to pay taxes, of course); on the other side, if your option was at 20, and the stock went *down* 5 points, you simply didn't exercise the option, and took no loss whatsoever. (I should point out that a manager's sale of his own company's stock, whether acquired by option or by purchase on the open market, is frowned upon, because it bespeaks a lack of confidence in the company's future and defeats the purpose of options, which is to create that "owner's mentality" in the managers.)

I have always been amused, and a bit annoyed, to see the change in attitude that comes over managers in a big corporation after they have completed a leveraged buyout of a division, or, for that matter, of the entire company: in the wake of the LBO, they start acting like owners! Why didn't they do that before, when they were still employees?

One common misconception is that after the management team in an LBO has acquired the company, they have no boss. Not true. The team has traded the standard set of bosses for a group of bankers or other investors whose loans are at stake—and this group can be even more demanding than a board of directors, since the investors' monies are at risk whereas the usual board of directors looks after the interests of that large and disparate set of owners known as the shareholders.

There are many reasons for the new owner-managers' changed behavior, but the heart of the matter is the way they are compensated and the amount of personal risk they bear. When managers work for a large corporation they generally do not have their own money at risk and usually earn a combination of salary, bonuses, and stock options. In this situation, their income can vary based on their and the company's performance, but the value of their stock options doesn't always correlate directly with their performance since the stock price is affected by so many other external factors such as fluctuations in the value of the dollar, the strength of the economy, and so on. The management team of an LBO has a different pay scheme, one that generates rewards in big numbers only through the managers' ownership of the business—and this is what drives the managers after an LBO to operate with a different mind-set.

Without the risk of losing something, there is little feeling of ownership. In recognition of this factor, private investors and investment banking firms involved in LBOs now insist that when executives of a public company buy it for themselves and take it private, they must bear considerable risks. The executives are pushed to remortgage their houses and take out other loans that put them at substantial personal financial risk. Since their money buys them part ownership in the company, they have become real owners. An atmosphere is created in which the executives are constrained from leaving the newly purchased company for some time, often until it has again been taken public or sold to another concern. The whole idea of this is to tie their future to that of the company.

It's amazing to see the transformations that take place in executives after the execution of an LBO. First of all, *they are no longer concerned with job security;* as owners, they have to instantaneously develop a "must win" attitude. Second—and, for some, an even more important consideration than security—*they are freed from the demands of the bureaucracy.* They don't have to write weekly or monthly reports or make endless presentations at countless meetings. Now they are the ones who determine what level of bureaucracy will be permitted in their company; suddenly, time becomes precious, and every dollar counts. They find less need for a heavy complement of finance, human resources, and legal cadres; they begin to question the value of some staff activities that only days or weeks earlier, before the LBO, they might have sought additional funds for, and which they never fought to eliminate. Now they aggressively cut back on every expense item. Is that visit to London really necessary? Should elected officers travel first class even on short trips? Do we really need a company airplane? They begin to seek out all areas in which (by their new standards) money is being needlessly spent, whether on expenses or on capital investments, and to cut back on such outflow of money, because they now see clearly that a dollar saved correlates directly with their own short- and long-term financial success. Proof of the pudding is in the numerous studies that demonstrate that in a privately held company the number of staff people and the level of expenditures are almost always less than what they are in a public company that has the same dollar volume of sales. Another important fact: when break-up artists examine a company with an eye toward taking it over and reselling it, they search for one whose stock is undervalued, and in which the resale price of the various units is higher than that of the company as a whole—they zero in on companies where management is not running the show well enough to give full return to the shareholder; in short, they look for a target in which the executives are not acting as owners.

What does this say about publicly held companies? And about the manager's versus the owner's mentality? One clue lies in the configuration of the staff. To my mind, an "efficient corporate headquarters" is an oxymoron, a contradiction in terms. In a corporate headquarters, you find many people who are the business equivalent of servants, people who are supposed to provide support to the operating units, and make the operating managers' lives easier. Some are just passing through on the way to or from line jobs in divisions, or acquiring seasoning; others are nominally ambassadors from or liaisons to the divisions—but all, or mostly all, are or become paper-shufflers. Very often, senior management doesn't know chapter and verse of what these middle-level employees are doing; when senior management permits it to happen, the staff *creates* bureaucracy, and staffers are very good at rationalizing to superiors the reasons for their continued existence. It is they who demand reports from people in line positions; it is they who hold most of the meetings, and who visit facilities where they demand that presentations be made to them. Supposedly in existence to provide service and support to the line managers, they do precisely the opposite—they get in the way of those line managers, often and repeatedly.

For instance, many staff people like to travel. Bored with the office, they invent reasons for escaping it. "Here I am, the liaison to headquarters in charge of Asia, and I've never been to Japan." The staffer then cooks up a reason why he must visit that subsidiary ("We need an on-site inspection of progress made at the new distribution center, and an analysis of its shortcomings."), gets his bosses to sign off on the request, and goes to Japan. He often travels first class, stays at an expensive hotel. And like many people in companies, he doesn't wish to travel alone, so he brings a few others with him; they are, of course, "experts" on various areas who are needed to evaluate what's going on in the subsidiary. The company people in Japan do not want to be boorish, or, God forbid, to act in such a way as to result in these visitors writing a bad report which would only generate a second wave of visitors, and so they wine and dine the visitors, and, what is just as time-consuming, interrupt their usual work to get an elaborate presentation ready for the dignitaries from headquarters.

The value of many of the trips by headquarters people is questionable. Their objectives are often fuzzy, the agendas ill-prepared. Most of the work done on them could as easily be done by telephone, mail, fax, and other less expensive ways of communicating. But in most large corporations, such trips are the norm, because the managers who can say yes or no to them are not acting as owners; they don't weigh the benefits of such trips against how much of the shareholder's money will be spent; they don't treat the company's money as if it were their own.

A good manager should always act as an owner would. One must continually question the necessity of having excess overhead, and evaluate all general and administrative (G&A) expenditures. For instance, what company executive really requires a suite in a hotel? Very few, because invariably meetings are not held in such suites but, rather, at company or customer facilities. You generally don't entertain guests in a suite; you go to a restaurant for dinner or to the lounge in the lobby for a drink. In a company, if it's axiomatic that everyone above a given job level gets a suite when he or she travels, then it must be recognized that the top executives, who have agreed to such a policy, aren't themselves interested in riding herd on expenses to the degree that they might be if shareholders' profits and return on equity were their main concern. The legal though wasteful abuses of company monies that I have observed during my career are too numerous to list; suffice to say that opportunities for belt-tightening of expenses exist in almost every large corporation.

So many managers act in a profligate manner that if you act in the opposite way, as an owner would, it will be noticed. In fact, *it's doubly important for a manager to act as an owner because it is behavior that is not expected.* If you are constantly trying to keep down wasteful expenses, to eliminate redundant jobs and departments, to travel only when it's necessary and then to do so in a modest way—it will come positively to the attention of senior management. For instance, there were times when because of my rank in a company I was allowed to travel first class, but I flew tourist class; often, there would be other executives from my company on the same plane. Word would get back about such incidents, and soon other executives would act in a similar way. Lead by example, and others will do as you are doing. Conversely, when I was at Burroughs, and we were having a tough year, I recall that the corporate controller had all of the controllers for our various divisions go to a business meeting in Jamaica, in the Caribbean; he even showed me on paper that because they were going to Jamaica out of season, and because people would have to fly from all over the world no matter where the meeting would be held, it was no more expensive for the controllers to meet there than at headquarters in Detroit—but to everyone else in the company, it looked bad. Here we were in a tough year, and the people in charge of the numbers were sunning themselves in paradise. I knew that wasn't really accurate, but the problem was how it appeared to other employees. By contrast, that year I took a group of executives to Oshkosh, Wisconsin, where we worked long days on some key business issues without the distractions of headquarters, telephones, and other interruptions while looking at the drifting snow; word got out that Stern and this group were really serious about business, particularly since on our return we announced sharp cuts in expenses and other similar actions. Further, the next year, when I took a group to Palm Beach, it was bruited about in the company that this group really must have done well for Stern to reward them with a meeting in the sun.

It's essential to try to inculcate the owner mentality in corporate America, and to replace a management culture that cultivates excess. To encourage the owner mentality, some companies have introduced profit sharing on a scale that brings truly meaningful sums to workers and executives when the companies are profitable. I've mentioned earlier that stock options can be part of the solution but are not the most effective way to help people feel they are owners, since the number of shares distributed in this way is insufficient to imbue a sense of ownership; however, they are a step in the right direction. There are other ways for employees to share in the company's profits, such as short- and long-term bonuses, but these are usually awarded only to a select group of managers. When the sense of sharing in the company's success is felt by all employees, and they can see a direct correlation between their efforts and the rewards they earn, attitudes will change. When this occurs, the inevitable result is also increased participation by employees in every phase of the company's activities. Not only do managers look at all expenses with a hard eye, but all employees are apt to chastize their co-workers whom they find not doing an adequate job—because they've realized that the excess staff or workers who slow down the line are elements that take money out of their own pockets. A second idea, really a variation on the first, is to recognize and reward those employees in a company who think in a proprietor-like manner. Make heroes of employees who are the most thrifty with the shareholders' money, and very soon the company will be realizing greater financial returns than it had previously.

In terms of making a career, when one is examining a company with the thought of taking a job within it, try to ascertain who owns it. For instance, how many shares in the company does the CEO have? *Business Week* (October 21, 1988) suggests that only seventy-seven of the top one thousand CEOs in the United States own a significant fraction of their company's stock. Although I think this figure is misleading because it doesn't take into account those executives' as-yet-unexercised stock options, it is significant. If your prospective CEO doesn't have much of a stake in his or her own company, relative to his personal assets, the chances are low of your being rewarded for thinking like an owner. Similarly, look up figures for how many insiders—here defined as elected officers and board members—have bought or sold the company's stock in the recent past; they are allowed to do so legally only during certain specified times of year. These figures may define not only the feeling of ownership among the company's top people, but also their sense of the direction in which they feel the company, and therefore the stock, is going. What you want is a company where all the insiders own shares in the company and are betting on its future, and where your own proclivity to act as an owner will stand you in good stead.

"BEING TOUGH"

In addition to having been characterized throughout my career as a manager who acted in the way an owner would, I've also been labeled a tough manager. I didn't seek the appellation and don't particularly like to think of myself in that way because of the connotation that being tough has to many people. Unfortunately, to the general public, tough managers are seen as nasty and heartless. I'm not nasty and I'm not heartless. But if we can redefine the concept of tough, I might accept the label, because toughness may well be the proper attitude for a manager to have. "Demanding" is the description I prefer.

In managing, there are plenty of arduous decisions to be made, for instance, where and when to construct a new factory or site a new building, but no one considers those to be tough decisions; rather, it's a pleasure to wrestle over where to site a new plant, or how many new people to hire. The tough decisions involve unpleasant matters such as layoffs, firings, demotions, plant closings, organizational consolidations. Most bad news in corporate terms means people losing their jobs, communities hurt by the loss of jobs and tax revenues.

There are managers who can make those tough, or what I would more precisely describe as difficult, decisions, and it is also said of them that they are compassionate. I think I fit into that category. Conversely, there are other managers who actually avoid making those unpleasant sorts of decisions, but people nevertheless say of them that they are tough. In my view, the latter group are *not* good managers, but, rather, people who have managerial styles inclined to meanness, intrigue, mistrust, and the generation of politicized environments.

In short, there's a difference between making a difficult decision and being a tough guy. Here are what I consider unpleasant decisions:

—*The manager has to tell a subordinate that he's doing a bad job at the moment and will have to improve or be fired.*

—*The manager who makes the decision to reduce expenses and takes actions that may result in the loss of jobs, salary freezes, or even cuts.*

—*The manager who makes a decision to close a plant or a regional office, a closing that will affect many employees and the communities in which they live.*

All of these actions are perceived as negative, and many managers avoid making similar decisions because they don't want to hurt anyone. In my view, however, the manager who refuses to make these decisions isn't compassionate, nor is he properly performing his duties. In fact, he is compromising the performance of the company and therefore placing an even larger number of jobs at risk.

Let's face it: some of the tasks of management are onerous, but they are part of the job. Driven by Wall Street, the American business environment enforces a focus on the short term, on achieving results *in this quarter and in this year*, and there's a lot of pressure put on a manager to deliver. If you as a manager have committed to keep expenses at a certain level, to meet certain delivery schedules, to achieve certain sales quotas, then it's your job to do whatever is necessary to deliver what you have promised, even if it means making the onerous decisions. It's your job to separate the performers from the nonperformers, to encourage the former and weed out the latter. One separates employees to build an effective organization, to deliver results time after time with the least amount of expense. To do this as a manager helps develop your own reputation, one that distinguishes *you* as a performer from other managers who don't or won't deliver results. A manager must raise the standards of performance for his organization to higher and higher levels.

As I've said in previous chapters, I believe in warning people repeatedly when their performance is substandard, and working with them to help them improve; but I also believe in separating them if they don't heed the warnings or make an effort to change their behavior. Unfortunately, there are some managers who will not fire people in person, but will do so through intermediaries or who will make their life difficult in the hope the individual will quit. Managers who use such tactics aren't tough; rather, they are cowardly, mean people who lack personal integrity.

A curious coincidence: I've observed that the manager who won't sit down with a subordinate and personally carry out the unpleasant task of separating him or her is the same one who will rather easily make the decision to close a plant, a closing which may affect hundreds of people. I'm no psychologist, but my guess is that the manager's behavior in this instance has to do with his need to deal with people and communities in the abstract, and his unwillingness to confront people as individuals. That manager doesn't want to see individual faces or hear individual pleas.

Managers who won't personally terminate the employment of an individual, and who close plants without taking into account the consequences for the employees and their communities are not tough, they're simply irresponsible and not to be trusted. Here are some other characteristics the mean manager displays.

Bad Example #12: I Hate My Walls . . .
The mean manager is the one who invariably sets difficult goals for his subordinates to attain, and then doesn't put in the time and effort to lead the organization to success; he comes to the office late, departs early, and is often absent from the company altogether. The mean manager often drops by the offices of his subordinates to needle them about their performance. He never accentuates the positive but harps on the negative. Some of the breed even try to establish their toughness by being rude to underlings who can't fight back without placing their future employment, or their careers, at risk. Upon taking a new job, mean managers will complain about the decor of the office or the inadequacy of the phone system. These actions often signal that they will not concentrate on the real objectives, the business problems at hand; their priorities are out of order. Because of their bankrupt attempts to communicate to those around them that they have power and aren't afraid to use it, subordinates fear them but do not respect them. They *are* to be feared, because they're usually in a position to harm a lot of people and seem not to care if they do so.

I never enjoyed firing anyone; in fact, I always felt bad about it even when I believed deeply that it was for the good of the person being fired as well as for the good of the company. Perhaps the most difficult separations are of those people who have reputations around the office as likable employees. These popular men and women are good-natured, thoughtful, kind, and friendly—but are often nonperformers. I terminated some of these office characters when, after an extended period of time, it had become clear that they weren't currently reaching nor was it likely that they'd ever reach the standards of performance which we had set for the company. It's entirely possible that if these people had been working for a manager with a style different from mine they might have fared better, but my insistence on excellence as the major criterion for employment was unshakable, and I had to judge everyone by similar standards. Not incidentally, it's the firing of such likable employees that often earns a manager the reputation of being mean, when, in truth, he or she is being *fair.*

Let me state this quite clearly: being tough takes backbone, but it pays off in respect. Employees respect managers:

1. who are honest with them about their performance;
2. who will go out of their way to give warnings about inadequate work; but
3. who are not afraid to fire—in person—subordinates who don't perform up to requirements.

The ones I'd gladly call tough are those who will insist on performance from their subordinates and separate those who won't deliver. Their distinguishing characteristic is that they are *demanding,* not mean. Most career-ambitious people prefer working for this sort of tough guy, because the likelihood is that he'll be in charge of a winning team. Very senior executives want to have such tough managers work for them because it makes the senior management's job easier, for they can rely on tough subordinates to produce results.

How does the demanding manager apply toughness to everyday work? Here are a few ways:

1. *Set aggressive goals.* Whether at annual budget time, during quarterly business reviews, or in the individual appraisal processes, agree with your subordinates on goals that are not easy to reach. Know where the potential cushions in a budget are, and agree to more ambitious goals. When they succeed, reward your people accordingly, through special recognition, salary increases, and, where appropriate, bonuses.

2. *Demand excellence.* Be involved with the details of your operations. Check with subordinates often on what they're doing and how close to schedule or budget or quota they are. Quarterly, readjust goals and objectives. "Yes, I know you've been doing well, but you seem to be coasting a bit. Let's do better—and you'll be an even greater hero." Always keep the pressure on for achieving higher and higher goals; it's the only way to make sure they excel.

3. *By your own example, create a fast-paced environment.* Arrive early, stay late, do a lot of productive work—and expect the same commitment of your subordinates. I was always in high gear, never

in neutral. I demanded as much or more of myself than I ever did of anyone in my organization. My subordinates knew that I'd read all correspondence, reports, and key documents without delay; when I was in town, my mail would always be answered within twenty-four hours. They knew I had a good information network within the company, and that it was in constant use. They knew that I was comfortable in all the disciplines needed to perform my job, no matter what the level I might then have reached, and that I was highly regarded by my own bosses, which gave me considerable latitude in my operations. There were no known or visible chinks in my armor, so, in order to stay abreast of me and be part of my fast-moving team, they had to perform.

Most people in corporations don't like this sort of pressure. These laid-back people complain that certain ambitious managers are too tough. But real performers thrive in the pressurized, fast-paced, demanding environment I've just described, principally because they know that it produces results and a winning team. Morale is always high when an organization is successful, and this, in turn, adds adrenaline to the team's members. One man who came to work for me had been a marathon runner in his spare time; although he kept running, he had to give up training so many hours a week in order to stay in harness with me, but he didn't regret it. Neither did another fellow who could no longer continue his many hours at his hobby, woodworking. They realized that sacrificing some of their outside activities on the altar of high performance would bring greater rewards from the company, and adjusted their priorities accordingly. Not everyone can make the same commitments or is willing to do so—but in most cases the ambitious, upward-oriented manager does it, because he recognizes that he is thriving in the pressurized environment, and that it is helping him shine and become known to higher-ups.

My people were betting that my rapid progress would create opportunities for those who could keep up with my pace and style. It did. Furthermore, I'm proud to say that when I switched companies, many people who'd worked very hard on my teams wanted to go with me, and, although I made it a rule not to raid previous employers for the benefit of my new one, eventually some of my former colleagues did join me in bigger and more senior jobs—even though they knew we'd work equally as hard again in the new environment.

The idea is a general one, not specific to me as a manager.

Everywhere, people want to be with a winner. Employee surveys in dozens of large companies, taken over periods of many years, invariably show that areas that report good results are also those that report high morale. Hard work that pays off in results for people is never really viewed as such. The best managers have a feel for how fast and hard to drive a team of people; they feel it in their fingertips and know how to demand enough to get results, but not so much that the pace would destroy the spirits, drive, and ambitions required to forge and sustain a winning team.

> You can be demanding without losing the admiration of your subordinates; in fact, the more demanding you are, the more respect you get.

There are negatives to this style of management. The demanding manager often keeps subordinates on a tight rein—a style that is more objectionable the further up the ladder you go. It results not only in grumbling from those subordinates, but also in being seen as unwilling or unable to delegate properly. The demanding manager's intolerance of mediocrity and his perpetual state of never being satisfied can backfire; you can get the reputation of being too much of a stickler, and unable to be one of the guys, which can impact on communication with those around you. Yet I think it is never right to tolerate mediocrity. On the whole, the positives of being demanding outweigh the negatives. It certainly worked that way for me.

BUILD A COCOON TO PROTECT YOUR PEOPLE

When one is a tough manager one must also be fair and equable to his people. Sometimes being fair involves protecting them when you first become responsible for a new area within a company. When taking over a new area, especially a troubled one, the last thing you want is anyone to hinder your efforts. Such interference often arrives in the guise of outsiders to the unit trying to help you, or in the form of those wishing to measure your progress before you're ready to have it measured. During the crucial months when you're just settling in, all too often corporate staffers will ask you for more presentations and reports than are necessary; and there are superiors who will inquire weekly (if not daily) as to how things are coming along. If the entity you're shepherding is an integrated business unit, you could tell these inquirers to wait for the next quarter's results, or until six months have passed, but if it's one that provides a product or services to other units within your company, "customers" who are heavily dependent for their success on your unit's health may be constantly inquiring why products or services aren't being delivered more quickly or with higher quality. All such inquisitors are like gardeners who are willing to pull the immature carrot out of the ground to see how it's growing. You know that in time you'll satisfy all the garden inspectors with lots of healthy vegetables, but you also know that it will take six months or even a year to get your patch of land in shape.

One of the first tasks of a manager upon coming into a troubled area is to build a cocoon around the organization, to shield it from excess outside pressure.

You do this in order to *buy time for the organization, and to protect your subordinates and colleagues so they will be able to assist in the reshaping.* Sometimes you can only buy a few months, which isn't a very long time, but every day can be made important. Generally, when one comes into a troubled area, there are problems with employee morale—they think of themselves as losers. For months, perhaps even years, outsiders have been sniping at the organization. Lateral units have been pointing fingers at your people, naming them as the cause of bottlenecks in production, lagging sales, poor customer service, and so on. Your task as a manager is to turn the unit around. In order to do so, you must first buy time to uplift morale; in buying that time, you also help yourself by establishing a bond with your subordinates, because they'll realize what you're doing and recognize it as a signal that you're all in this together and that you will rise or sink together.

How and when do you buy time? There are several ways. The first, and by far the most important way, is to *make a pact with your immediate superior at the time that you take the job.* This is the moment when your negotiating power is at its height, and you should use it. They need you to fix a mess, and you know it. So you make your acceptance conditional on being able to build that cocoon. "Look, I'll take over that unit, but I want your agreement that you won't bother me weekly for interim reports. Give me ninety days, and I'll show some substantial progress; and please spread the word at headquarters that for ninety days I'm not to be pressed for information so I won't have to deal with the corporate staff either. After that, I'll provide weekly reports if you need them." Recognize that the amount of time you can buy is a function of the expectations of your superiors. If your boss believes that the unit can be effectively altered in a year's time, you'll get a year—or, possibly, only nine months, if he or she is the type that likes to manage at a deliberately heightened pace.

After your superiors have agreed to leave you alone for a specified amount of time, *keep your bosses informed anyway on a regular basis—but on your own terms.* Give directions and progress reports, not hard figures. Assess the resources, the problems, the chances of success in impressionistic language, not with hard facts. Say that "Bill seems to be a hard worker, but needs a fire lit under him," rather than, "Bill is 20 percent under quota for this period."

In this same vein, *consider making an interim progress report that will scare your bosses.* "This unit is worse than even you or I expected it to be." I call this tactic the write-down mentality, because we most often see it in concrete form when a new CEO takes over a troubled company, looks at the figures, and asks the board to ratify enormous write-offs (say, of products on the warehouse shelves that ought to be declared obsolete rather than carried as slow-moving inventory); the write-down alerts the board and buys that CEO a platform on which to build and to get the company back on track. Just as preventive medicine is often much less dramatic though no less effective than life-saving surgery, the write-down strategy (a certification of corporate ill health) allows the CEO to be even more of a hero when he or she brings the corporate profits and growth back to health. In your smaller unit, you can philosophically write down your new unit in a memo to the boss (and to the files) about the conditions you find on entering; later, you can point to how far you've come.

An allied strategy is to *come back to your superior later in time, say, halfway through your grace period, with revised impressions.* What you want to do in this instance is to tell your management that the problems have been addressed, and they are now less problematic than they were. Again, no hard facts or figures unless you're ready to show them. Impressions are best. If, as often happens, you have addressed the sorts of difficulties in this new unit during your previous assignments, it will be easier for you to keep your superiors satisfied, because you know their concerns. At several of the companies for which I worked where I developed a reputation as a Mr. Fix-it, during a grace period I'd go to my immediate manager with a short checklist on the status of the unit and briefly explain where we were on such obvious concerns as costs, schedules, personnel, etc., in enough impressionistic detail to get that executive to let me continue my work to upgrade or rescue the unit—by myself, without his involvement, and especially without the involvement of his staff.

Now, how does one work inside the unit to reinforce that cocoon? The most important thing is to make everyone in the unit believe that the problems can and will be addressed, and that they will be solved. Set clear, achievable, and measurable short-term goals. When the group is able to see that progress is actually being made, morale will rise and confidence will return, accelerating the healing process.

I wouldn't tell my unit that I'd bought time by my pact with my superior—but they'd find out soon enough, because the dunning from outside would subside. My subordinates would understand that my bosses had enough confidence in me to give me the latitude to change things my way. Then, of course, I'd have to show them what my way was. I'd try to address difficulties in terms of the problem, rather than the people. I'd avoid saying, "You didn't do your job." Rather, I'd ask, "How are we going to change this low sales outlook? Cut or control expenses in a better way? Make a new marketing plan?" By discussing the task in such terms, I hoped to maintain the focus where it ought to be, on the problem to be solved rather than on the personalities involved. Of course this wasn't always easy, but I tried hard to inculcate the right attitude, the spirit of winning.

Frequently, after an early meeting with my staff in which I'd asked them to present me with a clear understanding of how their respective areas were doing, someone who had attended the meeting would ask to see me privately, and in that private chat would say that a colleague who had presented hadn't given an accurate picture of "what was really going on." I usually thanked the person for the information, but asked why he hadn't spoken up in the meeting.

"Well, I didn't want to hurt his feelings." I'd tell the person that I expected him to speak his mind at all future meetings, and that if he didn't he'd be in trouble—and that if his colleague gave me inaccurate information in another meeting, I'd come down hard on him, too. I made sure that everyone in the organization understood my philosophy on this subject. Now, all of this was in service of the objective of building a coherent team, one that reflected my management style and goals.

Invariably, in those early meetings with the staff of a new and troubled unit, I'd find myself saying, "*We* are going to fix this problem. We'll work as a team, although I'm in charge and will shortly determine precisely who is going to make up that 'we.'" I left no doubt in anyone's mind that we were going to succeed, and that results would be the final measure of success. The cost of nonperforming could be the loss of our jobs—but we'd all work as a team to get the job done so that there would be no losers at all in the situation.

Another strategy to help the unit cohere and to keep outsiders at bay is something I've mentioned before in other contexts: an insistence on professionalism in those aspects of the unit that are outwardly visible. I would take pains to insure that phones were answered on the second or third ring; that every document that went out of our unit was correctly and legibly copied; that the magazines and other informational material in the reception areas were appropriate, up-to-date, and helpful; and that customer inquiries received immediate and courteous responses. Soon, people outside would be spreading the word that Stern's organization had cleaned up its act, and was a force to be reckoned with—even before we'd actually finished tidying up the Augean stables.

It was always a joy to see that when the cocoon had been properly established, and when a unit that I'd taken over was starting to turn around, something else often happened: another shell began to form inside of the one I'd built. I recognized that this shell had been formed when I saw that when an outsider attacked someone in the unit, the colleagues of the person under siege would come to the rescue and deflect the attack. When I saw that kind of "one for all and all for one" behavior, I knew that the team was coming together, and that we'd have a good shot at solving the organization's problems.

PART THREE

Case Studies

17

Quality

EQUATE quality in managing with professionalism in everything that a manager does. At IBM, Braun, Burroughs, and later at Unisys, I was continually concerned with upgrading our processes, products, and operations; we in higher management tried to put the company's money and muscle into achieving greater quality in all aspects of our operations. How does being a quality manager impact on a career? Some managers will accept the idea that championing quality is all well and good for senior managers, but believe that being for quality at lower levels won't help their careers. They argue that instituting reforms that insist on quality costs a lot of money and will have a negative impact on their bottom line, and they know they are being judged on the basis of that financial bottom line.

To define the meaning and discuss the implications of being a quality manager, let me first make some points about quality in business. In the past decade, quality has become a buzzword. Some people in the corporate world believe that in the 1990's companies that improve the quality of their products will have an edge in the marketplace. I don't think so: customer expectations of quality have been rising and will continue to the point where having high-quality products will become a condition of being in business. Similarly, becoming a quality manager will be necessary to reach the high rungs of corporate ladders.

A few years ago, an article in *Business Week* suggested that "Managing for quality means nothing less than a sweeping overhaul in corporate culture, a radical shift in management philosophy, and a permanent commitment at all levels of the organization to seek continued improvements." I agree with that judgment, and want to back it up with some figures. In the early 1980's a study by the Strategic Planning Institute of Cambridge, Massachusetts, analyzed 2,700 businesses to try to assess the strategic importance of quality as measured by those businesses' customers. John M. Groocock of TRW reported in his 1986 book, *The Chain of Quality*, that:

1. Businesses that ranked in the top quarter for quality had an average return on investment of 32 percent, while the businesses in the lowest quarter returned only 12 percent.
2. Businesses that ranked in the top quarter for quality had an average return on sales of 13 percent, while those in the lowest quarter returned 5 percent on sales.

In another study of 1,712 businesses by the same institute, quality and productivity (defined as value added per employee) were assessed, and the findings were equally impressive:

3. Businesses that ranked in the top one-third on both the measures of quality and productivity had an average return on investment of 24 percent, compared to an average return on investment of zero—yes, zero—percent for businesses which ranked in the bottom third on both measures.

Drawing from these and other studies, the institute came up with some conclusions about quality:

1. When compared to other factors such as market share, product cost, service, and so on, *superior relative quality was the only company attribute that always correlated positively with good return on investment and good return on sales.* Low or failing relative quality was a sure sign of a business that was losing market share.

2. In terms of the costs of doing business, *there was no correlation between relative quality and direct costs.* That is to say, *businesses that put out higher-quality products and services did not have correspondingly higher direct costs.*
3. There was a positive correlation between having relative quality and charging higher prices to customers: *businesses that ranked in the top quarter on quality were able to charge customers 8 percent more for similar products than businesses ranked in the lowest quarter on quality.*
4. For businesses that were rated as having relatively poorer quality, *attempts to gain a larger market share by such tactics as spending more than competitors on marketing, or on research and development, or by introducing new products more quickly than other companies did not pay off.* In fact, such strategies only served to drive return on investment lower, rather than boost it.

Despite the obvious implication of these studies—that companies must increase the quality of their products, services, and operations—many companies, and, in particular, American-based companies, are resistant to achieving increased quality. This is a big problem, because American industry faces formidable challenges from overseas competitors. It's not a question of having the economic or human resources; rather, it's where and how we apply them. The Organization for Economic Cooperation and Development (OECD) recently ranked the United States first among the twenty-two industrialized nations in terms of our people, labor force, managerial skills, and motivation—but rated us eleventh in terms of outward orientation and sixth in invention and innovation. In the last twenty years or so, R&D as a fraction of Gross National Product rose 14 percent in Russia, 16 percent in West Germany, and 19 percent in Japan, while in the U.S. it *decreased* by 19 percent. A generation ago the share of U.S. patents issued to foreign nationals was 13 percent; now, it's 33 percent. The percentage of scientists and engineers in our labor force has been declining since 1965, while it has doubled in Japan and Germany; interestingly, many of those new scientists and engineers abroad are trained in the United States: half of all new engineering doctorates awarded here now go to foreign nationals—and this at a time when the American Electronics Association reports a shortage of about 100,000 qualified candidates for engineering jobs a year in this country.

While we can try to turn around some of these figures by spending more on R&D—at Burroughs, when our new team took over, we doubled the annual budget for engineering and kept it at that increased level from then on—the long-term way to change them is by insisting on, and working for, higher quality in everything that our companies (and we as managers) do. Quality is important, then,

> —*to keep up with our competition;*
> —*as an antidote for the short-term focus* that too many U.S. companies adopt;
> —*as a way of increasing customer satisfaction* with our products and services; and, finally,
> —*as a goal in itself,* a way of being in the world.

Unfortunately, many managers have not accepted the necessity of raising the quality level of their products, their services, and their own professionalism. They think that somehow quality may be fine as an idea, but that it won't pay off for their organizations or themselves. This is outmoded thinking, and career-conscious managers need to rid themselves of a series of myths about quality that are dead wrong.

Myth Number One: Quality can't be precisely defined, and can't be measured. Some aspects of quality can definitely be measured; conformity to specifications, for instance. One can make a product that doesn't fall apart, that works as it's supposed to, that lasts. Management techniques such as "process capability" and "statistical process control" allow executives to track production and insist upon quality controls that will result in error-free products. But conforming to engineering specifications isn't the sole guarantor of a quality product. For instance, the Edsel car and IBM's PCjr home computer conformed to specifications, but they failed to sell well enough in the marketplace. Their failures are evidence of a lack of quality controls in another important area that some people think can't be measured—customer demands and satisfaction. Managers believe this is composed of intangibles. But surveys among customers can reveal customers' feelings about the organization that sells the product, the cachet certain products have of being on the cutting edge of technology. These elements, too, can be made subject to the manager's control.

Myth Number Two: Quality costs more. The problem here is that people think of quality as an absolute, when it is really a relative term. Quality should be defined as the degree to which a product or service meets customer needs and expectations, conforms to specifications, and is competitive in price and delivery schedule— relative to what else is available to the customer. When looked at in this way, it can be understood that spending more money wisely on a product can be a good thing, but that unlimited spending will not necessarily result in the highest quality. Think of quality as a relative goal, not an absolute one, and you'll have more flexibility in where you spend money to upgrade.

As a consequence of the first two myths, some companies and managers, in straining for quality, make the following mistakes:

1. *Overdesign of the product.* Because of their uncertainty about the customer's real wants and needs, they build in more safeguards, gadgets, or other functions and features than are necessary to win market share, and their products end up costing so much that customers won't buy them.

2. *Overpromised quality.* This, too, is a consequence of the manufacturer's uncertainty about the customer's real needs, as exhibited by delivery and price schedules that are unrealistic, yet that have been agreed to by both manufacturer and customer.

3. *Incapable manufacturing processes.* I define these as processes that are not able to produce the product as designed.

4. *Inferior purchased materials and supplies.* Bad supplies lead to inadequate products.

Now—couldn't you as a manager do something about each one of these factors? All of them are subject to control by managers determined to provide quality, and you'll want to keep tight rein on them.

Here is a third myth that is equally as devastating as the previous two:

Myth Number Three: Quality problems are the fault of workers, particularly manufacturing workers, and are not the fault of management. This mistaken belief persists because the costs of defects, rework, scrapping bad products, providing extra service and repair at customer sites are usually associated with the manufacturing process. These costs are huge: *Business Week* reports that 15 to 20 percent of every sales income dollar is currently spent on reworking, scrapping, repetitious service, inspections, tests, and fulfilling warranties. Corning Glass CEO James Houghton, in an article in *Fortune* (October

24, 1988), estimates the cost of "preventing, detecting and paying for errors" even higher, at 20 to 30 percent of sales.

Again, a manager can't escape responsibility for quality in this area. The blame can't be placed only at the level of the factory floor. Quality experts have shown that only about 20 percent of quality costs can be traced to things that go wrong in the manufacturing process. About 80 percent of the costs can be attributed to problems in the design-development phase, to purchasing policies that yield defective materials or components, and to other mistakes in marketing and management. When a marketer presses the production side to hurry up and issue an incompletely tested product onto the market, or commits to putting product features on a machine that the design and manufacturing people can't complete in the time allotted before delivery—the result is high-quality costs without high-quality products. All of these problems can be considered management mistakes.

Good managers can work in such a way as to prevent these sorts of mistakes, promote quality throughout their own organizations, and help their own careers while doing so. At Burroughs, starting in 1981, we started organizing for quality from the top down, by instituting a Senior Management Corporate Quality Board with broad responsibilities. Shortly thereafter, we set up Production/Quality Councils or Teams at the group, region, and subsidiary levels. At the same time, we spent many millions to build and open an employee development and training center near Chicago, and spent more millions to open others near London, Paris, and Tokyo. In the course of a single year, we sent a thousand managers to quality awareness training courses at these facilities.

In our awareness programs, what we tried to do was change the managers' understanding of the corporate culture, to lead them to recognize that we at the top wanted high-quality products, services, and employees; that we wanted them to take pride in the company and what it produced, and to have a deep sense of personal involvement in championing quality, and in making every aspect of the work in their area of responsibility as good as it could be. After the programs had been in place for three years, our internal surveys showed us that more than 90 percent of Burroughs employees queried believed they have a personal impact on quality in the company, and more than 70 percent believed that the company was more significantly committed to achieving quality than it had been before the program began.

We spent a lot of money on attempting to improve the quality of the company's products and its management processes. We were aware that such investment might not pay off right away—but we knew it would pay off eventually. Our goals were to develop a corporate culture of doing jobs the right way the first time, and to have the quality of our products and services make a positive impact on how our customers perceived our company and its people.

Let me take a moment to detail how our quality program came into being. When I came to Burroughs, there was no organization within the company that was driving the idea of quality. We had a centrally managed Technical Information Organization (TIO), whose chief reported to Burroughs president Ray Stromback. The TIO jobs were at technical locations throughout the company; when one of our machines at a customer's facility had problems and the Burroughs field engineers—the servicemen—couldn't solve the problems themselves, they called the TIO person at the engineering/manufacturing facility responsible for that particular piece of hardware (or software), and if the TIO couldn't help, the TIO would then go to the design engineers who knew the product best and try to come up with an answer. In short, the TIOs were low-level troubleshooters who had no reason to push for quality in manufacturing, style, service, or anything else. They were ex-repairmen who, in general, had had nothing to do with the development of new products.

I had striven to introduce ideas on quality in the fifteen months that I was executive vice-president for Engineering and Manufacturing, but it wasn't until I became president of Burroughs in the spring of 1982 that I was able to put into practice a new idea for a company of our size, the notion that our company should have a vice-president for quality who should report to the president.

What I wanted was an organization of people at all locations who would report to a staff officer of mine, somewhat in the manner of a CFO or human resources VP reporting to a CEO, but with a different structure underneath. Whereas a controller of a division reports directly to the head of his division, and only tangentially to the CFO at headquarters, I wanted the VP/Q's people at all the locations to report directly to him, and *not* to the heads of the locations. And I wanted the quality people at these locations to be responsible for much more than making sure our manufactured products adhered to our specifications and standards; I wanted them to be the guardians of, and cheerleaders for, quality in every phase of our operations. Quality has no end objective. As Corning CEO Houghton says, "Quality applies to everything we do. This is a life-long journey, not a destination." Similarly, quality is not solely the province of top management—it's a process, one in which every employee can take part. Within a company, every employee has customers, the engineer, the secretary, and the janitor no less than the CEO. Quality must show up in the manner and in the alacrity with which the phones are answered and the physical plant made to shine, as well as in the professionalism of the managers and in the effectiveness and reliability of the products.

I made sure that the VP/Q had some real power to enforce the idea of quality. Through the observations made by the on-site quality people, the VP/Q would, for instance, receive information on adherence to specifications at every step of production. If standards weren't being met, the VP/Q could actually stop a production line or override the marketing division's pressure to develop a new product more rapidly than he thought warranted.

Of course he didn't stop anything at first. As a cheerleader for quality he gave speeches, encouraged others to do the same, and involved CEO Mike Blumenthal and me in an innovative poster-and-logo campaign for quality; we signed a credo and invited others to join us in searching for ways to enhance quality. Soon the Q logo was appearing everywhere in the company, and people were taking pride in earning it. We set up special awards for quality, awards that sometimes included money, though in this instance money was less important than recognizing the employee's work. People were soon competing to win these awards.

Fortunately, the man I chose for the job of quality czar was sensitive to the nuances of command and control. When the heads of factories or departments had problems, he often didn't report them to me, but worked to help the people solve the problems; they all knew he had my ear if he wanted it, and the threat that he could "turn them in" was generally enough to force compliance.

I remember the first time that the VP/Q had to shut down a production line. It was after he had issued several warnings, of course, but it still came as a shock when he stopped production of an ATM (automatic teller machine) for banks because it had failed to measure up to our specifications. Both the manufacturing and marketing sectors howled. When a plant's production line is closed down, the inventory of materials begins to mount; this is reported to headquarters, and almost immediately affects the division's cash flow, to which the manager's bonus is usually tied. Marketing was alarmed, as well, because the ATMs had been promised to customers. The problems were soon corrected, and production began again—but this episode succeeded in winning the attention of virtually everyone in the company, and heightening their interest in achieving better quality.

After the VP/Q had established his organization and made it effective, he and we could turn to long-range strategy on quality matters. He wrote white papers on quality, did industry-wide evaluations to determine where our programs stood in relation to those of our competitors, made the equivalent of internal audits for quality, and took charge of our enhanced training program for all employees. He looked into such usually neglected areas as how we were distributing our products. Was there too much time wasted between receiving an order and shipping to fulfill it? How could the process be accelerated?

It took several years for our insistence on quality to make a quantum difference in our goods and services, but when the impact showed up, we made the most of it. Our marketing people used our quality emphasis as a sales tool; they could impress customers with stories about a VP/Q with the ability to stop a production line.

Within the management team, we tried to instill a sense of determination to strive for excellence. We linked quality with ambition, and tried to promote those managers who demonstrated by their deeds their own commitment to quality.

Here's an example of an innovation for quality. We had one division that was encapsulated geographically and because of its customer base—it sold and maintained computers for nonmilitary customers in the federal government, principally in the Washington, D.C., area. I wanted to try to see if we could introduce a new field service organization. Often, within a company, field service people are viewed as drudges because they don't have the more glamorous tasks of sales or development. We put a whole new phalanx of these people into professional garb. We asked them to wear jackets and ties, and, more important, to go through some special training for their jobs, training that emphasized pride in service. We gave them special vans with telephones and beepers to keep in touch. A field service rep would be sitting somewhere, and his beeper would sound—just as if he were a doctor on call, they would tell us with some satisfaction. We gave the field service people more responsibility, too, for instance, the latitude to manage inventories of spare parts. This made good sense, because by being in daily touch with the customers they knew better than some desk-bound manager what parts were most needed and when. In short, we helped this particular field service organization realize that it was an elite group, and pushed it toward becoming a voice for quality within the company.

It was an experiment that I would have liked to see replicated throughout Burroughs, but just as the results were becoming clear, senior management became so involved in the acquisition of Sperry that it consumed nearly all of our time and focus.

How can an emphasis on quality directly affect a career path? I've given some instances earlier in this chapter, but it's important to recognize that an emphasis on quality can help you right from the start. As a new hire into a company like Corning or Burroughs, you could quickly discern the emphasis on quality, and hop on the leader's bandwagon. When you make innovations, do so on the quality frontier, since that's where the company's interests lie.

Now many people see improving quality as a long-term goal; that's true, but there are some things you can do to make a short-term quality impact. As a middle-rank manager, I could have instituted that revamping of the service organization noted just a few paragraphs above. Recognition events are important in the quick enhancing of quality, and are an idea that can be put into place by middle managers rather easily, because their cost is relatively small. Think of the smiles and goodwill that "chauffeur of the week" or "engineer of the month" may bring. Such pats on the back are a way of turning the attention of your employees toward quality. (Invite a manager several levels higher than yourself to come and present the award; that won't hurt you with higher-ups, either.) As soon as you come into an organization, take cognizance of, and fix, the small but outwardly noticeable things that may be awry— shoddy housekeeping in your offices, copies that are badly printed, phones that ring too many times before being answered. By striving to replace sloppiness with perfection in all endeavors, you put your own subordinates on notice that you will not tolerate mediocrity in anything that is representative of your area; this, in turn, will quickly raise the level of professionalism in your organization.

Make your place a showplace. Quickly raising the quality level in your area will enhance your image with your superiors.

If yours is the service department, engineering facility, factory, or divisional headquarters that is presentable—that shines—superiors will bring customers to view it or in other ways will trust you to interact with the buyers of the company's products. That will create more opportunities for you to impress them, and to advance.

Managing for quality and scoring points thereby is yet another instance of my main theme in this book: that your corporate life can be managed. Quality has to do with one's attitude toward one's work—and toward oneself. When you're pushing yourself ahead on a schedule, you can't afford too many mistakes. Where do you put your time and effort? Into those matters that will get you noticed, that will differentiate you from other managers. Many people can plan every complicated detail of the production of a new product, or their annual budgets down to the number of employees and the costs associated with them, but they won't put the same thought and energy into the details of planning their careers, or into paying attention to enhancing the quality of what goes on in their corporate areas of responsibility. Plan what others don't even think of planning, and you'll be likely to have a higher-quality organization and a higher profile.

The manager who is thought of as being passionately committed to quality is generally also thought of as being above the crowd of competitors. Managing for quality can be applied to one's own career by thinking of your personality, skills, and area of responsibility as a product to be designed, engineered, and kept on a delivery schedule. You'll want to make sure that your plan (to become an accomplished professional manager, frequently promoted) is solid, that your suppliers (the people you're managing) are giving you the best they have to offer, that you are always on schedule and have the proper reality checks at every point in the production line to gauge if everything is proceeding properly. You are making a product that is essentially a reputation; your "quality" is everything that you are as a manager.

18

Braun

W*HEN* a headhunter first telephoned me at IBM about a "general management opportunity" with a company whose name he would not immediately disclose, I was intrigued enough by his description to meet him for dinner—and then I was knocked over when he told me that the assignment would be in Germany with the electrical consumer products manufacturing firm called Braun. I knew very little about the company except that one of my favorite uncles raved about their electric shavers. I tried not to let my surprised reaction show to the recruiter, and agreed to a meeting with Braun's major shareholder, Gillette, at the venerable company's headquarters in Boston. There, in the course of a day, I met a number of senior executives including the chairman and CEO, and it became clear to me that the decision-maker was going to be an executive vice-president in charge of what they called the Diversified Group, which included Braun, S. T. DuPont (maker of expensive lighters and writing instruments), and several other companies. This man immediately addressed me in German, both to determine my fluency and to see how I'd react. I evidently did well in that test, because I could immediately sense a change in tenor of the interviews: now it was Executive VP Tom Singer who was trying to sell me on the job. I was not yet convinced, but agreed to accompany Singer to Braun's corporate headquarters in Kronberg, Germany, just outside Frankfurt, to meet selected executives of Braun.

On my visit to Kronberg, a wealthy suburb of Frankfurt, I met some members of the *vorstand*, the board of management that ostensibly ran Braun, including some Americans, a Canadian, and several Germans. Then Tom took me to lunch at the luxurious Blue Room of the Schloss Hotel, where I was interviewed by an American headhunter who lived in Germany, and the VO member for personnel. We all hit it off and drank plenty of wine. The prestige of IBM was very high, and I was a man who had done well at IBM and was reasonably fluent in German. After more meetings in Boston, a job offer was made. I would become a member of the *vorstand* in charge of all technical operations, a newly created post. The recently appointed chairman of the VO, an American who had worked for Gillette in Boston as well as for Braun, had his sights set on returning to the U.S. and to higher management at Gillette, and it was made reasonably clear to me—though never stated openly—that if I did well at Braun, I would have a good chance of succeeding him. I accepted the job, mostly because it was a terrific opportunity to become a real general manager whose responsibilities included clearly defined financial bottom lines. I also looked forward to obtaining hands-on international management experience while living overseas, to being part of a management team made up of people from many lands, and operating what was in its own right a multinational firm. Having already discerned that the Braun people liked to think of themselves as independent of Gillette, I didn't want to be wrongly branded by my new colleagues when I first came to work, and so tried to position myself with both Gillette and Braun people as this terrific IBM-trained manager being brought in because of his competence rather than because of any close ties to specific executives at Gillette.

In the 1960s Gillette had bought the holdings of two brothers who had a controlling interest in Braun AG, and thereby acquired the company, although some shares remained in other hands and the stock continued to be traded on the Frankfurt Exchange. The United States Department of Justice, concerned that this acquisition might enable Gillette to unreasonably dominate the dry (electric) shaver as well as wet (blade) markets in the U.S., had forced Gillette to sign a consent decree that would keep the Braun electric shaver brand name out of the United States for several years. Those shavers were then sold in the U.S. under the name of Eltron, through a Connecticut-based distributor. The government, however, allowed other Braun products—clocks, coffee grinders, coffee makers, lighters, kitchen machines, everything but shavers—to be sold under the Braun name in the U.S.

When I arrived at Braun in January of 1976, the company was profitable but not performing nearly up to its potential. Braun had product cost and quality problems in some of its key product lines, while other lines were losing money and presented opportunities to control product costs and expenses and thereby improve profitability. Braun's great strength had always been its industrial design. Braun products had the image of being the best in their field—not just the best-designed, but of the highest quality. Its image had long been bolstered by the company's stylish and forceful corporate communications: the product literature, product packaging, company publications, annual reports, and other public relations materials were always well done. Moreover their total presentation was orchestrated in such a way as to give to the company an image of being unified, quality-conscious, and on the leading edge of technology. Unfortunately, when I came on board the public's perception of Braun's quality no longer matched reality; actual quality had slipped, and we had many disappointed and aggravated customers. Nonetheless, in Europe and especially in Germany, the company's image remained strong and prestigious. Surveys revealed that most people thought Braun was a much larger company (in terms of sales volume and total employment) than it actually was.

Despite the company's strengths, there was a feeling, common to the Braun line employees and the German management, that for the past few years the company had been declining—and that this decline could be ascribed to Gillette's ownership. Detractors believed that in an effort to generate revenue growth and sell more units, Gillette had enforced for the company an overly commercial objective, with the result that the quality of Braun products had been allowed to deteriorate. For instance, Braun had recently gone into manufacturing hair care products (dryers and curlers) as well as oral care products (electric toothbrushes and waterjets); some old-timers at Braun considered these products unseemly companions of the company's sophisticated traditional products, and felt that they contributed to the sense of declining quality. Braun old-timers also resented the appointment of Gillette people to higher management at headquarters and in some subsidiaries; so much so, that by the time I arrived, the fact that several members of the executive inner circle were Gillette men had begun to generate a negative backlash toward the Boston-based owner. As I soon learned, quality had indeed declined in some product lines, but it had little to do with Gillette's control of Braun. Rather, the causes were complex, and had as much to do with changing times as they did with changing ownership. Some of these causes will become apparent as I discuss individual segments of the business.

There was no question that Gillette had placed greater emphasis—and thus, more pressure—on the financial performance of Braun than had been the case before the change in ownership. Their scrutiny had brought into the light three Braun business segments that were troubled and had little hope for recovery in the foreseeable future. Among these was the photo business, which produced and marketed sound movie cameras, projectors, and electronic flashes for cameras. Braun had been the first company to miniaturize flashes for use on amateur cameras, and it had been a very good business for the company until dozens of competitors entered the market. Another problem cropped up with the 8-mm sound movie cameras, which were highly sensitive and sophisticated products: it cost a lot per unit to produce these cameras, due to relatively small production runs and the high cost of their high-quality components, such as Schneider lenses. The gross profit margins on the products were slim to begin with, and whatever profit was left was eaten up by the demands for customer service within the guarantee period. It was not that Braun's cameras were bad, but customers would purchase these highly expensive and sensitive instruments, and then treat them as if they were indestructible—dragging them from ski slopes to resort beaches, for instance, without a thought that the mechanism that had functioned well in the cold might need an adjustment before being taken into an environment of heat and salt water. The best thing that could be said of the photo division and its wonderful high-end products was that it was entirely concentrated in Munich and could possibly be sold as a self-contained business unit.

The hi-fi division had some similar problems; its headquarters was in Frankfurt. Radios had been one of the original products of the Braun company, and expertise in radio had soon spawned allied lines of phonograph equipment, which included high-fidelity components, tuners, amplifiers, turntables, and some of the finest loudspeakers in the world. With the exception of the speakers, the hi-fi equipment was overly designed; that is, it was more finely tuned and expensive than the market would bear. Production was inefficient and costly. The products aimed at a very small, high-end market, and, just as with the movie cameras, there were problems when customers abused the products and then wanted them repaired under the guarantee. By 1976 the hi-fi products sold almost exclusively in Germany.

The third headache, not yet as large as that of photo or hi-fi, but careening in that direction, was the lighters business, which produced and sold moderately expensive and very beautiful pocket and table lighters in the traditional Braun colors, black and steel. These were technically advanced products utilizing piezo ignition systems; some were true classics, exhibited throughout the world, at the Museum of Modern Art in New York, for instance. Unfortunately for Braun, the market in lighters was polarizing at the low and high ends. At the low end, there were the throwaways, such as Cricket and Bic; at the high end were the lighters that were almost pieces of jewelry, such as those manufactured by S. T. DuPont, Dunhill, and others. Products in the middle—such as Braun's—were being squeezed out. (It is interesting to note that Gillette then owned Cricket as well as the S. T. DuPont lines.) I'll come back to these problems later on, but first I want to complete the profile of the firm's businesses as I found them in 1976.

In financial terms, the most important segment was the electric shavers business, which made everything from battery-powered shavers to rechargeable cordless ones, electric shavers with cords, and similar shavers for women. These shavers had very high market shares in most European countries as well as significant shares in the Middle East, South America, and Japan, all of which combined to allow very high volumes of manufacturing and sales, low product costs, and high gross profit margins. One of the things that I did during my tenure at Braun was to introduce total vertical integration in shavers; over a period of four years we automated factories to the degree that they could operate around the clock with 50 percent fewer people while their output increased 250 percent.

A second important and profitable product line was in kitchen appliances. These were the coffee grinders and coffee makers, as well as some other kitchen machines and a few products that were country-specific, that is, manufactured for special uses in particular countries. The factories of this division were in Germany, Spain, Argentina, Brazil, and Mexico. Although profitable, they presented an opportunity for me to introduce new product ideas to modernize and expand the lines, while at the same time improving the profitability of the ones already being manufactured. A third profitable division was hair care, which was growing at a tremendous rate as a result of capitalizing on outstanding design and utilizing the talents of powerful marketing and sales organizations. A fourth product line, on which Braun had recently embarked, was wall, table, and alarm clocks of various kinds. Because Braun's design was always exceptional, these clocks had already found their way into homes and offices around the world. However, an allied entry into the digital wristwatch field had proved disastrous. When I got to Braun, however, the watches were still on the market, and losing money for the company at a phenomenal rate; when I became chairman, I shut down the production of watches, and today the only Braun watches to be found for sale are highly prized collector's items.

At the campus of Braun's corporate headquarters in Kronberg was the building that housed its world headquarters, and also a household appliances division factory, that division's headquarters, and the site of the famed Braun industrial design facility and its product development and engineering. The area was basically residential, so Braun's factory was virtually the only one in the immediate vicinity; however, the famous five-star Schloss Hotel was only about ten minutes from our campus, and, I discovered, it was a favorite watering hole of Braun's senior executives.

As a Gillette expatriate, I was provided with a company house of our choice for myself and my family, including utility, telephone, and other house-related expenses; company cars with drivers; private schooling for my children at the Frankfurt International School; club memberships; and so on. This was quite a change from life at IBM, where practically no perks were ever given to managers; I remember that I often gave a ride home to my immediate boss at IBM, Paul Rizzo, who was the company's CFO, a corporate vice-president and a member of the board of directors. In comparison with the salary I had been earning at IBM, after deduction of expenses, my total net income at Braun was significantly higher, and with that and the numerous perks, our lifestyle changed dramatically. As I later understood, it was now on a par with that of *vorstand* members of other companies in Germany, and with that of my own VO colleagues.

When I pulled my company-bought car right up to the front door and my assigned parking slot at the Kronberg headquarters, I was both abashed and amazed: the place looked like a Mercedes-Benz car dealership. Executives' cars were lined up right at the door, while parking for employees was at some distance from the building. Parking for the handicapped was reserved and near to the main entrance, but not as convenient as the spaces for the VO. That parking lot, and the contrast it made with IBM's no-nonsense image and approach to management, was a fitting symbol of what struck me most forcibly during my first few days at Braun: the distinctive corporate culture.

I was part of an eight-member *vorstand*; six of us had offices on the top floor of the three-story headquarters building, while the chiefs of the photo and hi-fi divisions were in Munich and Frankfurt when not meeting with the rest of us. We were four Germans, two Americans, a Canadian, and an Englishman. All the officers were formal with one another; first names were seldom used, and everyone behaved with exaggerated decorum. On the other hand, there was a feeling at headquarters that all Braun employees were like members of a closely knit and proud family. The formality carried over into the physical plant of headquarters. All the offices were lined up along white corridors; when all the outer doors were closed, as they usually were, there was a deafening silence and an equally off-putting lack of people in the halls. I kept getting the feeling I was in a hospital. The managers were all behind double closed doors; to get to see someone, you first had to go through a door from the corridor into the secretary's office, then maneuver your way past the secretary and through a second closed door to see the manager. The managers seldom visited one another except when they had an appointment. The day's highlight was the festive lunch served in the executive dining room, a facility with its own kitchen and staff, used exclusively for members of the VO and a few other high-ranking individuals, ten or twelve in all. To go to lunch was an important matter here; fine cuisine and wines were served, with the selection of the day's wines a subject of some discussion and an occasion for the executives to show off their expertise. At IBM wine and liquor had been forbidden on the premises, and at company-sanctioned functions even when held at a restaurant, so the Braun executive dining room was a new experience for me. If you didn't like the menu of the day you could request nearly any special dish you wanted. Lunch table conversation rarely dealt with business, but, rather, was taken up with bantering about recent trips, hobbies, vacations, politics, food, or family. After lunch, due to the wine and good food, the afternoon's work proceeded at a more leisurely pace.

Executive meeting rooms were always decorated with fresh flowers, and to facilitate discussion coffee or tea would be served in china cups and saucers—no Styrofoam cups here, and no doughnuts haphazardly stacked on a paper plate either, since the coffee would be accompanied by exquisite pastries and linen serviettes.

Then there were the celebrations. Birthdays, anniversaries, engagements, weddings, divorces, German holidays, American holidays—every event was an occasion to hold a party, and each party reflected the magnitude of the event. Some were held on company premises, others at the nearby Schloss Hotel or at other equally distinguished hotels and restaurants in the area. When I had occasion to visit Braun subsidiaries, I noticed that the spirit of giving parties had spilled over into these far-flung operations as well. These parties, usually accompanied by beer, wine, and other spirits, would start in the late afternoons and often continue on into the night or even the early-morning hours. Not all took place on Fridays, and the next morning's long pale faces were testimony to those who had been the most festive. On the occasion of a *vorstand* member's round number birthday or anniversary—thirtieth, fortieth, fiftieth —processions with gifts and flowers began first thing in the morning, and culminated in parties starting immediately after lunch. Many of the gifts were elaborate, and some were handmade by one of the company's famous machine shops—at company expense, of course. As the day progressed, the celebrating executive would be "surprised" by visits from out-of-town and even out-of-country employees who had flown in (at company expense) for the day to attend the party. The size of these parties, and the quality of refreshments and gifts generally varied with the rank of the executive or of the power of his unit. It was a sign of acceptance to be invited to parties given by the industrial design department, which was located behind locked doors and was known for its creative approach to fun as well as to industrial design. "King" Richard of Waldurn, a plant manager in this outlying town who had operated his plant himself for many years before selling it to Braun, gave one of the company's most elaborate annual picnics, and an invitation to this event was similarly sought after. Every year several busloads of people from Kronberg, including *vorstand* members, would take a two-hour ride to give honor to King Richard, and to engage in the pursuit of sausages and beer at his picnic. Such events fostered the feeling of Braun as a family, and the co-herence, team spirit, and loyalty of Braun employees was a definite asset of the company. But the essence of the family had become its ability to carouse, rather than its fight to outperform competitors and produce results.

It took me a while to get adjusted to the different, and quite seductive, lifestyle of the Braun executives, which, I soon discovered, was similar to that of executives in other German companies. But after settling myself and my family in a house, getting the children to the International School, and so on, I was ready to turn my attention to the reason I'd been hired: to help Braun get going again.

The challenge to us in senior management at Braun was clear: to maintain the unique character and spirit of the company while improving its performance and market share throughout the world. We needed to make significant improvements in product quality and product costs; we also had to either make the problem divisions of photo, hi-fi, and lighters more profitable or find ways of winding them down or divesting them. To contribute my share, I had to learn the business quickly, gain the confidence of the management and the employees, and at the same time initiate actions that would take me toward my own goal of reaching the top rank, even if some of these actions might prove initially difficult or unpopular in some quarters. I wanted to make my mark, and make it fast. My fluency in German afforded me ready acceptance into the ranks of the Ger-man management team at various levels; the Germans were clearly numerically in the majority, though not in the top management. I had another advantage: I was viewed as not having come from Gillette. Many of the old-timers at Braun viewed the Boston com-pany as the enemy, and not a few hoped that Gillette would divest Braun, as a result of its lackluster performance. To move easily between the Germans and the people whom Gillette had brought in required balance, and some risk-taking.

It was essential to change the employees' attitude, to have them believe we must all work together to revitalize the company. Greater trust had to be established between old-timers and newcomers, be-tween German speakers and those who chiefly spoke other lan-guages. Because of my fluency in German, and also because I had come from IBM, which was universally respected for its manage-ment practices, I was able to help meld the various factions. It quickly became known that I had a tremendous capacity for work, remembered everything, and—perhaps most important—that I truly cared for my people.

In the United States, I had been able to demonstrate my caring for people rather well; in Germany, I found it was not so easy. Most European companies are conservative and formal; German ones are even more so. But I persevered. It had been critical at IBM to build bridges to the people who controlled the power centers of that company, and it was equally necessary at Braun. For instance, I worked hard to gain the confidence of Albrecht, the vice-chairman of the VO, a man who had been with Braun for decades, and whose line responsibilities included overseeing marketing and sales for Germany, Austria, and Switzerland. Albrecht was a very formal man, with what we in the United States would describe as a Prussian demeanor; he had even been a highly decorated fighter pilot in World War II. He would usually be found only behind the closed doors of his office, and would never meet anyone without his suit jacket. At the start of a meeting he would shake hands, and he always stood up when a VO member, or even his own boss, entered a room; he preferred holding discussions in German, and had difficulty with English. Through persistent attention, I discovered that Albrecht, a man in his late fifties, had a very young son around whom his world revolved; he loved to talk about the boy, and since my children were of similar age, we had a common topic of conversation and a common bond. Once I had won his respect and confidence, everything changed, and he proved willing to take direction from me—who he considered one of the Americans.

I focused on forging such relationships with both the German and the non-German members of the management team. I was not always able to do so; one English VO colleague resented me in many ways—he didn't like my aggressive management style, my less formal and less bureaucratic way of doing things, my youth (I was then not yet forty), and the fact that Gillette had brought me in from the outside. Things came to a head with him at one of our VO lunches, after I'd been at Braun about eighteen months. The two of us were the last to remain in the dining room, and he took the occasion to vent his rage and frustration at me. If I continued in my ways, he insisted, my days at Braun were numbered and my future business prospects bleak. He was wrong. Within a few weeks I was appointed Chief Operating Officer and shortly after that became Chairman of the Board—and his boss. Despite his outburst, he worked well with me when I took over these top positions.

Beyond cementing my working relationships with individuals it was also imperative to link the enclaves within the company; often, these operated as if they were separate from the company as a whole. For instance, the Central European team headed by Albrecht were mostly Germans, and shut out the English-speaking management. Similarly, there were plant managers whose primary concern seemed to be preserving the work load at their locations, and who were not lending necessary support for a newly built factory in Ireland. Fortunately our major factory in Barcelona was well run and stocked with talent, and other factories in Argentina, Brazil, and Mexico produced lines sold in Central and South America and could operate more or less independently. The photo and hi-fi divisions, which were self-contained within Germany, did not require technical and marketing support from corporate headquarters; on the other hand, however, they suffered because those parts of the Braun organization responsible for sales and marketing outside of Germany did not give hi-fi or photo the time of day, and as a consequence these businesses had been losing market share in countries other than Germany for many years.

To bring all these disparate elements together, and to get them to work as a team, I traveled extensively during my first several months. I found that the style of managing of most of the facilities was so interwoven with the acute stratifications and concerns of European society that it had gotten in the way of the company's ability to manufacture and sell its products. The chains of command had been so narrowly defined and strictly enforced by the organization that middle managers would only communicate to their superiors in the hierarchy, and never laterally to their counterparts. At IBM I had been accustomed to a less-structured environment wherein managers would often seek help from colleagues on all levels, in all functions, across departmental and divisional lines, and for almost any reason.

To break the rigid chains of command, and to challenge the cultural taboos, I thought the best approach would be what I called managing by walking around, talking to people at all levels, and by doing so introducing a faster pace that would force managers to work in my new style. And so I walked the hospital-like corridors of the headquarters building, often dropping in on people unannounced; I did the same at factories, workshops, subsidiaries, warehouses. For convenience sake I adopted the celebration culture as a means of getting to know people and to develop mutual respect. Soon organizational barriers began to crumble and the stiff formality started to melt; then it was time to build new structures.

For instance, I began a series of meetings to which engineering employees and plant managers from all over the company were invited. I took the German managers to our facilities in Barcelona and Ireland, and brought the international management team to Frankfurt, Munich, and our other domestic locations. Strange as it may sound, plant managers had never met together before; they had been kept each in their unit, unable to discuss common problems—or to suggest probable solutions to one another based on their experience. Another change: I introduced the concept of product program managers for each product line, so that, for example, one manager had responsibility for everything that had to do with shavers, another for kitchen appliances, a third for hair care products, a fourth for lighters, and so on. These program managers became the ones who talked to, and resolved the differences between, the technical organizations and the marketing entities. Further, these program managers, whose responsibilities went beyond geographical boundaries, stayed on top of their product lines and gave us, for the first time, a view of how shavers or hair care products were doing worldwide; previously, it took quite a bit of digging into the numbers provided by many separate subsidiary operations to understand that. It also helped force the diverse organizations to communicate and cooperate.

As I worked to increase the effectiveness of the program managers, I was also putting pressure on to reduce costs and to make significant improvements to our balance sheet. With the increased pace and the new ease of communications, important business issues were surfacing more quickly, and so was the willingness to do something about them. For instance, it became painfully apparent that our table and pocket lighter factory at Nuremberg was not competitive; labor cost per unit was very high, and the quantities produced were not large enough to justify automating the plant. It had previously been obvious to management that this factory was a money drain, but they had been reluctant to shut it down. Program management, by focusing on specific product lines, made the factory's shortcomings not only obvious but also showed just precisely how it was hurting us, and that it must be shut down. A recommendation was made to the VO that the Nuremberg plant be closed, some of the products discontinued, and work on the others be transferred to our factories at Kronberg and Ireland. The VO accepted the inevitable.

Then the decision had to be submitted to the *Aufsichtsrat*, the supervisory board of the company on which labor representatives had key roles ("codetermination"). During the course of several lunches and dinners I spoke personally to these labor representatives; although they understood and even agreed with our analysis, there was no way that they could vote in favor of closing down a plant in Germany. The management votes prevailed, we announced our decision, and I immediately drove to Nuremberg to describe to the employees there what our policies would be in regard to severance settlements, outplacement assistance, retraining, and so on. This was my first experience with a unionized labor force (there would be many more in the future). I was met at the gates by striking employees whose banners and placards hung from every fence, window, and doorway, and by a cluster of press, including television. Inside, the union representatives threatened a lengthy strike. I countered—and concluded the negotiations—by telling them that lost workdays beyond the end of the current week would be deducted from the generous severance package we were prepared to pay. A settlement was soon reached, and we phased out the factory over the next few months.

This first and highly visible action in a belt-tightening campaign was noted throughout the company; in its wake, other factories and whole divisions began to reevaluate their own operations. Dramatic cutbacks in employment and production were taken in the photo and hi-fi divisions; unfortunately, even these could not bring them to the level of profitability we desired, and both divisions were later sold.

As a result of good progress in many parts of the company, I was appointed chairman and CEO, and my predecessor was promoted to a position at Gillette in Boston. We continued aggressively to automate our already profitable shaver factories and vertically integrated their operations so that we only had to buy raw materials, and no longer even purchased such items as packaging or small screws from outside suppliers. By producing everything ourselves, we were rapidly bringing costs down. Soon we were making three times as many shavers per day with half the number of employees. Also, as a result of our lower costs and an aggressive marketing campaign, we were gaining market share for the shavers in every country. We made important investments in the kitchen appliances factories in Germany and Spain in order to reduce costs and to improve the quality of the products. We erected a new office building at the Kronberg campus; it included an outstanding cafeteria and a health center for the employees.

For the most part, by the time I took over as Chairman and CEO, the news was good and getting better, and we had the makings of an excellent management team—but there still existed a barrier between the VO members and the rest of the company. Now, while I had the support of the rest of the company, it was time to work on the top layer. Only if the revolutions I was introducing were put in place at the top would they have a chance of surviving more than a little while.

I decided to radically alter the Braun executive style in a way that would have an immediate and highly visible impact. I ordered the maintenance staff to work over a weekend and remove all the doors on the executive corridor, every one of them except that which led to the legal department, which was retained to protect the company's secrets. No more doors to the secretaries' offices, no more closed doors to the executives' inner sanctums; now anyone would be able to feel more at ease walking into these areas. I also fiddled with the parking slots. I had the slots for the handicapped moved closer to the front door of the building, and shifted the slots for the executives' fleet of Mercedeses. Then—in the eyes of some, the unkindest cut of all—I ordered the executive kitchen and dining room closed. Henceforth, we executives would all eat lunch in the new employee cafeteria, where we would be accessible to employees at all levels, and our lunches wouldn't be quite so liquid nor consume so much of the day's working hours. I also issued orders to scale down the innumerable birthday, anniversary, and holiday parties, and insisted that those that had to be held would only begin after regular working hours.

The senior executives were initially taken aback by these measures; of course, that was one of my objectives in making the changes. Within weeks, as I'd hoped, managers from all levels were roaming the executive corridor, talking to one another and interacting with their superiors; even the VO members were actually conferring daily with their counterparts instead of only confronting them at formal meetings. Rather than remaining in their offices and dealing only with a limited aspect of the company's business, the VO members were beginning to be in touch with the details of the entire operation. In the cafeteria, approached by many people, we executives got to hear more of what was actually going on in the company, and to know more about problem spots and employee concerns.

For me, the change in attitude was exemplified at its best in an open house Christmas party that was originally suggested by my wife. For the first time at Braun we held a party in celebration of no particular event or anniversary, but just in honor of our employees and in particular for their families. The idea was for children and other relatives to see the Braun workplaces. This was an astounding notion to many, for most of the families had never been inside the factory or office in which the father, mother, or grandparent worked.

Our many foreign workers—Turks, Yugoslavs, and Italians, chiefly—had little sense of community with the other workers of the company; this party helped rectify that situation as well. We pulled out all the stops, with great spreads of food, entertainment, a visit by the German equivalent of Santa Claus and another by the company's fire trucks, presents for the children, and so forth. We distributed pads and crayons and asked the children to sketch their impressions of the family member's workplace; later, these artworks were judged and the winning sketches were exhibited on the walls of the headquarters building. The exhibit was so successful that it then traveled to our other facilities all over the world.

The open house party, the removal of the doors, the redesignation of the parking slots, the executives eating in the cafeteria were all in service of what I call deformalizing the structure of the company. "Communicating with the troops" was a style with which I felt comfortable, and one that I worked assiduously to make viable. Having found Braun too formal, too sterile, too uncommunicative, my solution was to head it in the other direction. Soon my American slang expressions—"Go rock the boat," "This place is a zoo"—were adapted and repeated by other members of the management team. To Americans they would have seemed pretty tame, but to the employees and management of Braun they were emblematic of a new era and style in management. One of my expressions became a byword throughout the organization. When I really wanted some action, I had developed the habit of saying, "Let's hit it," meaning, let's get the job done. Braun's managers learned that when I said, "Let's hit it," some fur would soon be flying, and they came to like the excitement presaged by this innocuous phrase.

My other stock phrase was "We're in this together." Of course I'd been preaching just that since the day I'd arrived, but now the Braun people were ready to hear and understand its implications. They knew now that I put a great deal of effort into my own work, and that I would not ask more of them than I would demand of myself. But I did, now, ask them to do a great deal, and steadily reinforced the notion that Braun's future depended on a team effort that encompassed the efforts of the VO, the middle management, and the employees. This idea that the company's fortunes would rise or fall based on all of our joint efforts—and that, therefore, we should all work hard together—was revelatory. To back it up, I instituted systems whereby we could regularly measure our results more easily, and in a more timely manner.

It is not my style to write internal letters or memos, and the amount of memo-writing in the executive offices fell off sharply; people started communicating by telephone and by dropping into one another's offices to chat about everyday matters. I was happy to see communication outside of official channels, a sure sign that the less-formal structure was facilitating the work of the company. When I wanted information, I never liked to go through channels; rather, I wanted to go directly to the person who had the information; doing this at Braun encouraged that lower-level person to query me directly when he or she wanted or needed something in return. This style began to be followed by other senior managers. Reaching down into the corporation thus also had the effect of allowing junior managers to get to know the people in upper management, and to be encouraged to come forth with that most precious of all business products, new ideas. Because the juniors were more regularly and closely in touch with the seniors, the upper management came to know them well; this enhanced the career possibilities of the capable ones, and allowed us also to find and weed out the nonperformers.

My style, which fostered egalitarianism throughout the company, was well suited to imitation. As others replicated it, they had also to adopt my aggressive tactics and drive for results. And, of course, as our results got better and better, there was more and more enthusiasm about the new style and its demands—because nothing breeds enthusiasm or uplifts the spirit of company cohesion like continuously improving financial performance and success in the marketplace.

By the time I was ready to move from Braun, in 1979, the

company was healthy, positioned well for the future, and had an executive team that was better prepared for the more modern ways of doing business.

As for me, I had found that being at Braun was one of the greatest learning experiences of my life. I was fortunate to have the opportunity to acquire a lot of knowledge and experience while at the same time being able to use my talents to deliver solid results. Before going to Braun I had never really had to worry about cash flow, and had never truly had my performance measured on a real financial bottom line, that is, pre-tax profits. At Braun, the question was not "Did he make his budget or schedule?" but "Did he direct the company in such a way that it could pay the quarterly dividend?" I learned for the first time what it meant to prepare for, and chair, a shareholders' meeting, to deal with outside auditors, public relations matters, even with banks. At the level of management I had reached at IBM, the concept of residual inventory had little meaning for me; at Braun, moving goods out of warehouses into the hands of retailers and eventually into those of end users—customers— was a continual concern. I had to be able to grasp the notions of product pricing, discounts to wholesalers, to maneuver about in the world of currency fluctuations and multinational operations. I learned to live with codetermination—to manage a company that had labor representatives on its board. I also learned about the favorable impact of advertising on market share, and how good market share allowed a company to be more daring in its future planning.

To sum up: the difference was between knowing and doing. Previously I had known how to read a balance sheet or a profit and loss statement, but I'd never before had the opportunity of planning and executing a complete one.

Yet by year's end of 1979 my tasks at Braun had become repetitive. I had accomplished virtually everything I set out to do. I had changed fields, from computers at IBM to consumer products at Braun, and had performed well. I had gained international experience with a multinational company, had fulfilled my P&L responsibilities, and had even helped raise the company to higher levels of profitability. My progression had been rapid, from VO member to COO Chairman and CEO in about twenty-four months. I was now past my fortieth birthday, my children had outgrown the International School in Frankfurt, and I wanted very much to return to the United States and to work in a senior executive position for a high technology company much larger than Braun. My predecessor, Al Zeien, had gone on to higher positions at Gillette, but in my view my prospects at Gillette were limited: senior management in Boston all had had some operating experience with their main line of business, razor blades, and I had none of that. It had always been my rule of thumb to work in the mainstream of a company's business, believing that that was the only way to reach the top. Gillette was no different than other companies, and so I concluded that going to headquarters in Boston would not further my career. So I looked elsewhere. When a good offer from Rockwell International came along, I quickly took it—a jump that would later prove to have been made too precipitously, and that almost derailed my career.

19

Burroughs/Unisys

*A*LMOST from the moment I started at Rockwell International, I was unhappy there. It wasn't my kind of company or environment, and I should have known better than to go there. But I had gone, and now I was looking to get out. A Chicago-based executive recruitment agency contacted me for a search they were conducting on behalf of W. Michael Blumenthal, the new chairman of the board of Burroughs, who was looking to hire a new management team. I had been out of IBM and the data-processing field for six years; however, during my time at Braun and at Rockwell I kept up with the field by reading industry publications and the like. At IBM, we had known Burroughs as one of our main competitors. The company was viewed as technically innovative but unable to take advantage of its leading-edge ideas. For instance, around 1970, the industry was in awe of its "2.0" major software product release, but the company had not made much of a dent in IBM's dominance from that innovation. Similarly, Burroughs had developed "virtual" memory (a storage capability application), only to have IBM make a market out of it. There were also stories of the same kind about its stacked architecture for systems, and many other industry firsts.

Burroughs had a marketing problem, as well as a reputation for poor customer service.

I knew that Burroughs was on the low side of the average in the amount of money it spent on research and development, but I also knew that despite its limited financial resources, Burroughs had nevertheless pulled off many technological innovations. Its technical people were viewed as dedicated, creative, and efficient in the evolution of ideas. Even so, by the late 1970's Burroughs had become known as a company that needed help. It was profitable, and earnings per share had climbed to a peak in 1979, but its products and balance sheet had significant problems. Burroughs was thought not to be capitalizing on its installed customer base that had been generated over a period of decades by its excellent technical innovations and products. Beyond that, it had a reputation for poor competitiveness in terms of its price/performance ratio—how their products performed for the dollars spent, versus how other companies' products performed.

As for the management, it was viewed from the outside as an inbred company that would not go beyond its own ranks to fill management positions. Blumenthal was the exception to the hire-from-within rule. He had been the chairman of Bendix before becoming secretary of the treasury in the Carter administration, and was viewed by some as a strong executive. However, he had no experience in data processing, and this was considered problematic because the DP industry was one whose technology and marketing concepts took years to learn. Also, it was unique in that the leader in the field, IBM, was ten times the size of its nearest competitor. The industry was once known as "IBM and the Seven Dwarfs" or "IBM and the BUNCH." The BUNCH consisted of Burroughs, Univac (Sperry), NCR, Control Data, and Honeywell. IBM's great size and market dominance directly impacted the marketing and sales strategies of its competitors. Customers, as well as financial analysts, knew that the computer industry was capital and R&D intensive— that, to stay abreast, companies had to spend what in other industries would be considered a high percentage of their sales and income on R&D and new product development. As a result, smaller companies were always being asked questions as to whether or not the dollars they had available for development of new generations of computers were adequate, and about their long-term viability vis-à-vis IBM, a company that annually spent billions of dollars on

R&D. Such questions arose because once a customer had chosen a particular system architecture—that is, bought and installed main frames from one manufacturer—it became expensive and disruptive to change, and so customers would always want to know about a DP company's long-term capabilities before committing to go with that company's products. For all these reasons, within the computer industry it was unheard of to recruit top executives who didn't have DP experience, since executives lacking in such experience were considered to be at a disadvantage in a highly competitive marketplace. I discounted this a bit when learning of the hiring of Blumenthal, though, because when I'd gone from IBM to Braun, people had said that wouldn't work because I was an outsider who had no consumer products experience—and I'd been able to cope without undue difficulties with the problems at Braun. To go from, say, consumer products to computers, however, was viewed as a much more difficult proposition.

When I went to meet Mike Blumenthal at an airport hotel in Detroit, I did so mostly because I was curious to meet a former secretary of the treasury, not because I wanted an offer from Burroughs. Having done my homework, I knew that the company was in trouble, and I wasn't sure I'd even entertain a job offer from them.

Blumenthal was a cigar-smoking, long-winded man who could be charming when he thought it was necessary and to his advantage. He knew he needed help and was out to reel in the most appropriate managers to get that help. He was direct and frank about the company's difficulties, to the degree that he understood them. Looking back now, I know that we both had seen only the tip of the iceberg. He told me he was determined to recruit managers from outside Burroughs and to replace an extremely high percentage of the long-serving senior management currently in place at the company. He also said that he planned eventually to move the company from Detroit to Princeton, believing this to be a more appropriate location for a high-tech company, though he didn't say when he might do this. He left the impression that it would be done only after the financial performance of the company had been greatly improved.

Mike wanted me to handle the technical operations, be responsible for the products; there were problems everywhere—with quality, costs, schedules, inventories, and so on. On the one hand they had facilities with idle capacity while on the other they were building new facilities. Overhead was similarly growing faster than sales.

This was work I had done before, at IBM, at Braun, and a bit at Rockwell. I'd solved product problems at IBM and at Braun, and the basic elements of these—dealing with suppliers, looking at costs, analyzing labor—would essentially be the same at Burroughs, even though the products were different. As I listened to Mike, it became clear that he knew relatively little about the problems and issues facing him. He'd only been at Burroughs about a year, but I had not only done my homework, I'd been aware of the company for years; it was possible that I then knew as much about the health and potential of Burroughs as he did.

Mike was enthusiastic about me, and wanted me to meet his vice-chairman, Jerry Jacobson, whom he had brought in from Bendix. Jacobson, who was in charge of long-term planning and deal-making, was Blumenthal's confidant and had worked with him for many years. Before meeting Jerry, I was able to find out who my competitors for the job were. When you reach the senior management level, DP has a relatively small circle, and most of the leading executives know one another, and they—as well as headhunters—tend to talk more than they should. I realized that I had greater strengths and credentials than the other candidates, principally because I had international experience, spoke German and Spanish, and, in addition, had had P&L responsibilities for a number of years. In fact, Blumenthal had no real way of judging what I knew about data processing. He would be gambling if he hired me, and we both knew it. However, he had the good sense to discern that I was the most suitable candidate for directing the engineering and manufacturing activities at Burroughs. He also recognized that I had the potential to assume much broader responsibilities.

I had planned to go to the rollout of the space shuttle at Cape Kennedy in December of 1980, and had combined that with a vacation, taking my wife and three children to Disney World. Jacobson was also then in Florida, and we arranged to meet in my hotel room in Orlando. Both of us were in bad shape at the meeting—I, with a flu that made me shiver, and Jerry, who had so thoroughly injured his back playing tennis that he'd recently been hospitalized, couldn't drive, and couldn't really walk properly. We spent the first part of the interview comparing ailments. The rest of the time, he asked questions about my views of the DP industry—questions that were, from my perspective, naive. I had significant doubts about going to Burroughs, but when I get in these situations I sometimes try to see if I can get a job offer, just to test my market value. I played to the audience well enough to be next requested to meet Mike in San Francisco, where I had gone on yet another Rockwell business trip. At this meeting I was told that I would be asked to come into the company as executive vice-president in charge of technical operations, and that I would report directly to the president of the company, Ray Stromback, whom I hadn't met.

Our fourth meeting took place in Detroit. Although the Burroughs drivers had been told to take visitors via the most attractive route to the Burroughs headquarters from the Detroit airport, the trip through what I thought were some of Detroit's bad areas didn't give me the best picture of what it would be like to move to Motor City. At Burroughs headquarters, I met my first real Burroughs employee, Ray Stromback. He was as nice a man as one could ever meet, had been with the company for more than thirty years, and seemed tired. I suspected that Ray was not the decision-maker on the matter of whether to hire me. In fact, Mike pointedly told me, "If you have problems on the job with Ray, come to me. Don't worry about him." I had voiced my objections about that to Mike; it was, I avowed, contrary to my management philosophy to work for someone but to be asked to go around him routinely in order to get the job done. Were I to accept an offer from Burroughs, I said, I'd do my best to work with Stromback and to keep the lines of authority clear.

After seeing Ray, Jerry whisked me downtown to the Detroit Club, in whose august confines I had drinks with Mike and with what I told myself were "the three wise men," who had been on the board of Burroughs for many years. Two were lawyers and the third was a banker, and all were Detroit-based. I'd already found out that Mike and Jerry knew very little about Burroughs' two main lines of business, data processing and defense. Well, I thought, they were both new. But then I listened to the questions put to me by the Burroughs board members, and was surprised again. Their questions about the industry were less than penetrating. Perhaps they were just being polite. They didn't know how one company in the field compared to any of the others. In fact, they didn't know what questions to ask, and I doubt they understood the answers I gave to the ones they did put to me. It was easy for me to dazzle them with my expertise; they were not there to evaluate my technical skills anyway, but, rather, my personality and feel for the business.

After more courting—dinner with the Jacobsons and the Blumenthals, complete with their spouses—Mike extended an offer that included salary, bonuses, stock options, and the usual things associated with a high position such as house purchase guarantees, mortgage rate guarantees, club memberships, and a company car. Mike realized that I understood that he didn't know the DP industry, and so he offered me a two-year contract as insurance in case I came to Burroughs and found a complete disaster. That offer was made at his home in Ann Arbor, on a Saturday morning, after which I was flown back to Pittsburgh, where we were then living. A phone call from Mike followed me to see if I'd arrived safely. He, too, knew how to properly court a candidate.

Many factors were stacked against my going to Burroughs. It was a sick, inbred company, headquartered in a city that, at first glance, I hadn't liked. I'd be parachuting into the middle of a mess, and would have to fight continuously against people who'd been with the company since the Crusades. The assignment wouldn't add to my portfolio of skills, and the compensation, perks, and benefits were in line with industry standards, but were not especially attractive, with the exception of the stock options, which later turned out to be valuable.

On the other side was the incontrovertible notion I'd been forming that the president, Ray Stromback, was extremely vulnerable, and that I had an enormous opportunity to move up quickly into the job of president and chief operating officer—a position in which I could have a major impact on the company. It was likely that with this move I would reach my objective of being at the top of a very large company, able within a relatively short time to increase further my already existing financial independence. (In corporations as you go up the ladder, the salaries, bonuses, and stock options climb exponentially, so that even one step further up the ladder, from executive vice-president to president, would bring with it significantly higher income.) I knew I could exploit that opportunity by making an impact on Burroughs very quickly. I knew further that because the chairman—and vice-chairman—and the three wise men of the board—appeared *not* to comprehend the technical and product aspects of the company, even though the company was riddled with problems, my actions would be doubly impressive. Their lack of experience in DP would make Mike and Jerry very dependent on me, and that would therefore accelerate my promotion to the presidency of Burroughs.

When I'd asked Mike about Ray Stromback's future, I'd received what he used to call a pear-shaped answer, one that has no rough edges and is too beautifully composed to be believed. Mike hadn't said that Ray would stay until he was sixty-five, or that I would be his successor. Rather, Mike implied that if the top slot opened up, I'd be in competition for the position with other executives whom he was in the process of promoting or hiring from the outside. The prospect of competition didn't faze me: I knew that in the environment and with the challenges Burroughs was facing, the position of executive vice-president for engineering and manufacturing would provide a base for making the most immediate, most visible, and most measurable impact on the corporation. Recognition would surely follow if I achieved good results, and I knew that I could bring many skills to bear on producing those results.

By Sunday evening, I'd accepted the job. We worked out the details during the next week, and two weeks later on January 22, 1981, I started at Burroughs.

When I first came in I retraced Mike's footsteps in learning about the company through reading its own history. As viewed from the outside, Burroughs had been seen as short-term oriented; every quarter had been better than the same one in the previous year. But, as the industry had suspected and as I soon learned in detail, those results had been generated in some ways that were deleterious to the company's health. Accounting rules had not been particularly conservative. There had been clear directions from the top, but they hadn't always been followed. For example, the conservative approach to recognizing revenues holds that a sale to a customer be recorded only after his computer has been installed and tested and the customer has signed a release. At the other extreme—a perfectly acceptable approach—one could recognize the revenue when the computer left the selling company's shipping dock. But a large computer is a complex machine; a mainframe may come from one factory, fifty terminals from a second, disk and tape drives (storage capacity) from a third, connecting cables from a fourth—etc. Do you recognize the revenue on shipment of the whole system with all of its components? Or on shipment of the individual pieces? There had not been entirely standardized procedures in this regard, and, coupled with Burroughs' poor record of customer service, these partial shipments had resulted in having a lot of cash tied up in receivables and some of those receivables could not be collected because of customer dissatisfaction. Mike had tried to standardize the procedures, and had even set up a network of staging centers —centralized warehouses that would gather the components of the complete system order and ship them only after the system was complete. This was an expensive but necessary solution to gain control over revenue recognition timing, and, as important, to win back customer satisfaction and loyalty.

Mike insisted that obsolete machines be scrapped and written off; he had just taken a huge year-end write-off for obsolescence at the end of calendar 1980. However, that wasn't the end of the problem, and we took another such write-off at the end of 1982. Mike and I established ever more rigorous and conservative rules for inventory accounting, tracking everything from the raw materials through work in process, finished goods, and spare parts.

Another example of how the company's past practices were affecting everything we did: for some years, the company had been working on a high-end machine, the Burroughs Scientific Processor (BSP); it had been promised to customers, and was eagerly anticipated by the DP industry. When Mike had taken a fresh look at its development, costs, and potential markets, it had become clear that marketing had vastly overestimated the number of customers, while the engineers had similarly guessed wrong about the technical task involved, so that the machine made absolutely no business sense whatsoever. Mike terminated the project.

The most important problem, though, was the overall one of not having an effective management team. To encourage the long-serving senior management to leave quietly and comfortably, Mike had put in place a generous early retirement plan. At the same time, he was hiring aggressively from the outside. Many long-term Burroughs people saw what was happening, and took the opportunities presented to get out while they could, and before they would be forced out.

My own initial investigation of Burroughs showed me that the problems were broader, deeper, and more pervasive than I had thought. There was good news: Burroughs' customer base was loyal, and this would buy us the required time to revamp the company. Another piece of good news was that the engineering people were, indeed, terrific. But there was an awful lot of bad news. I was appalled at the chaos, sloppiness, and ineptitude I found in almost every area of the company. Meeting the managers, visiting many locations, I was stunned by the executives' lack of discipline and the company's lack of investment in its physical facilities. There were far too many executives who were simply unable to handle their own jobs; I guessed that they had risen through the ranks because of their longevity with the company rather than because of their contributions and competence. They didn't understand the products that competed with Burroughs' own. Their delivery schedules were unrealistic: they had no serious milestones by which they could measure progress, no effective review mechanisms, no quality assessments, no realistic business plans. Inventories were out of line, costs were out of control, forecasting was a shambles. Furthermore, at the facilities, roofs were literally falling in. The marketing people were at war with the technical people. Corporate finance was tearing its hair out. Human resources executives were still working with files that were on paper—this, at a computer company! Burroughs seemed to be held together by rubber bands.

To me, the worst aspect was the warring tribes. I've never been sympathetic to turf battles inside companies—after all, we're supposed to be working together, rather than against one another, aren't we?—but this was ridiculous. The most furious battles in this war took place at quarterly planning meetings attended by four of the company's major sectors: International Sales and Services, Domestic Sales and Services, Engineering and Manufacturing, and something called Corporate Program Management. The war pitted the two sales sectors against the manufacturing sector, with the program managers acting as referees.

This meeting was a complicated scene that needed a Daumier to properly cartoon it. Let me try to give a verbal outline. For several days running, some forty to fifty people gathered in a single room, in a meeting whose ostensible purpose was to forecast the next quarter's and the next year's supply and demand figures for each of the company's myriad products. In the weeks prior to the meeting, there would be internal haggling over these forecasts. Mr. International would ask Mr. Europe for a figure on, say, terminals for banks, and, receiving it, would shade it up or down depending on Mr. International's assessment of Mr. Europe's knowledge of his own customers, his previous success at forecasting, and so on. Mr. International would then report this figure to the person in the Corporate Program Management sector who was responsible for the overall program in the area of bank terminals. He, in turn, would have spent weeks talking over what this figure might mean with the person in Engineering and Manufacturing who would have to staff a factory and order raw materials in order to produce the terminals during the next quarter—if demand was down, to lay off employees and cut down on incoming supplies of materials. Based on what the program manager learned and "felt" because of his years of experience, he, too, would alter the forecasts.

So: the sales people would come up with demand numbers, numbers that the program managers would second-guess because many of them had previously worked in sales and knew how unrealistic the forecasts were—and then they would argue these with the supply side who would try to translate them into ordering components and staffing facilities. Imagine a meeting in which this process of adjustment has to go on for dozens and sometimes hundreds of different products. The engineering and manufacturing people want to be right so that they won't end up with too many unused components or excess inventory; on the other hand, the sales people also want to be right in order not to experience a sudden surge in demand and have no products to sell. "You ordered a hundred machines last quarter and only sold thirty-two—now you forecast a hundred more? Who are you kidding?" says Mr. Product Manufacturing. "You didn't make machines fast enough last quarter because you were afraid to staff up to do so—and we couldn't deliver, so our customers went elsewhere. Don't skimp this time," responds Mr. Sales. "He's being overoptimistic." "She's too cautious." "Your forecast creates problems for me." "Liar!"

Everyone gesticulates wildly, yells, and screams. You would have thought they were in the pit of the Chicago Commodities Exchange. There was lots of finger-pointing at supposed culprits. Lots of being caught up in the frenzy of the moment. Only one thing was certain: that *all* the conclusions to which this unwieldy group came were suspect, because none were based on real numbers. The figures were arbitrary, invented, and agreed to in this room without regard to what was real in the marketplace. Each product represented a problem and each received an unreal solution—this was even more pronounced when everyone was faced with having to project the demand for a new product about to be introduced.

All companies struggle with their market forecasts, but this was the worst I'd seen. The problem was that the man who ran the factory didn't care whether or not the sales organization could sell the products of that factory. He felt that he'd done his job in manufacturing them, and after that it was somebody else's problem. At my first big forecasting meeting, during one of the debates when there was a disagreement between demand and supply people, one man in the middle whispered to me in confidence that I shouldn't worry because "I'm on your side." What does side have to do with it? Weren't the factory manager and the sales manager drawing paychecks from the same company? Weren't they serving the same customers? Or the same shareholders? It didn't seem so. In these meetings, it was them against us at the favorite company pastime of assessing blame.

The blaming carried over into an astonishing amount of internal letter writing. Since the people in these sectors were at war and not speaking to one another, if a man on the marketing side wanted to get some information from or discuss a problem with his counterpart in technical operations, he didn't call that man on the phone or walk down the hall to see him. Instead, he'd write a memo about the problem to his boss, who would pass it to the head of marketing, who, in turn, would pass it to the head of manufacturing, who'd then send it down his line to the proper recipient. This ensured that decisions would not be made quickly (if ever), and that problems would never be jointly addressed by both sectors. The company wasn't pulling together, it was pulling apart.

These sorts of difficulties were not only relegated to lower levels. I had a hard time convincing the head of marketing or the president of the international group and the head of U.S. sales to work directly with me instead of constantly sending memos about problems to the president of the company. Fighting with one another, assessing blame and writing protect-your-rear memos had become the way of existence at Burroughs. The executives had bad habits that had developed over time and that were now encrusted with the added weight of tradition; such habits were extremely hard to alter. Nobody trusted anybody else. No one had confidence in anyone not of their own tribe, and certainly not in strangers who had just entered the company from the outside. Many of the managers derived pleasure from others' failure. In those who were marginally competent, their animosity toward one another transcended what talents they had. Were one to have made a movie about Burroughs' warring tribes and the chiefs and braves within them, it would have had to be a comedy.

I soon found wars similar to those that characterized the Marketing versus Technical sectors also were going on within my own area. Mr. Components would snub Mr. Terminals in the halls; Mr. Large Systems only spoke to Mr. Storage Equipment through intermediaries. There was an additional problem: nearly all of these managers, including the presidents of groups, though they were competent in technical matters, knew very little about business; the system at Burroughs had not encouraged them to be businessmen who thought in terms of overall company goals, but, rather, to act as if they were lower-rank supervisors in charge of a bunch of laboratories and factories.

I had a first round of staff meetings with my direct reports and asked them to brief me about the organization, products, and financials of their groups or divisions. As I listened to their reports, it became obvious that very few of the managers understood cash flow, or, for that matter, how to read or manage the elements of a balance sheet. They didn't know their own head counts, that is, how many people were working in their facilities; some hadn't even visited all of the facilities in their areas of responsibility. They didn't talk about product costs; when I asked questions about costs, they had to search for answers. All of them had their controllers in attendance and when it came time to talk about numbers, they'd simply turn the presentations over to the controllers—who, it developed, were scarcely better at the numbers than the managers. It scared me to realize that I knew more about the elements of finance than some of the financial managers.

In between my first and second round of staff meetings, I set out to visit all of the facilities for which I was ultimately responsible. There were sixty-three of these, and although I didn't get to all of them right away, in the first few weeks and months I saw enough of them to discover patterns of neglect. (I did visit them all within six months of coming to Burroughs.) It was a rare thing for someone as senior as I was to show up at such a remote facility as a factory in Scotland, Winnipeg, Canada, or Hollywood, Florida, but my visits were instructive, if difficult. At a factory in Scotland I found a large number of computers on the loading dock. I pointed to ten at random and insisted that they be uncrated and retested before they were shipped. Seven of the ten failed the inspection. A couple simply didn't work, and one lacked a plug, but most failed inspection because their exteriors, or skins, were damaged and unsightly. The people at the factory were aghast at my insistence that a computer with a damaged skin should not be shipped; to them, if the computer worked, it didn't matter what it looked like, because new skins could be shipped when they became available. I made them retest all the computers they were completing so that the quality of their machines was high enough for them to be shipped without embarrassment. In such on-site inspections, I was determined to send the message to our employees that we would not tolerate mediocrity in our work or products.

As I had done throughout my business career in other companies, at Burroughs I insisted on maintaining high standards in everything that I did personally, and in all that I expected from people around me. For many Burroughs people, my style was a revelation—and a challenge.

At corporate headquarters, I had been given a large and beautiful office with lots of wood paneling. To try to comprehend the organization for which I was now responsible, I decided to analyze the company thoroughly. Taking down the nice oil paintings, I replaced them with row upon row of charts that I made myself, by hand. Pretty soon these charts covered every available inch of wall space; only the windows were left uncharted. These charts were basically organizational diagrams that had a great amount of detail. I traced operational lines, reporting lines, what each location produced, the names of key individuals, ratios of various kinds such as overhead to direct labor. I used different pens and color dots to make codes, for example, if I put a blue dot next to someone's name, it meant that the person was a corporate officer. I differentiated domestic and overseas facilities, products such as large machines and small machines. Here and there I'd note the direct versus indirect labor costs at a facility, or how much in direct cost dollar value each location produced and shipped. What I was trying to understand, of course, were patterns and trends in the sixty-three facilities and tens of thousands of people under my command: why did the ratio of direct to indirect labor costs vary from location to location? How come manager A could function with level X of staff support while manager B needed level Y? What was the expense budget at location L as opposed to what it was at location M? How many people reported to group president N or to his counterpart in group Z?

I'd made the charts for my edification; it was part of my way of learning, memorizing, and understanding my area of responsibility. But I discovered that the charts had an interesting effect on people who came to my office. A manager would enter, look at the charts, and invariably ask what the color codes meant; I'd tell him that the charts were just my notes and that the codes were meaningless. No one believed me—but no one said so. Instead, the managers worried that, for instance, a blue dot meant a particular person was slated for removal or promotion. I let my visitors draw their own conclusions. They worried. After all, Stern was known as an aggressive manager. Was he thinking of a reorganization? How big was his hatchet?

It came time for the second round of staff meetings, and they were not much better than the first batch. After listening carefully, I went on the offensive. I laid out for my people all my impressions: the warring tribes, the managers' ignorance of their own numbers and their unwillingness to communicate. I told my direct reports that the next time they presented, *they*, rather than their controllers, would be responsible for presenting *and* explaining their financial results and forecasts. Each manager would have to completely understand every aspect of that part of the business of which he was in charge; of course they could bring along their controllers, but it would be the managers themselves who would present and who would have to answer questions. It was time for them to assume the leadership positions, and time as well for them to be fully accountable for the performance of their organizations.

I also announced to the managers that they were going to have to learn to communicate and work directly with one another. No more writing memos to avoid making decisions. No more appealing to the boss to mediate the constant disputes. No more assessing blame rather than addressing problems. "I don't care if you like each other or not," I said, "but you do have to work together. Go home and think about it, and come back in a week and give me an answer—in person. If by that time you decide that you really can't work with these other people, then I'll help you with early retirement or to get another job outside the corporation. If, on the other hand, you tell me that you will work within the new system of cooperation, I'll expect you to do so from then on." I didn't have to make explicit the threat that I'd fire anyone who slipped back into the old style of doing things, but everyone understood the implications of not performing.

One man actually came in and told me he couldn't stomach his colleagues and would be better off elsewhere; I respected his honesty, and helped him find a job. Many of the others took early retirement on the relatively generous terms that Mike Blumenthal had instituted for this purpose. But several said they could work together happily ever after; that wasn't so, of course, and in time I had to force some of them out. I remember vividly two of these. One was a man who had been head of a division at Burroughs; his management skills were so inadequate to the level on which he currently worked that when he took a job at another large corporation his best job offer was as manager of a single department. Another man, who communicated in a hushed voice, also had the annoying habit of always jiggling the change in his pocket when presenting. At first, I asked him to stop the clanging and when he couldn't, I actually had to request that he take the change from his pocket and place it on a table before starting to talk. His habits were indicative of a larger failure: he was afraid of being heard because, as I discovered, he had no understanding of his area of responsibility, a division whose performance was exceedingly poor and whose prospects were dim.

A great many people left Burroughs during this time. Mike and I had targeted something like 250 top managers for early retirement, and nearly all of them took it. As for those who stayed, I at first held them on a much tighter rein, and had more people reporting directly to me than should have been the case, given our organizational structure. This annoyed some executives who were used to being watched less closely, but I wouldn't let them have greater freedom until they proved to me that they now knew more about what they were doing than they had previously shown. I also got rid of some staff people by lateraling them to corporate headquarters. In most companies, operating divisions are located at some distance from corporate headquarters, and so there is a reason to maintain some independent staffs for HR, legal, and other functions. But at Burroughs, the headquarters of some divisions which I headed were physically within the corporate headquarters building. If I had a need for HR or legal work, I could obtain the service and support from the corporate staff contingent. So I did what is usually unthinkable in the corporate world: I gave back resources. Usually, managers are expected to be turf-builders who seize every opportunity to expand their empires. By slimming down my organization, I sent an important signal to senior management and to the rest of the company that we intended to operate in a lean manner even while moving ahead rapidly.

The departure of so many managers left multitudinous holes in the organization, only some of which could be filled by new outside hires. Financial performance was poor, the company was being sued by several customers for various product problems, facilities were being closed and people laid off. Even though many of the Burroughs old guard agreed with the wrenching changes that new management was putting the company through, morale was low. It was time to show tangible evidence that our new management team was optimistic about the future. It became essential for our new team to identify high-quality people already within the company, take risks on them by promoting some to key senior management positions. Burroughs' pay scale was low, out of line with that of other DP companies. To attract outsiders we had to break the existing salary guidelines by large margins, but by doing so we created two distinct pay groupings within the company, the relatively low-paid old-timers and the competitively paid newcomers. We moved to correct this by awarding large salary increases to deserving and long-serving Burroughs managers and employees. Various benefit programs such as medical and retirement plans were brought into line with those of comparable companies; however, this could only be phased in over a period of years, since the company could not afford to implement all the changes at once. Incredible though it might sound, Burroughs lacked many programs that had become standard throughout the industry in the previous fifteen years. We put in place employee recognition programs. An employee suggestion plan was greeted with some skepticism when it was first announced, but shortly thereafter, when a retiring customer service employee received $100,000 for one of his suggestions, everyone began to pay attention. Ideas began to flow in by the thousands. Several $50,000 awards followed. As one can imagine, these suggestions saved the company millions. We also instituted both formal and informal recognition events. One such event recognized people for outstanding achievement, mostly in engineering. A Corporate Fellows program recognized others for technical prowess; Corporate Fellows were treated similarly to corporate elected officers, except that the Fellows were an even more select group. We started paying employees for patents, and adopted a Legion of Honor for the top sales people, whom we would annually take (with spouses) to Bermuda, the Bahamas, or Hawaii where we would entertain them royally and present plaques and other awards. Typically, eight hundred to a thousand people would be brought to these events from all over the world.

From the charts in my office, I discovered many areas where we could consolidate or reorganize to effect savings. In short order I closed facilities at seven locations, and combined several others. One location that I eventually shut down completely was that luckless factory in Scotland; even after I'd so vividly insisted that they clean up their act, the people at the factory had been unable to change their ways.

While these consolidations were taking place I began a "phase review" process throughout the company that provided review and control mechanisms to management for products as they proceeded from idea through development to production to market. One of the key areas I dealt with was quality in every phase of the company's activities, as I described in an earlier chapter.

My organization was on a roll, and my expectations were being realized: I was making a visible and significant impact on the company, fast. By the time a single year had gone by, I had produced tangible results. I had a management team that was a blend of outside hires and old-timers, quality was improving, product costs and inventories were coming down, the consolidation of facilities was well under way, and—most important—my people had started feeling like winners. We could have moved faster, but the president, Ray Stromback, didn't like the speed at which change was taking place, and didn't agree with my methods; through holding back approvals that I required for certain actions, he was succeeding in slowing us down. On several occasions, all with his knowledge, I went around him to see the chairman and got my approvals; at other times I simply went ahead with what I thought was right and worried about approvals afterward. It was clear to everyone that the management team of Engineering and Manufacturing had its act together, was firing on all twelve cylinders. The results were becoming irrefutable. The work load was greater than I had ever handled before but that was my own doing because I compressed our objectives to meet an abbreviated timetable. The people I had hired—from IBM, Xerox, and other companies—were all young, aggressive, and impatient. We worked hard and complained incessantly, but we were having a lot of fun.

In March of 1982, fourteen months after I'd started at Burroughs, Mike Blumenthal and I were alone in the company airplane on our way to the Bahamas to visit with our first Legion of Honor winners. He informed me that at the May meeting of our board of directors he planned to recommend that I be appointed president and chief operating officer of the company. The first thought through my mind was that the assumptions I'd made on deciding to come to Burroughs had been proved absolutely correct. I had read Blumenthal, Stromback, the board, the business status of the company, and the requirements for my own success perfectly. At the May 26 meeting the board ratified Blumenthal's recommendations and I was elected president and COO; Ray Stromback was elected vice-chairman for special programs, with the tacit understanding that he would retire at the end of the calendar year. Finally the career plan that I had begun sixteen years earlier had come into full flower, and it was time to reap some of the benefits. I had achieved complete financial independence and could do whatever I wanted to. What I wanted to do right then was drive Burroughs to greater and greater successes.

Just after my presidency was announced, one of my first actions was to send a letter to all members of management at Burroughs. As this letter set out my philosophy and what I planned to do, I think a slightly edited version bears quoting here at some length:

> As I begin my new job, I would like to share with you my vision of our company and of its mission, as well as my understanding of the important tasks that we must carry out together. As I do so, I will be answering two fundamental questions: *(1) What kinds of standards should we set for ourselves? (2) What will I be doing to help move us in the right direction?* The mission of Burroughs Corporation is to design, build, market, and support the finest, most cost-effective line of information systems available anywhere in the world. And this, of course, will lead to the sustained, profitable growth that our shareholders expect.
>
> I believe that an organization will always reflect its leaders. And as our partnership gets under way, I will try, through my own behavior, to set a clear example of how our corporate goals and expectations are to be fulfilled. Management and supervision, in other words, are not so much the achievement of things—but the development and motivation of people, so that they themselves can achieve and in turn teach others to do so. Another important principle is that it isn't what you know about management that counts—it's what you do. Mediocre managers let things happen; successful ones make things happen. What, then, should we be trying to make happen in the months ahead?
>
> Very high on the list is quality. Those of you who know me from Engineering and Manufacturing will realize that qual-

ity has been one of my prime concerns ever since I came to Burroughs. The kind of quality I'm talking about is a property of the entire organization. It begins in the mind, when people resolve to themselves that they are going to do it right the first time, with no errors, no inaccuracies or defects. It then translates into specific actions, because people with the quality mind-set are results-oriented. They're governed by what they have to do to get the job done, not by the desire to merely follow orders or to get out by quitting time. Quality is a commitment to high standards. But commitment as an organizational goal means setting objectives—in sales, in marketing, in service, in forecasting—and then doing what has to be done to meet them. You set your targets as high as possible—or, as someone once said, "Always take a job that is too big for you." Then you stretch to attain them.

One of our most important objectives will be to remain aware that we are all one company. There is no competition between one discipline and another, between one operating group and another. Engineering and Manufacturing, for example, needs good forecasting from Marketing in order to keep costs down and quality up. And sales people need those low-cost, high-quality products, delivered in a timely manner, if their marketing campaigns are to be successful.

Teamwork implies loyalty—but not blind loyalty. The good of the organization demands that we communicate. It demands that we listen to one another's ideas. It demands that we managers explain what our goals are and how they are to be achieved. And it demands that problems not be swept under the rug, but rather brought to the attention of someone qualified to evaluate and fix them.

You can build a successful organization in two ways—and both involve a process of elimination. On the one hand, you identify those individuals who can and want to do the job. You train and develop them, then promote them to new challenges and responsibilities. And on the other hand, you identify those people who cannot or do not want to perform at our high standards—and you deal appropriately with them. Both kinds of elimination are crucial. We are already on the way. But there is still much more to be done. And in this undertaking, the people who will be the greatest help to us—and who stand to gain the most in terms of personal success—will be those who subscribe to the basic ideals that I have outlined. What the chairman and I are asking from you is not easy, but it is no less than what you can expect from us. Together we can—and, I expect, will—achieve the excellence of which I know Burroughs Corporation is capable.

This short summary of the philosophy that I have discussed in much greater detail throughout this book was revelatory to the Burroughs managers—perhaps because the notions I expressed were so different from those to which they'd adhered for so many years. The long-term Burroughs employees were amazed that upper management would want their ideas, would insist on high quality in all endeavors, would ask them to set high goals and evaluate and promote managers on whether or not they achieved those goals, and—good heavens!—would demand that they communicate and work with one another. But perhaps the most important thing that made the letter meaningful was that the management and the employees were able to believe the letter's contents because they had already seen that it reflected the style, pace, standards, and demands I had set during my first fifteen months at the company.

Because this is a book about careers, I want to make some observations about the opportunities to get ahead that surfaced during the transformation of Burroughs in the early 1980's. There was a good deal of scrambling going on. As I observed people jockeying for position, I felt as if I were watching an ant farm.

Prior to the time I became president, when some alert executives in other divisions saw what I was doing in engineering and manufacturing, and that my rapid change of the system had the blessing of the CEO, they began to position themselves in relation to me. Some tried to form alliances with me, since it was obvious to many that I was a key contender to take Ray Stromback's job. These career-driven people also hurried to institute changes in their own areas similar to those I'd put in place; for instance, people jumped onto the bandwagon of quality. They figured that if they had improvements in place before I became president, that they'd be a step ahead of the game. Naturally, after I became president we tried to carry over from engineering and manufacturing the same pattern and pace of change to the other sectors of the company. In that process—in that turmoil—certain insiders at Burroughs stood out and others did not. We were retiring many people and a lot of key management positions were open. Also, we were reorganizing, which created still more opportunities. The perceptive manager knew that the chairman and I were under pressure to fill the open slots, and that we would prefer to give someone the job rather than to put in an acting division head and later be forced to make a decision whether or not to give the acting manager the permanent job.

One guiding principle in times of reorganization is to know who the key players are. When the top managers are already insiders, the mid-level managers in a company will have been made aware of their idiosyncrasies, personalities, and styles, by virtue of having rubbed shoulders with them for some time. At Burroughs, though, Mike and I were relative unknowns; managers weren't sure how we thought or operated. Were we friendly? Hard driving? Decisive? People oriented or just interested in the bottom line? When did we get to the office in the morning? When did we go home? What were our work habits?

We in upper management had similar problems trying to evaluate the candidates. Our dependence on them was great—and those who understood this could leverage it. In a chaotic atmosphere, an anchor is needed even by the most daring skipper. We needed people to provide that anchor, and important concessions could be wrested from us by people who could provide stability and continuity. During this hectic period, if a manager accepted a big job, he or she could get from upper management a fair amount of latitude in managing their respective organizations. They could also negotiate significant increases in salary, as well as stock options, because we needed good people and wanted to keep them satisfied. We didn't want a manager to take a job, then become dissatisfied and quit, because that would create even more confusion, so we were willing to give in here and there. (This sort of leverage can be overused. I've encountered instances where a manager in this situation threatened to quit, and was placated with extra stock options and the like—but, a year or two later, when new management opportunities opened up, these were not offered to him, because his superiors had put in place a man who could do his job equally well at less cost to the company. In fact, such a manager could see his career flatten to the point where he would no longer be seen as pivotal to the company's operations.)

I can unequivocally say that the Burroughs insiders who got the good new jobs were those who:

1. *projected an image of willingness to change;*
2. *readily established a working relationship with the new executives who were brought in;*
3. *were careful to give us the impression that their presence would insure continuity with the best elements from the company's past.*

I must just as quickly add that in the long run, not all of the executives who got the good new jobs proved to be competent managers. Many survived the first round of early retirements and organizational upheavals on image alone, and later showed themselves to be unable to keep up with the pace and demands of the new environment. But they did shine early on. On the other side of the coin, I'm certain that some people who might well have turned out to be capable managers, but who were unable or unwilling to play the game of bringing themselves favorably to the attention of the new senior executives, were eased out because they didn't rise to the occasion. They hid their lights under bushel baskets or believed—naively—that given another year or two their essential superiority would become apparent. It didn't. We didn't have that year or two in which to take the long view; we needed changes accomplished right away.

One last group of people affected by the changes were those staff employees whom the old management team had put on relatively fast tracks and had labeled as comers. Because those labels had been applied by a now-rejected leadership, it was necessary for these staffers to once again prove their strengths and capabilities. Many weren't as wonderful as they had imagined themselves to be, and lost out. Some may well have been good, but refused to accept that they had to provide new evidence of their excellence or risk suffering the consequences; many of these, as well, got knocked off track in one way or another.

To sum up: A time of chaos is the ideal moment in which to position yourself to leverage a career. Old-timers can reintroduce themselves to new management; outsiders can obtain important concessions; staff can make a new impact. Here are some guidelines:

1. *Identify the power players*, and get yourself near to all of them, not just to one favorite, because more than one champion may emerge from the fray and you don't want to be linked to the wrong one.

2. *Check the priority of the problems.* Learn how these are viewed by the new upper management. Is the difficulty in forecasting? Revenue growth? Need to close facilities? Expense control? What is now the management's focus?

3. *Be positive.* There are a lot of negatives in the air—that's why a new team has been brought in. But don't be negative. "Yes, that area is a problem; I can provide part of the solution."

4. *Be aggressive in presenting yourself.* If the new management doesn't understand how wonderful you are—tell them. Better yet, show them some results.

5. *Demonstrate some impact, fast.* While all the new people are still getting directions to the washroom, do something in your area of responsibility that is dazzling—and then make it seem as if this is routine for you. If you have to pull profits into this quarter from the next, do so; you'll worry about how to make it up later, and chances are you'll succeed; but if you don't do it now, you might not be there later.

20

Mergers and Acquisitions

*I*N earlier chapters I've stressed the importance of getting to know
the personalities and business styles of the decision-makers who
can influence your career. This is especially important during
mergers and acquisitions. Great opportunities for advancement often
emerge in periods of turmoil, and there is no more tumultuous time
in the work environment than that occasioned by a merger or acquisition. The problem is that during such upheaval, time is not on
the side of the manager who wants to get a sense of the new decision-
makers involved in the amalgamation of the companies. Things
happen quickly. But individuals who are able to understand what's
going on in these turbulent times, and to play the game well, gain
a distinct advantage over those who are competing with them for
key positions in the new company.

I had participated in mergers and acquisitions while at Rockwell
International, but the opportunities and risks for advancing careers
were brought home to me during a series of acquisitions while I
was president of Burroughs. There were a half-dozen of these, ranging in size from the rather small to the acquisition of Sperry, which
was larger in sales volume and number of employees than Burroughs. I found that the greater the relative size of the companies

involved in the deal, the greater the potential opportunities for changes in careers. If the financial weight and number of employees in two merging companies is large and also relatively equal, there is the most likelihood that management in both companies will be seriously affected. If the acquiring company is a big one, and the company being acquired is much smaller, it is unlikely that management roles and responsibilities in the acquirer will be affected at all. In the big-swallows-small situation, the career-making opportunities and risks are solely in the domain of the smaller company. Typically, senior management of the smaller company looks after itself—if it can—during the negotiating period, at which time the acquirer is eager to make settlements in order to close the deal. Such settlements can be made in terms of career promises, monies paid to the executives at the time of the acquisition or in the form of "golden handcuffs" that make it financially attractive for the manager to stay on with the acquirer for an agreed-to period of time, after which they receive a large payment. In the acquiring of a medium-sized company by a big one, some jobs are affected on both sides; though here, too, most of the career opportunities are on the side of the acquired company.

For the purposes of this chapter, I'll divide the acquisitions we made at Burroughs into three categories, small, medium, and large. The small acquisitions were of companies whose sales amounted to less than 1 or 2 percent of Burroughs' annual corporate sales; the medium-size acquisitions were of companies whose sales were 10 to 15 percent of our own; finally, there was the multibillion dollar, unfriendly acquisition of Sperry, whose sales at the time were greater than those of Burroughs.

SMALL-SIZE ACQUISITIONS

Between 1981 and 1984, Burroughs acquired three small companies. Although in these acquisitions there was little movement of executives to the new parent, on the other hand the behavior of their managers (and of our own) during the acquisition was worthy of comment. Each of these companies was in a specialized business sector that interested Burroughs and whose acquisition fit into our objectives of emphasizing growth in these specific market segments. Each acquisition had a champion pushing its case inside the Burroughs hierarchy. This is always a necessary prerequisite, for a company should not consider a small- or medium-size acquisition unless there is a champion for it in the acquirer, and unless that champion is willing to be responsible for the new addition after the purchase is completed, and particularly if there is a chance that all will not go as well as planned. If there is no champion, no one will feel accountable for the acquisition. In each case at Burroughs, the projections that the champions and the acquired companies themselves made were greatly overstated and, it later turned out, unrealizable. I have learned from colleagues at other large corporations that their experience in the acquisition of much smaller companies was similar to ours.

So: in quick succession, Burroughs bought Systems Research Inc., or SRI, based in Michigan, whose communications products had an emphasis on what are called front-end processors; the Midwest Systems Group (MSG), based in Chicago, which produced educational software for kindergarten through the twelfth grade; and Graftek, headquartered in Colorado, which specialized in Computer-Aided Design (CAD). Common to all of these small companies—average annual sales of less than $50 million each—was an ability to operate with very low expenses and minimal capital investment, as well as the ability to make and execute business decisions quickly. Balancing these factors was an almost equal lack of formal business and organizational structure.

In two of these companies, senior management were the founders. In all three cases, the senior managers with whom Burroughs had negotiated the takeovers left the businesses and their new parent company within a year or two of the acquisition of their companies. Many of these executives hadn't planned to leave. All had been enriched personally by the Burroughs buyout, and they had grand notions of staying on and using the new financial resources and market presence of Burroughs to see their old companies flourish. But it didn't happen that way, and they resigned. Moreover, none of them left in order to enter higher management at Burroughs. Why? The answer reflects an interesting personal aspect to big business: many of them discovered, to their chagrin, that life under a new and large parent was not the same as it had been when they were independent. Now, as executives of a small part of a multi-billion dollar company, their actions were constrained; they started receiving more ''help'' from the parent than they wanted, and with this came a constantly growing demand for the entertaining of visiting corporate managers, meetings and more meetings—and, worst of all, an insistence on their filing frequent and endless reports. They had to conform their paperwork to that of a large corporate head-quarters, which had standards for personnel and salary reports, req-uisitions, travel expenses, budgets, and training which they found gratuitous and unnecessary.

On the other hand, once acquired, the managements of the small companies seemed overnight to change their attitudes on ex-penses and resources. What in the past had seemed significant sums of money now were labeled small change. Requests for adding staff and overhead went up dramatically. Concern about the business's survival vanished—if something went wrong, or if their plans and forecasts didn't materialize as projected, it wouldn't matter because Burroughs would foot the bill. (I must digress to tell the story of a small business unit within a large corporation of which I was a senior manager. During annual budget negotiations, the senior man-agers of this division were arguing with us at headquarters about the need for more staff and more resources in order to operate their business more successfully. Shortly thereafter, the managers ac-quired this division in a leveraged buyout to which we agreed be-cause we had wanted to sell it anyway. Next thing we knew, those same managers were busy cutting overhead and laying off staff to make their businesses more efficient. Now that their own money was at stake, the senior people were acting like owners, and had become better managers.)

Within two years after SRI, MSG, and Graftek were acquired, they and their managers were acting like the other small divisions in the Burroughs family. Those senior managers who in all cases had grown the businesses to the point where they were attractive to the acquirer had now gone, and the mind-set of their replacements was no better than that of other victims of the bureaucracy in big corporations. The new managers weren't good enough to attract the attention of senior management at Burroughs, and they weren't bad enough to warrant separation from the company. In general, they kept their heads down, and muddled through. By the mid-1980's, it could be seen that these small-sized acquisitions were not really profitable for Burroughs, nor did they achieve the market-share objectives for which they had been acquired. In fact, they had be-come headaches, taking up a disproportionate amount of the Bur-roughs senior executives' time and energy when compared to that devoted to significantly larger, more important business units.

MEDIUM-SIZE ACQUISITIONS

In 1980, Burroughs was a multibillion-dollar-a-year company whose main business was commercial data processing products which included computer systems hardware, software, and services. Burroughs had several secondary but also substantial lines of business—in the hundreds of millions of dollars annually—in services for the defense industry and for nondefense branches of the federal government, and another in forms and supplies commonly required by computer users, which included products such as paper, ribbons, toners, developers, and the like. Chairman Blumenthal had come into the company with a mandate for change, and, in the first years of his tenure, had begun clearing out whole phalanxes of middle- and upper-rank Burroughs executives who had been with the company for many years and who had presided over its slide into lower profitability. I mention this last fact because it underscores the idea that just then there were many important management slots available to be filled within Burroughs.

In 1980, senior management of Burroughs began to recognize the market opportunities for selling, installing, and managing what is called total system integration for information management systems. System integration means selling solutions, as opposed to boxes of computers. It involves the integration of hardware, software, services, and support that might initially come from different suppliers, including our own and those of our competitors, in order to solve a customer's problems. To build up the specialized skills and resources to go after system integration business ourselves would have taken several years and required significant investment. Instead, we decided to acquire them by buying a company in the field, one whose size was large enough to have critical mass and a reputation that delivered annual sales in the hundreds of millions of dollars. The System Development Corporation (SDC) of Santa Monica, California, had the reputation, skills, technical expertise, and experience in software, system integration, and services, as well as a significant knowledge of what sort of integrated systems federal, state, and local government agencies required. SDC had an excellent reputation in the marketplace, and the nature of its expertise was complementary to that of Burroughs, and Mike Blumenthal championed its acquisition. Among Mike's hopes was that SDC's expertise and resources would serve as a base on which to increase our own defense as well as our commercial businesses. Burroughs' Federal and Special Systems Group (F&SSG) had had a great deal of success in transferring the expertise it had developed in complex networks into a program called SWIFT, an international financial network which operates around the clock to transfer monies among most of the major banks in dozens of countries around the world. SDC's expertise would, he believed, be the basis for more successful integrations of that sort. In due course the acquisition proceeded smoothly and soon SDC became a wholly owned subsidiary of Burroughs. Blumenthal had promised during negotiations that SDC would have a new campus, and it was built in Camarillo, California; this and other major capital investments added substantially to SDC's overhead. In retrospect, we can now see that these new investments reduced SDC's profitability for many years.

The chairman and CEO of SDC became a senior vice-president of Burroughs, and a few other SDC executives also became elected officers of the new parent. The SDC chairman remained at Burroughs for three years, until his retirement. But other senior officers of SDC, including its president, resigned shortly after the acquisition, and their resignations were serious losses for Burroughs. Several of these men reaped substantial amounts of money when SDC was acquired, and their new fortunes allowed them greater independence and mobility: now they could go where they wanted and do as they wished.

Because SDC had become a subsidiary of Burroughs, there was no longer a need in its hierarchy for certain corporate functions that were replicated at Burroughs, and so these offices were dissolved and their people assigned elsewhere. The legal staff, for instance, was absorbed into that of corporate headquarters, and the former treasurer of SDC became my executive assistant. He prospered with the change, and is currently vice-president for corporate development (mergers and acquisitions, as well as strategic planning) at Unisys. Unfortunately, he was the only senior manager at SDC who worked his way out of the subsidiary and up the ladder in the parent company. A bright and competent executive, he would have done well at any large corporation.

As for the organizational merger, the union of F&SSG and SDC yielded very little additional management gold. The man hired from the outside to head the new subsidiary after the former chairman retired did eventually become president of the entire defense unit at Unisys, but other senior managers who were also newly brought in have since remained at SDC, rather than being able to rise in the ranks of the parent. Also, no managers from Burroughs or, later, Unisys, were able to transfer into the SDC unit in a way that significantly advanced their careers. In short, while SDC became a successful subsidiary of Burroughs, there were only a few instances of helpful movement within the management ranks in the wake of the acquisition. The opportunities for advancement were there on both sides, but only those few individuals who knew how to play the game were able to make the most of them.

On the heels of the SDC deal, at the end of 1981, Burroughs acquired the Memorex Corporation, whose main business was peripherals (disk drives and tape drives) used to store information within computer systems. Storage products, critical to the fluent functioning of computer systems, are based on complex technologies that are difficult to master. Memorex's two other businesses were the Communications Division, which produced IBM plug-compatible terminals and printers, and the Media Division, which manufactured floppy disks. In 1981, we at Burroughs decided it was too late in the game for us to develop independently the engineering skills and programs to effectively produce such storage products; our facilities were scattered throughout the United States, Canada, and Scotland, and they were making products that were not considered to be state of the art or as reliable or profitable as those of other manufacturers. We considered buying into an already existing joint venture with a group of other companies to develop our storage products, but decided instead to acquire Memorex, a company with an excellent reputation for technological expertise.

Memorex was available because it was in a cash crunch and unable to fund its business to the level required for long-term viability. The data processing business is very R&D and capital intensive, and Memorex was looking for a partner who could provide it with new financial resources as well as access to wider markets. Burroughs fit that bill. Immediately after we officially acquired Memorex on December 3, 1981, we sold off its consumer products division, and examined critically its three remaining business units. One division produced and sold floppy disks; this division was fast-growing and reasonably profitable. A second division, unrelated to storage equipment, sold terminals, controllers, and printers for what was called the PCM or plug-compatible market. These were products that were similar to IBM's and that were sold to IBM's mainframe customers at lower prices than IBM's terminals. Memorex's third division, the storage equipment business, also sold most of its products in the PCM market, to IBM's mainframe customers. The difficulty with the latter two business units was that their products were at the mercy of IBM's moves in the marketplace; with each new product, new price list, and new service agreement that Big Blue put out, Memorex had to scramble to adjust.

By integrating our own storage equipment division into Memorex, we were able to combine operations in such a way as to make deep cuts in staffs, overhead, and engineering; we closed several factories and laid off hundreds of people. Burroughs began to buy its storage products from its new subsidiary, rather than produce its own, which accomplished two objectives: first, it gave Memorex a large and recurring customer, and it allowed Burroughs, through Memorex, to develop and manufacture more reliable and less costly leading-edge products.

There were problems, of course. When we looked more closely at Memorex, we found that their engineering department was not meeting their schedules and had slipped badly in their ability to deliver the next generation of products. Nor was product quality as stable as we had hoped. As a consequence of both these difficulties, their current and future profitability was not as high as we had been led to believe it would be. These matters were ironed out over a period of five years, and today Memorex's technical expertise plays a key role in Unisys.

During the initial months when we were discovering that all was not well at Memorex, and we were trying to change that, the Burroughs and Memorex managements got to know one another extremely well—and fast. There were many trips from corporate headquarters in Detroit to California, and vice versa, as we tried to ascertain what progress Memorex was making and to provide the new subsidiary with corporate resources to get it back on track.

During the transition, there were a handful of important management moves. As with the acquisition of SDC, there was an elimination of redundant offices at Memorex, for example, the treasury. Their CFO moved to Burroughs headquarters to become our vice-president for finance, an important promotion for him. Today he is one of the top executives at Unisys. One man moved the other way. He was my executive assistant during the acquisition, and by the nature of his job was privy to much that went on. In fact, he so impressed the chairman of Memorex that when the deal was concluded, the chairman offered my assistant the position of vice-president for planning for Memorex. He later became CFO of Memorex and subsequently vice-president for manufacturing—a wonderful progession and a broadening of experience for him that resulted in a résumé that is the envy of many in the industry; he is a young man with great career potential.

The chairman of Memorex stayed on for three years as executive vice-president of Burroughs, reporting to me, and was extraordinarily helpful in making the integration of his company into Burroughs a smooth one. Upon his retirement he was succeeded by a Burroughs senior vice-president, whom I had previously brought into Burroughs from IBM. Other than these moves, there were, over the years, perhaps a dozen lower-level, administrative transfers from parent to sudsidiary and from Memorex into Burroughs, but no mass movements and no spectacular career moves made that can be directly attributed to the acquisition.

In fact, there were the same defections from the ranks of senior management as we saw with SDC—senior managers, now enriched, leaving Burroughs-Memorex for adventures elsewhere. In addition, over the course of the three or four years after the acquisition, dozens of middle managers drifted away from Memorex. I learned that such changes were not uncommon in Silicon Valley.

Did these people make the right decision in resigning from the big company? Had they been more astute in capitalizing on their opportunities during the transition period, would they have done better at Burroughs, as the former Memorex CFO did? Why didn't more managers from the parent company push to obtain management positions in the newly acquired subsidiary, which would have allowed them to gain broader general management experience?

There are no simple answers to these questions, but some conclusions about careers can be drawn from the SDC and Memorex acquisitions. Both SDC and Memorex, despite their size, were important but secondary businesses for Burroughs, whose mainstream internal growth was and continues to be mainframes, entry-level machines, microcomputers, and personal computers. As I've described earlier, it is rare (and rightly so) for senior positions to be filled by individuals who have not had experience in managing or made an impact on the corporation's mainline business unit. Knowing that this is the case, it would have been foolish for upwardly mobile executives at Burroughs to go into either Memorex or SDC. Of course, there are always exceptions to the rule, but if you look at the literature that gives you the backgrounds of the top executives at publicly held companies, you can see the evidence. The simple reason for this is that those who manage the mainstream business of a company are invariably in the mainstream of the company's action, information, and attention; they become the best-informed and the best-known candidates for the top jobs.

In the history of management movements to and from SDC and Memorex, I also see more evidence for my thesis that most people don't plan their careers or press them forward. For instance, both of the acquired companies were based in California, and many of the SDC and Memorex executives who might have had the chance to advance themselves would have had to move to Detroit to do so. Virtually none did, and I think that most of these consciously or unconsciously decided that their quality of life in California took precedence over going to Detroit and making progress up the Burroughs corporate ladder. This is a prime example of why ambitious managers who want to reach the top quickly cannot let location unduly affect their important career choices: refusing to go to Detroit limited not only the SDC and Memorex executives' progress, but their options for advancement. Another factor in the mix was the desire of the parent company to maintain continuity of management in the newly acquired subsidiaries, which kept some people in place in California who might otherwise have made a successful jump to Burroughs; then, too, Burroughs senior management didn't know the people in the acquired companies very well, and was therefore less inclined to bring such unknown managers into the parent corporation and was more inclined to send our own trusted employees into senior positions in the subsidiaries.

THE BIG ONE

During 1985 and 1986, American industry consummated what were at that time three of the largest mergers in industrial history, GE and RCA, Allied and Signal, and Burroughs with Sperry. As president of Burroughs, I had the good fortune to view this last "merger" at close hand; actually, as it wasn't a merger, but rather an unfriendly acquisition.

The data processing industry differs from other industries in many ways, not the least of which is, as I mentioned, the enormous disparity in size between the industry's leader, IBM, and its competitors. The industry is further distinguished by the rapidity of change in, and the complexity of, its technologies. These characteristics demand heavy and continuous spending in research and development, as well as in capital investment. Common ratios of R&D as a fraction of sales range from 7 to 12 percent—which represents substantial sums of money. Another determining factor in the industry is that when a customer decides to buy his computers from a particular supplier, he is making a critical purchase, one that will color all other possible purchases for some time into the future. That is because the system architectures of machines made by the various manufacturers are sufficiently different one from another that the application and operating system software packages of one maker are not easily used on another's computer. This means that software developed for NCR's computers would not operate on those made by Univac without substantial adaptations or, often, the development of an expensive and completely rewritten software package. For this reason, it can often be a lengthy, costly, and disruptive process for a dissatisfied computer customer to change to another vendor's hardware system. In recent years, changing systems has been made easier by the development of hardware and software communications products which permit the combined use of various manufacturer's products of heretofore incompatible machines; this allows different system architectures to coexist.

I've subjected you to this explanation to emphasize that when a buyer makes a decision to purchase a given manufacturer's hardware and software, this is a long-term commitment to that particular supplier. Accordingly, potential buyers look long and hard at the various suppliers before they make such major purchases; they evaluate the vendor's human and financial resources and the vendor's ability to maintain viability in the data processing marketplace far into the future—at the very least, past the time of the decision-maker's own retirement date. This makes for very loyal customers; indeed, what is known as the installed customer base of a data processing company is a very valuable asset, one that also generates large revenues annually from maintenance and service supplied by the vendor. It also makes for recurrent queries to even a $5 billion company about its long-term staying power in relation to the obvious solidity of $50-billon-a-year IBM. Those decision-makers who wanted safe bets usually went with IBM—even though IBM was *not* always the purveyor of the best products, nor of the most cost-effective system, nor of the products on the leading edge of new technology. After all, if they chose IBM, the industry leader, they could not be blamed if the products didn't work out well enough. On this note it is interesting that despite huge expenditures by IBM in R&D, their products have usually not led the BUNCH in terms of innovation; for decades, IBM simply overshadowed its competitors because of its exceptional talent in marketing, sales, and service.

By 1984, Burroughs, always a purveyor of leading-edge technologies in computers, had made great strides since the time I joined the company in early 1981. Our product lines were evolving nicely, our balance sheet was in good shape, and we had developed an outstanding management group that was the envy of the industry. Previously, we had decided that Burroughs ought to remain principally in two businesses: information processing and defense. Now, through acquisitions and internal growth, our sales were at the $5-billion-a-year mark—and yet potential customers and the financial experts were still habitually questioning our ability to compete with Big Blue, as well as our long-term staying power in view of our "small" size. We decided to grow in size by making a big acquisition, one that would be big enough for industry analysis and potential customers to conclude that we would be around for a long time, and would henceforth be a solid number two to IBM.

A small group of us at Burroughs analyzed a whole range of companies and by the end of the first quarter of 1985 had fixed on the Sperry Corporation. Excluding their farm equipment business, called New Holland, Sperry was slightly larger than Burroughs, but an analysis of the two companies revealed a strong potential alliance. First of all, the companies' histories were similar. Secondly, there was good geographic and industry segment fit. For example, Sperry was strong in Germany, Italy, and Spain while Burroughs' strength was greatest in the United Kingdom, Latin America, and South Africa; both companies were doing well in France, Scandinavia, and Japan. Sperry was much larger in the defense marketplace, but Burroughs, through our SDC subsidiary, had complex systems integration capabilities that complemented those of Sperry. In industry segments, Sperry did well with the airlines and the Bell telephone operating companies, while Burroughs' strength had historically been in sales to financial institutions, to health care providers, and to the education field. Both companies had done well in the safety and public sector marketplace, and in sales to companies that manufactured and distributed commercial products. Our analysis showed that there would be significant savings if we could consolidate technologies, entry level products, peripherals, terminals, service, staffs, procurement, and plants.

We held our first talks with the Sperry management in the late spring of 1985. At Mike Blumenthal's apartment in New York we met with Sperry chairman and CEO Jerry Probst and Joe Kroger, who was at that time executive vice-president. Both men were opposed to the merger, principally on the grounds of their belief that the two companies' systems architectures were incompatible, and could not be brought together at any time in the future. Kroger and Probst argued that Sperry's customers, believing that an attempt would be made to swing the Sperry user base to Burroughs' architecture, would flee to other manufacturers. They did not accept our argument that an effective campaign would convince customers that both system architectures would be continued forever. Discussions and negotiations continued in New York and involved batteries of lawyers and investment bankers on both sides. Despite the reluctance of Kroger and Probst, progress was made as groups of executives from both companies made presentations to the legal and financial experts. One of the most cooperative of the Sperry officers was their CFO. At this point, many of us felt that we were close to a deal for the merger of the two companies. Some people began to jockey for position and even to ask outright what slots they would fill in a new company.

In a small restaurant over dinner, Mike Blumenthal informed me that in order to close the deal, he needed the cooperation of Probst and Kroger, and he had decided that I might have to give up my titles of president and COO, and perhaps report to Probst in parallel with Joe Kroger. So enthusiastic was I about the possibilities of this merger that I encouraged him to proceed and not to worry about me (I knew he would have done so in any event). I told him I would definitely help with the merger and would later decide for myself what my next career step ought to be—with the new company or outside of it. Blumenthal's behavior that night told me volumes about what I might expect from him in the way of loyalty in the future.

The very next day, news of the potential merger leaked out, and the stock of both companies started gyrating wildly, so much so that we were forced to set a deadline by which the merger agreement would be consummated or called off. Shortly thereafter, the talks ended, and we went home disappointed. Within the next few months, the cooperative CFO left Sperry and Joe Kroger was appointed president and COO.

Toward the end of 1985, Blumenthal, myself, and three other senior Burroughs executives sat together nights and weekends to update our strategic plans and to make decisions affecting the company's future. At these discussions, it became more apparent to us than ever that the key to our future lay in getting together with Sperry—even if that meant acquiring them in what we expected to be a difficult, unfriendly takeover. We developed various financial models, based on several assumptions and on data made available to the public, as to what a combined Sperry-Burroughs company would look like, and what savings would likely be achieved; we used these calculations for the bases of probable prices for the Sperry stock, or what combination of cash and "paper" we would need to pay for the company, as well as what financial impact each combination would have on the future profitability and balance sheet of Burroughs. A paramount concern was the potential balance sheet of the new company and whether, within reasonable limits of risk, we would be able to service the debt we would incur by making the acquisition. We concluded that there were salable assets in both companies that were not in our main lines of business and which could be sold to bring our debt-to-capital and debt-to-equity ratios into acceptable ranges within eighteen months of the acquisition.

We presented all the information and our strategies to the Burroughs board of directors, and to investment bankers and legal advisers on the afternoon of Friday, May 2, 1986. Discussions continued through the day and on into the weekend, until on Monday, May 5, 1986, the management received the board's approval to extend an offer for Sperry. Among the many accomplishments of that long weekend was the absence of leaks; another was the preparation of communications that would accompany our offering, and would go to the employees and customers of both companies, to the financial community, and to legislative bodies in Washington.

Unfortunately, when our offer letter was delivered to Sperry on Monday, Chairman Probst was in Japan on a business trip. He immediately started back to the United States, but didn't arrive for some time. I spent the week in the nation's capital, where I met with various Cabinet officials, including the secretary of commerce, Pentagon leaders, executives from the Federal Aeronautics Administration, and other government agencies to explain our objectives and why the amalgamation made sense for the United States as well as for the two business entities. I reassured our governmental customers, and those of Sperry, that at no time, even well into the future, would this business move negatively affect their procurement and investment in or their ability to use the computer systems they'd already bought or those that were in the process of being developed. Many defense establishment computer users needed such assurances about the highly specialized programs to which they had already committed.

Sperry was determined not to be acquired by Burroughs, and they furiously looked for a white knight to rescue the company. They couldn't find one, but their action forced us to pay a higher price for Sperry than we had anticipated. Even so, the battle was concluded in just over two weeks. On May 22, 1986, the boards of Sperry and Burroughs held their first joint meeting, and the deed was done.

Now came the difficult and demanding task of merging two corporate cultures, two work forces totaling 120,000 people, and so on, while addressing customer uneasiness and the skepticism of the financial analysts, who were furiously writing negative reports disparaging the lack of wisdom displayed in this acquisition and predicting imminent disaster. We tried to ignore the doomsayers, considering that our most important and immediate task was getting the new company's balance sheet in shape so we could focus on our promise of increased profitability for the new company. We were certain that moving quickly was the key to accomplishing this complex task, and decided to integrate the two companies more quickly than had ever been done by any acquirer in the past.

To amalgamate Sperry and Burroughs we used a variety of concepts and ideas that we thought then were new and untested; later, I learned that they were remarkably similar to those used in the Allied-Signal merger. It was Mike Blumenthal's notion that even though Burroughs had acquired Sperry against Sperry's wishes, the amalgamation was to be treated as a merger. Both companies were to be seen as equals. History was to be ignored. This was fine in theory, but many Burroughs people still felt like conquerors who deserved more consideration than the management and employees of the vanquished party.

In the first few weeks of June, Blumenthal and I visited many of the Sperry facilities in the company of Joe Kroger and Jerry Probst. Probst had already announced that he would retire at the end of

1986. It was amusing for me to sit and listen to the glowing tributes to Blumenthal that Probst and Kroger would deliver to their employees as they introduced Mike to his new minions; only a few short weeks earlier, they had depicted the Burroughs management in the vilest of terms. I took this as a signal that the season of heavy jockeying for position in the new company had begun in earnest.

A merger coordination council (MCC) was established to oversee the process of bringing the two companies together. The MCC was chaired by Blumenthal and included both presidents (Kroger and me), as well as the CFOs for both companies, Ed Gilbert from Sperry and Jim Unruh from Burroughs. At our first meeting in mid-June we formed about a dozen task forces, each of which consisted of both Sperry and Burroughs executives whose jobs or functions and expertise were similar. These task forces were to gather information and recommend how we could reap substantial savings through the elimination of duplicate or unnecessary operations. They were to affix dollar figures to the operations and the potential savings, and recommend proposed organizational structures for the combined operations, where appropriate. Among the task forces were those addressing research and development, manufacturing, various product line offerings, customer service, procurement, corporate staff, and marketing. One of their objectives was to generate a list of which business units and idle assets might be sold to pay down our substantial debt. Under Mike's direction, consultants from Booz Allen & Hamilton participated in some of the MCC meetings, and Blumenthal also hired two industrial psychologists to guide the management through "merger stress and uncertainty". I don't know precisely what these consultants contributed to the success of the merger, but I am certain that they learned much more from being part of our process than they could have done in any other circumstances. At the very least, they watched us in senior management coping with the problem of running two companies at once, and doing double duty in order to achieve reasonable results in the remaining third and fourth quarters of the year.

In July, Blumenthal began discussions with Joe Kroger and me about the organizational structure for what he termed "Newco" in the absence of a formal new name for the company, which was yet to be chosen. He discussed various options, but it was clear to me, since I had observed his style for more than five years, that he'd already made up his mind. He needed to do something to keep both Joe Kroger and me aboard; he couldn't afford to lose one and certainly not both of us, and he stood a good chance of doing so unless he could keep both of us happy. He promulgated an Executive Office that was to consist of himself as CEO, Joe Kroger as vice-chairman, myself as president, and Jim Unruh as executive vice-president. This committee was to operate Newco, though as president I was to be responsible for the annual financial and operating plans as well as its quarterly profits. Since I am not a believer in committees, I didn't like this concept, and said so. I was prepared to leave the company, but was persuaded by Blumenthal and several of the Burroughs board members to give the Executive Office (EO) concept a try, and at least to stay for a year through the transition.

The EO had now to define the organizational structure for the business. Blumenthal wanted the notion of merit to govern our choices for this organization, who would lead the various parts of the new company. To achieve meritocracy, as he styled it, we would evaluate all candidates for the new positions regardless of whether they had been at Burroughs or at Sperry, and choose the best ones for the jobs. This made tremendous logical sense.

Unfortunately, meritocracy as a concept never had a chance. Although it was acknowledged in the industry that Burroughs had the superior management, when the job of dividing up the management positions was finished, and I tallied all of our picks for the important jobs, it turned out that half were from Sperry and half from Burroughs. Isn't that amazing? To have gone through the agonizing choice process only to come out of it with a 50-50 ratio? If the choices had been made solely on merit, there would have been many more Burroughs people, but, as I had feared, the selection of candidates was more political than based on merit.

Let's see who got chosen, and why. Remember that on the EO there was one former Sperry man, Kroger, and three from Burroughs, but our votes were certainly not equal. Mike was bending over backwards to be accommodating to the Sperry people, and often overruled choices made to the contrary. As Chairman Abe Lincoln said to his own cabinet, or EO, after a vote on an important issue in which the members' many nay votes were in opposition to his single aye: "The ayes have it."

In early September of 1986 the Merger Coordination Council met to review the final recommendations of the task forces. The two-day meeting, held in New York City, covered enormous amounts of material. The task forces had done outstanding work and many of their recommendations were accepted and implemented. The merger proceeded much more quickly than we had anticipated, and the savings to be effected were greater than we at Burroughs had projected—in fact, they were almost four times what we had expected. Officially the two companies became one on September 16, 1986, when shareholders of the two companies held back-to-back meetings in Wilmington, Delaware. After that we divested some businesses, sold excess real estate, and so on, to the degree that we were able to reduce our debt load to the planned levels one year ahead of schedule. The first full year of financial operations at Unisys was an unqualified financial and operational success, as we consolidated fifteen factories, eliminated many overlapping programs and thereby reduced overhead, amalgamated our two service organizations, organized our sales and marketing along lines of business (which streamlined them), integrated the defense businesses of both companies, and accelerated the development of new products. By the time I left Unisys, at the end of 1987, I was happy that I had been persuaded to stay through the transition and help oversee the birth of a viable Unisys and its emergence as a heavyweight competitor in the information and defense industries. By coincidence, Joe Kroger left the company at the same time.

Now, to deal with career moves during the amalgamation. At the Plaza Hotel in New York in September of 1986, as each task force presented their findings and suggestions to us, we had a chance to get some impressions of the presenters and other members. It was on these impressions, as much as anything else, that we later based our choices for fifteen or twenty key positions. Thus the presenting of those reports was a remarkable opportunity for an ambitious executive to further his or her career; the sad fact is that only a few recognized the opportunity and knew how to take advantage of the situation.

At that moment in time, everything was up in the air. Because of the union of the two companies, no one's previous job was safe—and there were plenty of opportunities for advancement, both in terms of titles and salaries, and in terms of budgets. For instance, the new head of the defense businesses would control an empire with $2.5 billion in annual sales, an amount of sales that is larger than some businesses whose sole enterprise is defense contracts. Similarly, the head of sales for Newco in Europe would have a very large fiefdom. Since the task forces were suggesting selloffs, consolidations, and reorganizations, we in the executive office would be inclined to assign the task of making those reorganizations work to the people who were recommending them to us. It was a matchless opportunity. In a sense, we were at the mercy of the task force members; they had the information, and we were eager to understand it and act on it.

How did they fare?

To begin, those Sperry people who had formed close alliances with Joe Kroger and had been part of Sperry's inner circle were in good shape. Joe took care of them; many got key jobs and were able to recommend others for second-rank positions. For instance, one was named head of marketing, sales, and service for the United States, and had quite a bit of latitude in making choices to head the operations in the various regions within his overall jurisdiction. Other candidates, perhaps as competent or even more competent, had not seen fit to make their talents known to Kroger and the EO, were not as well championed to the EO, and did not get big jobs. It is conceivable that some excellent Sperry people fell through the cracks as a consequence of their unwillingness or inability in this regard. Some of the Sperry people had also understood that Mike, Jim Unruh, and I would be excellent people to get to know and impress before this big meeting, and had spent the summer trying to show us just how cooperative, competent, innovative, and results oriented they were.

The second largest determiner of whether or not the task force members got big jobs was their attitude. We were looking at how people were presenting the material, of course, but we were also drawing conclusions based on how people presented *themselves*— through their dress and manner, their ability to communicate to us about difficult issues both in writing and in person, and, above all, by the way in which they made or did not make a good first impression. None of us even admitted to ourselves that these were criteria— but they were.

Beyond this were subtler questions of attitude. Plenty of people had a good appearance and presented their material well. But some differentiated themselves from the pack by their understanding of the game that was being played. As I look back on it, the winners were clearly those executives who made it their business to understand the mind-set of the EO members and other senior executives. They discerned the nature of the chairman's dream—an acquisition billed as a merger—and that the unification of the two companies was to be paid for by expense- and cost-cutting. They figured out also that Mike wanted peace among the tribes, and that he wanted managers who would know how to deal with the rank and file of the new company. Mike gave out hats at this session, baseball caps that said Newco on the brim. Bad marks were put down against those who used the terms "We at Burroughs..." or "We at Sperry...." Those who came out of this process ahead of the others were the ones who frequently used the name Newco in their conversations; most even went so far as to wear the hats while in meetings with us. (They looked wonderfully silly during these very serious discussions.) They exuded the positive, rah-rah fervor that the chairman obviously espoused. They talked about how they would cut expenses, but equally, about how they would soothe hurt feelings and make things at Newco go smoothly.

In the two years after the dust began to settle at Unisys, certain trends in careers became apparent. Those who had hoped that their talents would be discovered by the upper management, but who had made no effort to shine the light on themselves, remained hidden in the woodwork. Beyond that, the inherent talent and dominance of the former Burroughs management team members quickly came to the fore. Old Burroughs stalwarts who now held important jobs looked after the colleagues with whom they had previously worked, and, over time, the Burroughs graduates regained dominance in Unisys. This trend was accelerated by the short reign of the Sperry graduates in the key positions. A hefty portion of those former Sperry people who had obtained big jobs upon the strength of their presentation (and because of the chairman's proclivity for making a 50-50 split of those jobs between Burroughs and Sperry graduates) did not survive in the jobs. Many were unequal to them; others didn't like the new style of management. A large proportion of these former Sperry people have since been passed over for further promotion, lateraled into lesser jobs, or have resigned. Being good game-players in the midst of a grand upheaval had won them their jobs, but to keep the positions, they needed to perform well—and they hadn't done so. In the long run, performance was a more important determinant to their careers than political connections.

After Probst's retirement, my resignation, Joe Kroger's resignation, and the loss of some other members of senior management, the inner circle of Unisys added two men who came neither from Burroughs nor from Sperry. They were top executives of two companies recently acquired by Unisys, Convergent Technologies Corporation and Timeplex Corporation. Obviously, they received their positions as part of the deals which brought their companies into the Unisys fold. Given the sort of defections and disenchantments that usually follow such acquisitions, as detailed in this chapter, my question was how long these deal-made executives would stay in that fold. Today, they are both gone.

PART FOUR

Conclusions

21

The Essence of Making a Career

OF DREAMS AND *THE ARABIAN NIGHTS*

When I entered the corporate world, I had no inherited money, knew no one, and had no connections to the hierarchy, yet I was able to rise to power and fortune in these corporations. I am convinced that other ambitious people not wired in to the power structure before they enter the door can do the same. Above all, never lose sight of the goal; to get to the top must be a burning, ever-present passion in your life, the stuff of dreams. Though jobs and responsibilities change, the target remains constant—the achieving of financial independence through reaching top-level management positions at a large corporation—and the process remains the challenge of having fun while getting there. Anyone willing to work very hard and to unfailingly produce results can go straight to the top.

Throughout this book I have advocated being a quality manager, one whose behavior is *korrekt*, whose concern is for individuals and who always tries to act in the company's best interests.

Some worry that this notion is incompatible with ambition, that to truly get ahead in business a manager must be a ruthless game-player, that producing results counts for less in the game than playing by the political rules. To disabuse everyone once and for all of the idea that quality managers are doomed to failure, let's look more closely for a moment at the less-scrupulous competition.

Plenty of managers achieve entry into the upper echelons of corporations by means other than those I champion. Many aspects of corporate life lend themselves to exploitation by managers who play a good game. I've often been chagrined to see how easy it is to fool bosses—from those on the lowest managerial level right up to the CEO and board of directors. The upper echelon generally only knows what middle managers tell them, and doesn't like bad news. Many managers don't want to be shot for being the bearers of unpalatable truths, and therefore fail to communicate properly with their bosses. Now, I'm an advocate of presenting things to your boss in the best possible light, but I'm also a believer in keeping the boss fully informed, which means conveying bad news when he needs to know it; one must walk a fine line here. The same managers who prefer concealment to disclosure also are prone to using flattery to distract the boss from important matters, and they routinely promise what they know they can't deliver. Their behavior reminds me of a story in *The Arabian Nights*.

Once upon a time, a pair of thieves caught stealing horses were sentenced to have their hands cut off at the wrist. When the king appeared at the place of judgment astride a magnificent horse, the thieves complimented him on the beauty and intelligence of his horse; so fine was this horse, said the first thief, that he was emboldened to make a proposal: if the king would not cut off their hands for a year, the thieves—who, after all, did know a lot about horses—would guarantee to teach the horse to speak. The king thought the idea was terrific. He agreed to let the thieves keep their hands; however, if at the end of the year the horse (whose name was Budget 1990) wasn't talking a blue streak, the risk to the thieves was to be substantially greater than before. At that time, if the horse was mute, the thieves' heads, rather than just their hands, would be chopped off. The two thieves promised to deliver the miracle and led away Budget 1990. Once out of sight of the king, the second thief turned to the first and fearfully asked how he proposed to make the horse talk. "Look," said the first. "In a year anything could happen. The king could die. You or I could die. Budget 1990 could die. Or perhaps we could even teach the horse how to talk."

Many corporate horse thieves promise what they know they can't deliver because they are counting on not being held accountable for their promises. In a year, they or their bosses could be transferred, the objectives could change, there could be a reorganization—in short, even if the thieves fail to deliver, many things could happen to make the boss/king unable or unwilling to make good on his threats.

To my annoyance, horse thieves are invariably the same managers who treat subordinates badly, manipulate people shamelessly, politicize environments, and do all the other things I've decried in this book. Does their success mean the quality manager must plateau in the middle ranks? Not at all. Smart managers know that the environment in many companies is *always* political. To dismiss what's going on by labeling it political and having nothing to do with it is to miss the boat. Recognize that you must play certain games well—in meetings, presentations, and in the many other situations I've discussed throughout this book. Understand that the quality manager may need to work harder than the devious one to make an impression. For instance, while it's easy to flatter those above you, it's hard work to be nice to your subordinates. Quite a bit of effort is involved in attending a retirement party in a remote suburban location, sending handwritten notes, being sympathetic to personal problems—in doing those tasks that may not have an immediate impact on the race to get ahead, but which make you feel good and which build your own cadre of loyal people. I pride myself that throughout my corporate career I maintained the highest standards of integrity, never compromised myself, and never knowingly misled an organization or stole anything, not even a budgetary horse. I can't say the same for all my former colleagues. Some were outright horse thieves. Others wished to be thought of as good people, but their drive to get ahead permitted no scruples to stand in their way; more than a few said or did things that fell between the truth and a white lie—and some ended up totally losing their integrity.

> A continual push to achieve results and good performance, coupled with a reputation for integrity, can always make up for the edge gained by a competitor whose style has no substance behind it.

Many managers run into career roadblocks. Most simply live wiht these and don't try very hard to go above, around, or through them. Don't accept being stuck or stymied: do something about it —now! Go to your boss's boss. Resign. Get a transfer. Or spend your time looking for a new job or obtaining new skills that will take you further in your career. Whatever happens, never stop believing in yourself; keep looking for new opportunities, because no one is going to hand them to you—you have to go out and find them.

If you accept that roadblock as an obstacle that can't be surmounted or finessed, you've thrown away your career plan when such behavior is not warranted. With eyes firmly set on your goal, you can deal with setbacks because you can see clearly that the most important thing is to keep going. The most crucial management moments in a career may be those in which you struggle to get back on track after a derailment. Some people refuse to act when blocked, or when stuck on a career plateau, because they either don't have a career objective firmly in mind, or they won't make the difficult decisions that will force them to adhere to their own plans.

> When problems crop up, don't be an ostrich; keep your head above ground, figure out how to remedy the situation, and take quick action.

THE ROLE OF IMAGINATION

Very early in my career I made a chart that showed where I'd been in terms of jobs and income, and where I wanted to be in the future—in six months, a year, two years, five years—and when I expected to get my first stock options, my next promotions, and so on. The chart was similar to a product development plan with its associated checkpoints. I consulted the chart regularly, and let it spur me: if I hadn't achieved a certain salary level in the expected amount of time, I pushed harder, knowing that to achieve my personal objectives I had to keep on a fast track, and consequently that to remain in a particular job slot for a long time meant not staying on schedule. On a regular basis (and certainly each time the possibility of a new position arose), I asked myself: Where will I fit in? Do I want to take that job? Will it be good for me in the long run? What are the tools of the trade that I'll need to get even further ahead?

Recalling the exercise I completed at IBM about twenty years ago—the one in which we wrote down the details of a typical day in the future when we would be high-ranking executives—I now think that the difference between my pleasure in the exercise and my colleagues' unease at its revelations lies in the fact that I had frequently and repeatedly used my imagination in service of my objectives. Artists and athletes use their imaginative faculties routinely; Salvador Dali thought long and hard not only to create the image of the floppy timepieces in this most famous painting, *The Persistence of Memory*, but he also conjured up and relished the adulation that would come to him as a result of his having produced an unforgettable artistic image. Similarly, Chris Evert imagined herself holding aloft the champion's trophy at Wimbledon long before she was able to. Using your imagination to shape the future is an expression of the conviction that the events of your life are within your control. Need this be true only for artists and athletes? Of course not. Everyone has the ability to imagine; it is a quintessentially human trait. Yet *if there is one crucial factor that characterizes those who seem unable to master the corporate climb, it is this failure of the imagination, this inability to believe that one's own career is within the province of the individual to control.*

Unfortunately, most people in the corporate world seem to have put their imaginative faculties under wraps, and have come to believe that they have no control over their careers or their lives. They have developed some profound, and, to me, entirely negative convictions:

> —*that if they are blocked they can do nothing about it;*
> —*that they are puppets whose future is in the hands of others;*
> —*that "the company will take care of me";*

> —that promotion and security are gifts that the company or their immediate superior (in the manner of an arbitrary deity) may give or may take away; and, therefore,
>
> —that the company and the immediate superior must be propitiated in order for the individual to survive.

When managers come to believe that someone else will take care of them, they lose all perspective, initiative, and the ability to perform precisely those tasks that are critical to getting ahead, such as analyzing the information in their environment, picking their opportunities and targets, using their leverage. They stop asking those questions of themselves that I posed a few paragraphs above, and become passive; instead of acting for themselves, they come to rely solely on the hope that others will act for them. They trust that the employer will have their best interests at heart at all times.

MISPLACED TRUST AND THE FAILURE OF IMAGINATION

One doesn't really accept a corporate job on a handshake with one's new superior—you wait for confirmation in writing before resigning the current position. By such an action, you express a healthy distrust of the new employer that has nothing to do with the character of your new boss and has a lot to do with the nature of the world and the general relationship between big corporations and their employees. Most of us behave this way without thinking that we're expressing our mistrust. *We go to work and perform our tasks in ignorance of the consequences of having understood that our trust with our employer is far from perfect:* we don't admit to ourselves that advancement and reward will not come to us automatically, and therefore that we are going to have to take charge of our own future. Most employees fail to use their imaginations to make these important connections.

Analyzing the bargain between employee and company in the way I've just done is an act of the imagination—and you don't have to be an artist to do it. But you do need to seize control of your own career by examining and acting upon facets of life that others simply accept as part of the fabric of existence. When you take a new job, examine minutely the job's implications for your career, and gauge how it will help you toward your next position and toward your ultimate goal. You must be relentlessly realistic about each opportunity. When it ceases being good for you—or exciting —then maybe it's time to move on. If you won't judge your own progress in these ways, you resign yourself to reliance on a trust that all the evidence says is misplaced, and, as a consequence, give yourself over to operating in a climate controlled by fear.

As just one instance of how the failure of imagination affects managers, let me point out that many employees both fear and give their unrestrained trust to their immediate superior. Far too many people, believing that their boss is the key to advancement and continued employment, predicate their work on always pleasing that superior, and let themselves be bullied rather than speaking up for what they think is right. Such fears are groundless. Accept the idea that if you act aggressively and do what you think is right and that is in the best interests of the corporation, not everyone will love you or agree with you—but accept also that there will be people somewhere in the hierarchy who will recognize and reward your actions and attitude, or whom you can force to reward you. And, if you see that you are blocked, recognize that you can go to another company where your superior abilities will be more properly judged and appreciated.

> **Work closely with your boss, but do not tie your future exclusively to him or her.**

I recently saw a stark example of fear and lack of imagination: there was a reorganization at a large company in which I'd once been employed, and a number of high-ranking executives were "layered," that is, were asked to report to an intermediary figure rather than to the CEO. Although this was a political move and may have had little to do with those executives' competence, had I been dealt such a career setback, I would have immediately resigned or at least begun a hasty job search. But most of these executives, men in their late forties and early fifties, are choosing to stay in place, some to wait for early retirement, others because they don't want to take new risks. I believe they know in their hearts that if they looked for other jobs, they'd find them; it would be a matter of months. Some of these executives talked to me about lack of loyalty shown to them by the company, and complained bitterly about their lot in life, but, as best I could judge, none planned to leave the corporation. In my view they are unfortunately predicating their actions—really, their nonactions—on fear, showing misguided loyalty to the corporation.

Management manipulates people through their fears, and the echoes are felt throughout whole organizations, chilling them. *Fear and lack of imagination make for myopic managers who predicate their actions and nonactions on avoiding doing anything that might get them fired.* This results in conservative—that is, nonaggressive—business decisions that lead directly to corporate stagnation.

In private life I'm a conservative investor and not much of a gambler. I derive no pleasure from Las Vegas, Atlantic City, or even Monte Carlo—but I do take risks. Inside corporations I took them all the time, and never believed they would be fatal to my career, or unhelpful to the company, because they were carefully considered risks over which I had some control. If you're betting on the roulette wheel, you have very little control; but if you're gambling on whether to make a certain aggressive business decision, you have quite a bit of control. Why? Because the risk isn't very great. As an individual, if you make a bad decision and are punished for it by loss of your job, that's not so terrible because, as I've shown earlier, most managers who lose their positions are able to find new and more challenging jobs within three to six months, often at higher pay. Understanding the downside can similarly reduce the level of perceived risk in taking business gambles. If the factors affecting your forecast are beyond your control, such as a downturn in the economy, you can still do something; if revenues are not at the level you have projected, you can cut costs and expenses to achieve your quarterly or annual profit goal. Also, if the external factors are severe enough, the likelihood is that every company, including your competitors, will be similarly affected.

PROPOSAL FOR A QUIET REVOLUTION

The United States today needs corporations that can devise innovative approaches to the challenges of the years ahead in which our industries will face increasingly stiff competition from abroad. We won't evolve such corporate entities unless managers feel free to imagine more innovative approaches than are now being taken. But when a manager acts out of fear—doesn't speak his mind, or says only what he thinks the boss wants to hear, or makes conservative, low-risk decisions—there is little hope of generating imaginative ideas.

We want unafraid managers. We want people to feel that their coming to work makes a difference to their companies. We want open communications up and down the hierarchy, an environment in which managers feel that their time is not consumed by having to play political games, a company to which they can give their loyalty because it gives them a challenging, rewarding life and limitless possibilities for growth.

The principal deterrent to promoting such a good environment is the fear that reverberates through many American corporations, fear that expresses itself as overly conservative attitudes in corporate managers. As I've earlier suggested, this fear often crystallizes into worrying about the consequences of losing a job—the inability to pay the mortgage, to pay medical bills, to pay for the children's college educations.

Let's consider what other countries do about such fears. In Japan, whose companies' management style is now much admired, the fear of losing one's job has ostensibly been eliminated by the paternal ways in which the Japanese corporations operate. However, Japanese managers are often banished internally in a corporation, and have a hard time recovering; furthermore, they find it nearly impossible to leave the corporation because Japanese society frowns upon resigning and makes it difficult to obtain a job in another corporation. As a result, fear still operates in Japanese companies, though not always as visibly as it does in the United States. In Germany and in many European countries, when a company fires or lays off an employee, that employee must be paid through the ensuing twelve months, during which he or she will almost certainly be able to find a new job. Also, there is free education for the children at good universities, and free health care for families, so these fears are seemingly neutralized. But all these services are paid for by an extremely high rate of taxation on individuals; in most societies, when something is "free," that means *everyone* pays for it somehow. One would hope that society's removing of these fears would allow the blossoming of aggressive corporate executives—but my experience shows me that, in general, European executives are more conservative than their American counterparts, not less. Though freed of the fear of losing their jobs or being unable to pay for the necessities of health care or education, European managers have evolved a lifestyle that accepts the notion that one need not work as hard as their counterparts in North America to achieve and hold a position in a corporation, and that longevity, rather than talent and aggressiveness, is the key to advancement. This attitude is exacerbated by the managers' knowledge that even if they strive hard and make more money, the government will take most of it from them in taxes. The European corporations seem to demand less commitment from their employees, and to get less. In the Scandinavian countries, particularly Sweden, which has the most socialistic of European societies as well as the highest and most progressive of tax rates, since the government takes so much of each extra dollar paid to managers who are already in the high tax brackets, employers are almost entirely deprived of the tools they need to motivate the sort of hungry tigers who move companies ahead.

As opposed to these foreign examples, the structure and processes of American corporations don't seem quite so bad. In an American corporation both the incentives that a more capitalist society pays, and the operation of a bit of fear of losing one's job for nonperformance, are necessary and proper; these are the carrots and sticks that keep employees on their toes. (As a manager, one needs to be able to fire people who are not performing, just as much as a manager needs to be able to reward those who are producing results.) Of course, our corporations do a lot of stupid things, such as sending our brightest young managers to outside, university training and then not knowing what to do with them when they return; but on balance, we're not hopeless.

Part of our problem lies in a factor that differentiates American businesses from non-American ones, and this is the pressure that comes from Wall Street for our corporations to show good quarterly results, no matter what it takes to produce them; in practice, this often means that if results are slipping, American corporations believe they are forced to respond by doing such things as cutting expenses, which results in laying off people in order to come up with a properly profitable quarter. It's not simply the mentality of Wall Street that is wrong, but equally the willingness of American corporations to go along with the pressure to report good short-term results, often at the expense of the long term.

That pressure notwithstanding, the sum of all the factors leads me to conclude that the key to damping down fears yet encouraging managerial innovativeness lies in the reward structure. If junior executives could be free of their fears of being unable to pay medical bills, mortgages, and college tuition, they might be free also to speak their minds, to come up with new ideas.

One way to generate a lot of excitement in low- and middle-level managers might be by enriching them early in their corporate careers, rather than only when they have become senior executives. With financial cares out of mind, they could afford to be other than conservative in their thinking and actions. But their fear of the consequences of dismissal having been calmed, would they work as hard as we need them to? Some would, but some wouldn't. We don't want the money to encourage laxity, but it might. And so perhaps the early rewards ought to take the form of trusts that would only be activated after a manager had spent a certain amount of time in the company, or after having been deemed sufficiently innovative in his actions. Or we might award lower-rank employees stock options in amounts large enough to be meaningful—thereby encouraging them to take actions that will enhance the corporation's return on equity, and, as a consequence, eventually line their own pockets.

This concept is highly theoretical, and I don't have a precise formula for how to best reward these younger employees. There may be no easy answer to this complex question of motivation. One clue, though, lies in the nature of the contracts between employers and high level executives that are already common in American industry.

The usual rationale is that contracts are given to senior management because employers feel they'd be unable to attract proven talent without them. I see it differently. In my view, such contracts also are given as a ratification of what has been learned about the candidate in the interview and background check process, and to encourage new hires to do the very best work of which they are capable. When a company signs up a senior manager, it does so only after that person has been interviewed by a fair number of knowledgeable executives, after the candidate's record of performance in other jobs has been established, after references have been checked—both those provided by the candidate and others that key executives might want to ask about the candidate—and after extensive discussions have determined what is expected of the candidate once the job has been accepted.

As evidence for this view—and you can see this in the contracts that public companies give, which are part of their public documents—such contracts are invariably weighted on the side of the employee; they generally remove any lingering concerns that he might be fired for doing the job as he sees fit, and demonstrate unequivocally that the company will do as it has promised. That is because the contracts usually contain penalties that the company has to pay out in the event it wants to get rid of the employee before the end of the contract.

On the company side, the company takes these potential penalties into consideration—but counts on not having to pay them. In fact, it's rare for a company to have to pay out on such contracts (excluding golden parachutes that go into effect if a company is acquired and an executive is forced out) because the company has done its homework on the manager before hiring, and is convinced that things will work out as planned.

Companies go to great lengths for proven senior executives—but would they be willing to write such one-sided contracts with lower-rank employees who may not be deemed as crucial to the company's progress? Many companies shudder in horror at the idea, though I think it actually carries far less risk to them than is currently perceived.

If the hiring process for middle managers were as diligent as it is for senior managers, and if internal hires were subjected to as much scrutiny as those people joining a company from the outside, there would be less likelihood of a new hire not working out. If the company's only real fear is that it might have to pay out on a contract—and if this fear can be damped down by greater emphasis on getting to know the middle management candidate during the hiring process—then a contract with that middle manager would not be very risky at all.

Or there may be other solutions. You could have something short of a contract, say, an agreement, that if things didn't work out, the manager's salary would be continued for a year, and/or that medical benefits would be continued through a similar period. Wouldn't such things add to the corporation's cost of doing business? Certainly. But—and this is the point to ponder—such costs would be small when compared to the enormous sums that corporations run up every day by having managers who are more concerned with job security than with doing what might be best for the corporation. A good, aggressive decision by an employee could make or save a company millions of dollars—and this far outbalances the occasional cost of carrying for an additional year one of those managers who didn't work out.

For that matter, the contracts or agreements don't have to be written ones. Companies such as IBM, Johnson & Johnson, Digital Equipment (DEC), and Procter & Gamble are known for their high consideration of employees; in essence, they have *moral* contracts with their managers, unwritten agreements that encourage managers to do what they think is best and to know they'll be rewarded and promoted for such behavior. One of the benefits these companies reap from moral contracts is relatively low employee turnover. That, too, keeps costs down.

Remember, our goal is to get rid of fears that are unproductive, such as the fear of getting fired, in those who are, in good conscience, trying to help the company; if employees speak their mind, they should not be punished for doing so. Openness and candor should be celebrated, not discouraged.

Doubtless, one can write contracts or promulgate rules to help eliminate fear and foster aggressive business decisions, but a far easier way to control fears and encourage risk-taking is through leadership. Toleration for openness and the taking of risks that sometimes don't pay off begins from the top of a company and is an attitude that can be translated downward, all through the ranks. This, of course, requires leaders who behave in the demanding but caring manner I've detailed throughout this book, and who abjure politicized environments that create and thrive on fear, and push people to actions that fuel the environment's continued existence.

No matter where I worked, I tried to create an environment in which performance and results, not game-playing, were the key to advancement. And it seems to me now that my most important characteristic as a manager was that I believed in what I was doing, and was never afraid of my superiors because I had the conviction that my actions were always in the best interests of the corporation. I made mistakes, of course; everyone does. But it was always obvious to my managers that I was not afraid; that was one of the things that was attractive about me.

In fact—and this is the optimistic notion on which I want to close—I understand now that in my career *I was rewarded for not being afraid.* And I've learned that others who had this same attitude were also habitually rewarded. Somehow, though, the secret that the unafraid can and do get rewarded and promoted has been hidden behind the veils of corporate mythology. It has been replaced by the mistaken belief that only those who don't rock the boat will continue to be employed and to progress. That's not true. The system rewards those who *do* rock the boat, who take actions that can make quantum differences to their organizations and benefit the corporation.

So, at bottom, beyond enhancing the reward structure, and beyond proper leadership that encourages candor and risk-taking, the most accessible key to banishing fear in corporate life lies within the individual manager—within you. If you act out of the courage of your convictions and show that you don't fear the consequences of those actions, you are in control of your future. Nothing can stop you, not a boss who is unduly political, not a system that seems to tolerate incompetence, not the groupthink that pleads for you to keep your head low in order to remain employed and pay the bills. Take charge of your own career. By acting in the manner I've detailed in this book, you too will be able to reap the considerable corporate rewards on the fast track straight to the top.

Index